Knowledge Economy and the City

This book explores the relationship between space and economy, the spatial expressions of the knowledge economy. The capitalist industrial economy produced its own space, which differed radically from its predecessor agrarian and mercantile economies. If a new knowledge-based economy is emerging, it is similarly expected to produce its own space to suit the new circumstances of production and consumption. If these spatial expressions do exist, even if in incomplete and partial forms, they are likely to be the model for the future of cities.

The book first searches for some basic definitions, asking whether knowledge economy is a reality, dream or mere rhetoric, and looking for the theoretical relationships between society, economy and space. This is followed by an investigation into the changing nature of products, the emergence of knowledge as a productive capacity, the role of information and communication technology, the social organization of work and the new global division of labour. It then moves on to the sites of production and consumption in cities, where new clusters of activity are formed while others shatter and disperse, creating new places of innovation and new patterns of differentiation and stratification. It zooms in on the new spaces of knowledge, such as universities, science parks and cultural quarters, which are created side by side with the new spaces of consumption and new patterns of social inequality.

The book argues against some of the widely circulated misconceptions about knowledge economy: its immateriality and aspatiality; the determinism that comes with a fascination for new technologies; the idea of a post-industrial economy; the limited way knowledge is interpreted and used; the multiple and overlapping roles of science and culture; and the rise of a new social class. It offers fresh insights into the contemporary city for students and scholars who are interested in the relationship between society and space.

Ali Madanipour is Professor of Urban Design and a founder member of the Global Urban Research Unit at the School of Architecture, Planning and Landscape, Newcastle University. His books include *Designing the City of Reason* (2007, Routledge); *Public and Private Spaces of the City* (2003, Routledge); and *Social Exclusion in European Cities* (2003, co-ed, Routledge).

Regional Studies Association
THE INTERNATIONAL FORUM FOR REGIONAL DEVELOPMENT POLICY AND RESEARCH
The Association welcomes as members all individuals and organisations who are interested in the study and understanding of regions and regionalism

Routledge
Taylor & Francis Group

Regions and cities

Series editors: Ron Martin, University of Cambridge, UK; Gernot Grabher, University of Bonn, Germany; Maryann Feldman, University of Georgia, USA; Gillian Bristow, University of Cardiff, UK.

Regions and Cities is an international, interdisciplinary series that provides authoritative analyses of the new significance of regions and cities for economic, social and cultural development, and public policy experimentation. The series seeks to combine theoretical and empirical insights with constructive policy debate and critically engages with formative processes and policies in regional and urban studies.

1 **Beyond Green Belts**
Managing urban growth in the 21st century
Edited by John Herrington

2 **Retreat from the Regions**
Corporate change and the closure of factories
Stephen Fothergill and Nigel Guy

3 **Regional Development in the 1990s**
The British Isles in transition
Edited by Ron Martin and Peter Townroe

4 **Spatial Policy in a Divided Nation (April 1993)**
Edited by Richard T. Harrison and Mark Hart

5 **An Enlarged Europe**
Regions in competition?
Edited by Louis Albrechts, Sally Hardy, Mark Hart and Anastasios Katos

6 **The Regional Imperative**
Regional planning and governance in Britain, Europe and the United States
Urlan A. Wannop

7 **The Determinants of Small Firm Growth**
An inter-regional study in the United Kingdom 1986–90
Richard Barkham, Graham Gudgin, Mark Hart and Eric Hanvey

8 **The Regional Dimension of Transformation in Central Europe**
Gorzelak Grzegorz

9 **Union Retreat and the Regions**
The shrinking landscape of organised labour
Ron Martin, Peter Sunley and Jane Wills

10 **Regional Development Strategies**
A European perspective
Edited by Jeremy Alden and Philip Boland

11 **British Regionalism and Devolution**
The challenges of state reform and European integration
Edited by Jonathan Bradbury and John Mawson

12 **Innovation Networks and Learning Regions?**
James Simmie

13 **Regional Policy in Europe**
S.S. Artobolevskiy

14 **New Institutional Spaces**
TECs and the remaking of economic governance
Edited by Martin Jones and Jamie Peck

15 **The Coherence of EU Regional Policy**
Contrasting perspectives on the structural funds
Edited by John Bachtler and Ivan Turok

16 **Multinationals and European Integration**
Trade, investment and regional development
Edited by Nicholas A. Phelps

17 **Unemployment and Social Exclusion**
Landscapes of labour inequality and social exclusion
Edited by Sally Hardy, Paul Lawless and Ron Martin

18 **Metropolitan Planning in Britain**
A comparative study
Edited by Peter Roberts, Kevin Thomas and Gwyndaf Williams

19 **Social Exclusion in European Cities**
Processes, experiences and responses
Edited by Judith Allen, Goran Cars and Ali Madanipour

20 **Regional Development Agencies in Europe**
Edited by Charlotte Damborg, Mike Danson and Henrik Halkier

21 **Community Economic Development**
Edited by Graham Haughton

22 **Foreign Direct Investment and the Global Economy**
Corporate and institutional dynamics of global localisation
Edited by Jeremy Alden and Nicholas F. Phelps

23 **Restructuring Industry and Territory**
The experience of Europe's regions
Edited by Anna Giunta, Arnoud Lagendijk and Andy Pike

24 **Out of the Ashes?**
The social impact of industrial contraction and regeneration on Britain's mining communities
Chas Critcher, Bella Dicks, David Parry and David Waddington

25 **Regional Innovation Strategies**
The challenge for less-favoured regions
Edited by Kevin Morgan and Claire Nauwelaers

26 **Geographies of Labour Market Inequality**
Edited by Ron Martin and Philip S. Morrison

27 **Sustainable Cities**
Graham Haughton and Colin Hunter

28 **Regions, Spatial Strategies and Sustainable Development**
David Counsell and Graham Haughton

29 **Clusters and Regional Development**
Critical reflections and explorations
Edited by Asheim Bjorn, Philip Cooke and Ron Martin

30 **Regional Competitiveness**
Edited by Ron Martin, Michael Kitson and Peter Tyler

31 **Regional Development in the Knowledge Economy**
Edited by Philip Cooke and Andrea Piccaluga

32 **The Rise of the English Regions?**
Edited by Irene Hardill, Paul Benneworth, Mark Baker and Leslie Budd

33 **Geographies of the New Economy**
Critical reflections
Edited by Peter W. Daniels, Andrew Leyshon, Michael J. Bradshaw and Jonathan Beaverstock

34 **European Cohesion Policy**
Willem Molle

35 **Creative Regions**
Technology, culture and knowledge entrepreneurship
Edited by Philip Cooke and Dafna Schwartz

36 **Devolution, Regionalism and Regional Development**
The UK experience
Edited by Jonathan Bradbury

37 **Intelligent Cities and Globalisation of Innovation Networks**
Nicos Komninos

38 **Whither Regional Studies?**
Edited by Andy Pike

39 **Business Networks in Clusters and Industrial Districts**
The governance of the global value chain
Edited by Fiorenza Belussi and Alessia Sammarra

40 **China and Europe**
The implications of the rise of China as a global economic power for Europe
Edited by Klaus Kunzmann, Willy A. Schmid and Martina Koll-Schretzenmayr

41 **Globalizing Regional Development in East Asia**
Production networks, clusters, and entrepreneurship
Edited by Henry Wai-chung Yeung

42 **Manufacturing in the New Urban Economy**
Willem van Winden, Leo van den Berg, Luis Carvalho and Erwin van Tuijl

43 **The Impacts of Automotive Plant Closures**
A tale of two cities
Edited by Andrew Beer and Holli Evans

44 **The Futures of the City Region**
Edited by Michael Neuman and Angela Hull

45 **Migration in the 21st Century**
Rights, outcomes, and policy
Kim Korinek and Thomas Maloney

46 **Leadership and Place**
Edited by Chris Collinge, John Gibney and Chris Mabey

47 **Knowledge Economy and the City**
Spaces of knowledge
Ali Madanipour

Knowledge Economy and the City

Spaces of knowledge

Ali Madanipour

Routledge
Taylor & Francis Group
LONDON AND NEW YORK

First published 2011
by Routledge
2 Park Square, Milton Park, Abingdon, Oxon OX14 4RN

Simultaneously published in the USA and Canada
by Routledge
711 Third Avenue, New York, NY 10017

Routledge is an imprint of the Taylor & Francis Group, an informa business

British Library Cataloguing in Publication Data
A catalogue record for this book is available from the British Library

Library of Congress Cataloging in Publication Data
A catalog record for this book has been requested

ISBN: 978-0-415-55895-2 (hbk)
ISBN: 978-0-203-81614-1 (ebk)

Typeset in Times New Roman
by RefineCatch Limited, Bungay, Suffolk

Printed and bound in Great Britain by
CPI Antony Rowe, Chippenham, Wiltshire

Contents

Acknowledgements

Parts of Chapter 8 draw on a joint urban design studio with MIT (Massachusetts Institute of Technology) in 2004–05 on the theme of relationships between city and university. I should like to thank the Cambridge-MIT Institute and Newcastle University for funding the project, John Goddard for supporting it, the project tutors (MIT's John de Monchaux and Julian Beinart and my Newcastle colleague Bill Tavernor), all the outside speakers and the students from the two universities who participated in the project. Subsequent work at Newcastle University led to the publication of a paper in 2010 in *European Planning Studies* with Paul Benneworth and David Charles, now at Twente and Curtin Universities respectively, whom I thank for their collaboration. Parts of Chapter 9 draw on my 2010 chapter 'Living together or apart: exclusion, gentrification and displacement', in the book *Urban Design: Roots, influences, and trends: the Routledge companion to urban design*, edited by Tridib Banerjee and Anastasia Loukaitou-Sideris.

1 Introduction

Many consider knowledge economy to be a follow-up to industrial economy. The capitalist industrial economy reshaped cities and regions in several major waves of development and redevelopment, producing its own space, which differed radically from its predecessor agrarian and mercantile economies. Manufacturing industries reorganized access to raw materials and markets around the world, created and controlled transport networks, attracted large numbers of workers to cities, and set up rigid routines of work, all reflected in the patterns of spatial and social organization. If a new knowledge-based economy is emerging that is sharply different from the past, it is similarly expected to produce its own space through reshaping the industrial city to a new form that would suit the new conditions of economic production and their associated social habits and institutions.

This book explores the relationship between space and economy, the spatial expressions of the knowledge economy, and how these expressions contribute to the further development of knowledge economy. If these spatial expressions do exist, even if in incomplete and partial forms, they are likely to be the model for the future of cities. The book looks for a definition of the knowledge economy and its main characteristics, evaluating some of these features to see if and how they find spatial expression in the city. It aims at understanding the economic logic of current urban transformation: if a new knowledge-based economy is emerging, its spaces are being, or will be, created accordingly. The process of urban transformation that we are witnessing, therefore, is expected to coincide with the process of economic change.

The study first searches for some basic definitions, asking whether knowledge economy is a reality, dream or mere rhetoric, and looking for the theoretical relationships between society, economy and space. This is followed by an investigation into the changing nature of products, the emergence of knowledge as a productive capacity, the role of information and communication technology, the social organization of work and the new global division of labour. It then moves on to the sites of production and consumption in cities, where new clusters of activity are formed while others shattered and dispersed, creating new places of innovation and new patterns of differentiation and stratification. It zooms in on the new spaces of knowledge, such as universities, science parks and cultural quarters, which are created side by side with the new spaces of consumption and new patterns of social inequality. On the way, it finds some widely circulated misconceptions about knowledge economy: its immateriality and aspatiality; the determinism that comes with a fascination for new technologies; the idea of a post-industrial economy; the limited way knowledge is interpreted and used; the multiple and overlapping roles of science and culture; and the rise of a new social class.

The book is organized along the dynamics of production, inquiring into the nature of products, the organization of production, the factors of production, and the patterns of distribution and consumption. It is structured in three parts. Part I develops some basic definitions for knowledge economy, city and space. Chapter 2 investigates how knowledge economy is defined, measured and promoted. It is generally defined as the economic application of knowledge, drawing on information and communication technologies used by highly skilled workers to develop marketable innovations. The chapter problematizes this definition, to see it as a historical process rather than a sudden event, a bundle of different trends rather than a single process, emerging in a supportive social and institutional context rather than in a void. It argues against making false assumptions about the primacy of particular driving forces, forms of knowledge, classes of people, or places. Chapter 3 develops a theoretical framework that integrates political economy and cultural analysis to explore the close connections between economy, society and space. It offers a perspective of dynamic multiplicity that draws on the relational nature of space, its temporal dynamism, its social character, and embedded and embodied diversity of perspectives into its understanding. Cities are concentrations in space and time, congregations of people in search of mutual support, where economic relations find manifestation in spatial phenomena such as distance and location, creating a context for the beliefs and actions of individuals, households, firms and other organizations and groups.

Part II explores the process of economic production and charts the changes in the nature of products and the factors of production. Chapter 4 investigates the nature of knowledge products and how they are identified and measured. The symbolic and relational character of these products and their low transaction costs are used to characterize knowledge economy as post-industrial, immaterial, and aspatial. The chapter argues that knowledge products are indeed material processes, both by virtue of their own materiality and how they relate to the economic processes: they are mediated through physical objects, produced, exchanged and consumed through material processes. Cities are not becoming aspatial or weightless, but in fact gaining more weight through their own gravity within the context of the rapid growth of the world's urban population. Chapter 5 investigates the nature of knowledge and whether the phenomenal changes in the processing of information have caused an epistemic rupture. By engaging with philosophical and sociological discussions, knowledge is found to be embedded in socio-temporal-spatial contexts and embodied in intelligent human bodies, used as instrument, product, or productive capacity. While scientific knowledge is often given priority, knowledge economy in practice focuses on the accumulation and instrumental use of whatever passes as knowledge, as a new form of capital that still needs to be converted to money, creating tensions with the idea of knowledge as common good.

The emergence of knowledge economy is closely related to the development of information and communication technologies. Chapter 6 argues against technological determinism, as technological development and deployment are intertwined with the way society works. The chapter explores the relationship between technological change and economic cycles, the conditions of the mediated city, and the implications of digital technology for urban space through dispersion and agglomeration, as played out through spatial compression, temporal acceleration, social decontextualization, and functional augmentation. The creative and economic dimensions of the knowledge-based economy are enhanced and facilitated by new technologies, but they are not necessarily co-extensive. Chapter 7 analyses the social organization of production as another driver of economic change, searching for how changes in the supply and division of labour transform the global economy and find spatial manifestation. The separation of conception from execution, which had transformed cities, is now globalized, with globalization as a spatial process in which unification, stratification and differentiation are at work. The urban landscape is transformed to reflect these changes, declining and regenerating in the image of global division of labour, competing with others so going through both homogenization and differentiation, imitating others while struggling for recognition through symbolic transformation.

Part III focuses on the sites of production and consumption in the knowledge economy. Chapter 8 reviews the dynamics of urban economics, the growth of concentrations, spaces of encounter, and their role in innovation. It then studies different types and examples of knowledge economy clusters, formed either by public policy or by the decisions of individuals and firms, including universities, science and technology parks, creative economy clusters, and office clusters, as well as home-working. Clustering, however, may also be part of marketing strategies, the pressure for specialization may fragment urban space further, and the production of space may be only responding to the demands of the development industry rather than the knowledge economy. Chapter 9 balances the discussions of production with consumption, under two key themes of diversity and inequality, with considerable implications for society and environment. As an engine for the economy, consumption has grown, intensifying the chain of 'creative destruction', i.e., the modernist attitude with its readiness to transform the urban landscape in order to renew the productive apparatus. It leads to faster, shorter cycles of production and consumption with a higher frequency of obsolescence and disposability of products. It encourages social differentiation to facilitate the spread of consumption, and the reorganization of space to cater for the sense of status that comes from differentiated consumption. Furthermore, there is intensified stratification, whereby social inequality grows in partitioned cities and gentrified spaces.

Chapter 10 brings together the main discussions under the four spatial processes of dispersion, differentiation, connection and concentration. Knowledge economy refers to the economic application of knowledge, scientific as well as cultural, which aims to occupy the high end of the global division of labour, where conception, innovation, and production of high value-added products are based. The key features of the knowledge economy include innovation through the changing nature of knowledge to become a productive capacity and economic asset, facilitated by the changing organization of production and the use of information and communication technologies, transforming the nature of economic products. Rather than a coherent whole, however, knowledge economy is an umbrella term that groups together a number of different trends and various conditions, which is then used in a normative capacity by national and international organizations to advocate particular future directions. The spatial implications of travelling in this direction can be visible in the spatial processes through which people, activities and objects are uprooted and dispersed, differentiated, connected to one another, and re-concentrated in new ways.

Dispersion, from the global to local scales, is a spatial solution to overcome the limitations of time and space and of the factors of production, as facilitated by connections and movements made possible by new technologies. Differentiation becomes a new basis for social stratification, expansion of consumption, and competition between places, helped by aesthetic and spatial devices. Dispersion and differentiation respond to the pressure for individualization and social fragmentation. The economies of scale, however, require spatial concentration, hence regrouping the dispersed and differentiated elements into new clusters. Urban space is transformed accordingly, whereby the existing clusters of working and living that served the manufacturing sector are dismantled to be replaced by new clusters thought to be a better fit for the new production processes. Science and technology parks, cultural and creative districts, office clusters, gentrified neighbourhoods, and deprived ghettos are all different spatial manifestations of these processes. The major challenge for the advocates of knowledge economy is how to address the social and environmental consequences of these processes.

Part I

City and economy

Part I develops some initial bases for the inquiry into knowledge economy and the city, looking for definitions and conceptual tools to investigate knowledge economy in Chapter 2, and the city, economy and space in Chapter 3.

2 Reality, dream or rhetoric?

As a first step in our investigation, it is important to find out what the term 'knowledge economy' means, how this economy is structured, which sectors it includes, who are the knowledge workers, and how it is viewed by national governments and international organizations. Is there such a thing as knowledge economy at all? If so, what are its features? What sectors of the economy can be identified as knowledge-based? Who are the knowledge workers and knowledge firms? The chapter starts by asking whether it exists in reality or it is a dream that governments and international organizations pursue, or merely a promotional label, a way of packaging a number of economic trends. In search of an answer, it goes on to review the definitions of knowledge economy, the role of science and technology, as well as arts and culture, and innovation and creativity in its development, followed by an analysis of its constituent parts, and its pattern of distribution in centres and peripheries.

The dawn of a new economy?

The problem with labelling large-scale social and economic phenomena is that we may group a large number of dissimilar or unrelated issues under a banner, without any internal coherence to the constituent parts. We may decide to call the current or future phase of our economies as knowledge economy, hence appearing to give the concept a degree of coherence that it might lack. After all, knowledge has always been integrated in what humans do, and the notion of knowledge economy appears to claim it for now, and somehow deny that the different economies of previous generations were also knowledge-based. Producing, sharing and using knowledge is not new at all; these may have intensified in some historical periods and with the help of some new technologies, such as the invention of writing, printing and telecommunication (Burke, 2000). So a series of questions revolve around what distinguishes the new developments from the past.

A key question about knowledge economy is whether it is a reality or a dream. In other words, we need to establish whether it describes the actual conditions of some places, from the de-industrializing economies to the emerging industrializing economies, or that it points to a future to which these economies and others aspire. In other words, is it a descriptive or a normative term? After answering this question, we will need to establish what type of reality or dream it is, and whether as reality it differs substantially from the past, and as dream whether it is achievable or a mere motivating banner. Is knowledge economy a general empty slogan, a bandwagon that local authorities and investors jump on, used so widely that it may be almost meaningless? Is knowledge economy a glorified term for the widespread use of ICT or for the predominance of services in places from which manufacturing has departed?

The evidence for answering these questions is mixed and ambiguous. A number of writers have described our age as the knowledge or information age, as information economy and information society, or knowledge-based economy and knowledge society. For these writers, we have already passed the threshold into a knowledge-based society, particularly characterized by the widespread use of information and communication technologies. Indeed, the origins of this change are traced back to the 1950s and 1960s (Bell, 1973; Toffler, 1981; Bannock *et al.*, 2003), which suggests that by now we should have already moved into a knowledge economy phase. According to one commentator, 'historians of the future may well refer to the period around 2000 as the 'age of information' (Burke, 2000:1). The present US president seems to believe that knowledge economy is a current reality: 'the knowledge economy we're living in today', whereby 'new jobs and industries that require more skill and knowledge have come to dominate the economy' (Obama, 2005).

Meanwhile, we come across national governments, regional authorities and local institutions that set themselves, at least in their promotional material, the target of entering into this new age of knowledge and information. The US government makes preparations for laying the foundations for being able to compete in the global knowledge economy (Hass, 2009).The UK government's Business Secretary introduced the plan for Digital Britain as 'a strategy for building a knowledge economy' (DirectGov, 2009). The European Union's Lisbon Strategy and its successor 'EU 2020' promote the development of a knowledge-based economy for the future of Europe (EC, 2009a). Europe faces major structural challenges, which include globalization, climate change and an ageing population, exacerbated by the recent economic crisis. To meet this challenge, the aim is 'for Europe to lead, compete and prosper as a knowledge-based, connected, greener and more inclusive economy, growing fast and sustainably, creating high levels of employment and social progress', an economy 'where the key input will be knowledge' (EU 2020).

> Europe's knowledge economy is central to its future economic competitiveness. In a world characterised by strong competition, economic interdependence and low wages in emerging economies, Europe cannot rely on low wage, low value-added production in order to generate economic growth and create new jobs. Instead, Europe must focus its efforts on areas where it has a potential competitive advantage: the production of high value-added goods and services, embodying a high level of physical and human capital and knowledge.
>
> (European Policy Centre, 2009:1)

The World Bank has a programme of helping and encouraging countries to enter the knowledge economy (World Bank, 2009). Whether they have left manufacturing industries behind or are just embracing it, many national and local authorities seem to be anxious to move in the direction of knowledge-based activities. For them, knowledge economy is a dream to be realized, a target to be achieved, and a future basis for economic development. Transition to a knowledge economy remains an aspiration for many countries, and a powerful normative goal for policy-makers.

An economy based on knowledge

Defining knowledge economy, or knowledge-based economy, is not as straightforward or uncontroversial as it may appear, as knowledge itself and the role it plays in social and economic behaviour are difficult to define and measure (OECD, 1996). The roots of the idea of knowledge economy go back to the mid-twentieth century, when two distinctive features were noted: the growth of services and the increased role of knowledge in the economy. Employment grew in services far more than in manufacturing, mining and agriculture, while the growth in the economy far exceeded the growth of capital and labour inputs. The difference was attributed to advances in knowledge, and the notion of knowledge-based economy was born (Bannock *et al.*, 2003).

The knowledge economy primarily involves the economic application of knowledge. It is defined as 'an economy where knowledge is the main engine of economic growth' (Chen and Dahlman, 2005:1). This engine works with innovations by highly skilled workers made possible through new technologies, so for some the knowledge economy is 'what you get when firms bring together powerful computers and well educated minds to create wealth' (Brinkley, 2006:3). Its definitions are often related to the phenomenal development and spread of the information and communication technologies. The emphasis on scientific knowledge and the spread of ICT tends to keep the weight of the definitions within a science and technology framework. Therefore, knowledge economy has been defined as 'production and services based on knowledge-intensive activities that contribute to an accelerated pace of technological and scientific advance as well as equally rapid obsolescence' (Powell and Snellman, 2004:201).

According to the World Bank, knowledge economy is a term that signifies the importance of knowledge as a source of growth in the global economy; it is 'where organizations and people acquire, create, disseminate and use knowledge more effectively for greater economic and social development' (World Bank, 2008a). This reflects a 'knowledge revolution', which is manifest in closer links between science and technology, the importance of innovation for economic growth and competitiveness, the significant role of intangibles (R&D, software and education), and the global interdependency and connectivity facilitated by the ICT explosion (World Bank, 2008a). The application of knowledge is now considered to be one of the main causes of growth in the global economy. This application has been evident in areas such as entrepreneurship and innovation, research and development, software and design, and in the levels of education and skills. The countries that have pursued a coherent strategy to develop their capabilities in creating, accessing and using knowledge have made rapid progress, as exemplified by Korea, Malaysia, Finland, China and Chile (World Bank, 2009).

Research has shown considerable growth in new knowledge, as indicated by the rising number of patents in the US and other advanced economies in recent years, particularly in biomedical and information and communication technologies. Research has also shown a dramatic rise in the number of people employed in science and engineering. This shift may not have yet been translated into higher productivity gains, particularly at the country scale, which is probably due to the time it takes for new investments to become effective. Information and communication technology may be seen as a general purpose technology, adoption and effective use of which would depend on the institutional context. Without matching innovation in organizational structure and processes, productivity gains may remain elusive (Powell and Snellman, 2004). In other words, investment in knowledge is necessary but not sufficient. One of the key features of knowledge economy is the rise of innovation in organizational and presentational practices, which cover work practice changes, design and marketing. It is particularly important in knowledge management, which uses ICT to analyse, process and share information and knowledge among knowledge workers, leading to higher productivity in firms (Brinkley, 2006).

In their review of the subject, Powell and Snellman (2004:200) identify three lines of research on the subject of knowledge economy. A longer line of research has focused on the central significance of theoretical knowledge as a source of innovation and the role of new science-based industries in social and economic change. A second strand has inquired into the relationship between technology and productivity, the types of industries that are knowledge-intensive, and whether the knowledge economy is fundamentally different from the past in types of jobs and work organization. A third strand of research has focused on the role of learning and innovation inside firms, asking whether knowledge is codified or tacit, and looking for the kinds of social arrangements that are conducive to the generation and transmission of knowledge.

Driven by science and technology

What are the constituent parts of the knowledge economy? An answer may lie in what the various national and international organizations consider to be the key indicators of the knowledge economy. The way we measure and promote knowledge economy shows what we think it is and what its constituent parts are. One of the three key drivers of the European Commission's EU 2020 vision is 'Creating value by basing growth on knowledge' (EC, 2009a:5).This involves acknowledging knowledge as 'the engine for sustainable growth', energized through education and research, innovation and creativity (ibid). 'The aim for 2020', as the consultation document announces, 'is to achieve a genuine European Knowledge Area, underpinned by a world-class knowledge infrastructure, in which all actors (students, teachers, researchers, education and research institutions and enterprises) benefit from the free circulation of people, knowledge and technology (the 5th freedom)' (EC, 2009a:6). In this vision, the development of the knowledge infrastructure finds a special place, with a particular place of significance given to the information and communication technologies.

There is often a close connection between knowledge economy and digital technologies. The term information society is widely used for referring to the use of information and communication technologies, which is considered to be critical for its competitiveness as well as meeting the needs of the economy and society. Under the title 'What exactly is the "information society"? A guide for newcomers', the EU defines the information society within a technological framework:

> You are reading this page on the Internet. You may also have a digital camera, a mobile phone, an MP3 player. These are all 'information society' products, made possible by the convergence of computer, telecommunications and media sciences. In just one generation, information and communications technologies (ICTs) have revolutionized the way we live, learn, work and play. They have radically recast the ways in which people, industry, governments and society interact.
>
> (EC, 2009b)

The i2010 initiative, the policy framework for European information society, promotes 'A European Information Society for Growth and Employment – which seeks to boost efficiency throughout the European economy by means of wider use of ICT'(Eurostat, 2009:495). Its stated aim is creating an inclusive digital society by overcoming social and geographical differences. Therefore its three main priorities are announced as creating a single European Information Space that promotes an open and competitive internal market for information society and media services, strengthening investment in innovation and research in ICT, and fostering inclusion, better public services and quality of life through the use of ICT. The data about the information society, therefore, primarily revolves around monitoring access to broadband connections and use for households, businesses and government in different European countries and their comparison with Japan and the United States. In 2007, for the first time the majority of households (54%) in the 27 member states of the European Union had access to the Internet, but overall these countries were spending a lower proportion of their GDP on ICT when compared with Japan and the US (Eurostat, 2009:499–500).

The World Bank's approach to knowledge economy is also driven by science and technology. The Bank's Knowledge for Development Programme is devised to help countries around the world to identify where they stand and what the challenges and opportunities are for making the transition into a knowledge-based economy (World Bank, 2009). To encourage and measure this process, the bank has devised a benchmarking tool called Knowledge Assessment Methodology (KAM), which uses 109 structural and qualitative variables. These are grouped under four 'knowledge economy pillars', which are: economic incentive and institutional regime, education, innovation, and information and communication technologies. The benchmarking tool is used to measure and compare the performance of 146 countries on their 'knowledge economy readiness'. The four pillars are then aggregated to a single Knowledge Economy Index (KEI), which measures 'a country's ability to generate, adopt and diffuse knowledge and also whether the environment is conducive for knowledge to be used effectively for economic development' (World Bank, 2009). The bank describes the four pillars as:

> an economic and institutional regime that provides incentives for the efficient use of existing and new knowledge and the flourishing of entrepreneurship. An educated and skilled population that can create, share, and use knowledge well. An efficient innovation system of firms, research centres, universities, think tanks, consultants, and other organizations that can tap into the growing stock of global knowledge, assimilate and adapt it to local needs, and create new technology. Information and Communication Technologies (ICT) that can facilitate the effective communication, dissemination, and processing of information.
>
> (World Bank, 2009)

To take a closer look, we may consult the Basic Scorecard, which is a simplified version of the knowledge economy league table with 14 variables, grouped under the four pillars, plus the overall performance of the economy. The 14 variables are: The overall performance of the economy (average annual GDP growth, Human Development Index), the economic incentive and institutional regime (tariff and non-tariff barriers, regulatory quality, rule of law), education and human resources (adult literacy rate, gross secondary enrolment, gross tertiary enrolment), the innovation system (royalty and licence fees payments and receipts, patent applications granted by the US Patent and Trademark Office, scientific and technical journal articles), and information and communication technology (telephone users, computer users, Internet users).

There are many ways of interpreting these pillars and the effects of such a process on different countries, with all the potential controversies and shortcomings that league tables have when trying to squeeze a large number of issues into single numbers. The scoreboard shows encouragement for countries to improve the skills and education of their workforce and support innovative practices by embracing the information and communication technologies. It also shows encouragement to join the globalization process and free trade, which is embraced by some and criticized by others. It shows a preference for science and technology, with a potential disadvantage for different forms of knowledge, which may not have economic application. The indicators show that the gap between low-income and high-income countries is very wide, and for the low-income-countries the notion of entering the knowledge economy may appear to be beyond reach, where no amount of benchmarking could help them overcome their substantial economic and institutional problems. Furthermore, it seems to advocate a single model for all, while the diversity of contexts and conditions would mean that there would inevitably be different paths to economic development.

Therefore, a brief look at the EU's and the World Bank's notions of knowledge economy shows it to rely on the expansion of the information and communication technologies, privileging science and technology, enabling innovation and encouraging the development of knowledge and skills through research and education. These are, however, the prerequisites for the emergence of a knowledge-based economy. What are the conditions in such a society, and how are those conditions different from ours? In what ways is a society based on knowledge economy a better one than the current or previous societies? Is it a society in which new products and services are continually created, encouraging a faster cycle of consumption and a more disposable attitude towards the natural resources? Is it a knowledge society in which wisdom as well as information grows, hence enabling its members to use the earth's resources with more care and attention? How does it deal with the distribution of resources and the problems of social inequality? What is the nature of innovation that would be the linchpin of such a society?

Culture, creativity and innovation

Science and culture, which have been separated for long in minds as well as in practices, have given rise to different labels to describe the desirable shape of the future economy: knowledge economy or creative economy. Under the banner of innovation, however, the two are united, as they both involve finding new pathways for economic development. The European Union's strategic documents group them under the umbrella of knowledge-based activities. In a green paper published in 2010, the EU acknowledges the significance of the cultural and creative industries (2.6% of EU's GDP) with high potential for growth. It identifies cultural industries as those engaged in the development of cultural expression irrespective of their economic value, and creative industries as those that use culture as input and have a cultural dimension, but their output is mainly functional (EC, 2010:5–6). This distinction seems to run parallel to a distinction between art and design, which sees art and design as 'useless' and 'useful' activities respectively, even though the boundaries are always blurred (Sudjic, 2009).

The creative industries, according to the UK government's Department for Culture, Media and Sport, are 'those that are based on individual creativity, skill and talent. They also have the potential to create wealth and jobs through developing and exploiting intellectual property' (DCMS, 2009). The department lists the sections of these creative industries as advertising, architecture, art and antiques markets, computer and video games, crafts, design, designer fashion, film and video, music, performing arts, publishing, software, and television and radio. In some of these areas, namely advertising, computer and video games, design and publishing, this department's responsibilities are shared with the Department for Business, indicating the overlap between creative activities and economic concerns. Over the past decade, the creative economy has grown at twice the rate of the economy as a whole, accounting for 2 million jobs and contributing £60 billion (7.3%) to the British economy. The DCMS launched a Creative Economy Programme in 2005 as a government strategy for the development of creative industries. The vision of the government was that 'of a Britain in ten years' time where the local economies in our biggest cities are driven by creativity' (DCMS, 2008: 6). To achieve this dynamism, the development and nurturing of creative talents was thought to be the key, alongside support for research and innovation, business growth, intellectual property rights and the development of creative clusters. The emphasis in the promotion of creative industries is on the development of talents, in other words on the embodied knowledge and skills (see Chapter 5), as well as the use of information and communication technologies.

The creative economy, therefore, overlaps with those parts of the economy that draw on science and technology. Art and design, as well as science and technology, are both seen as engines of economic growth. In the UK, they are dealt with as overlapping areas, jointly addressed by the government departments for business, culture and higher education. In the European Union, creativity and innovation are addressed as part of the overall knowledge economy. In the first debate in the European year of creativity and innovation in Brussels in February 2009, the central significance of creativity and innovation in achieving the Lisbon Strategy's ambition of developing a knowledge economy for the future prosperity of Europe was emphasized (European Policy Centre, 2009).

The EU studies in innovation have acknowledged that investment in R&D (research and development) is not the only route to innovation. Other paths to innovation include technology adoption, incremental changes, imitation and reconfiguring existing knowledge. In particular, the role of design and creativity in innovation is recognized: 'Creativity and design are important features of a well-developed knowledge economy spurring innovation and having a favourable impact on people's well-being and business performance' (EC, 2009c: 28). In 2009 a Design, Creativity and Innovation scoreboard was devised that included new indicators (EC, 2009c). In the development of the scoreboard, creativity, design and innovation were defined: creativity as 'the generation of new ideas', design as 'the shaping (or transformation) of ideas into new products and processes', and innovation as 'the exploitation of ideas, i.e. the successful marketing of these new products and processes' (Hollanders and van Cruysen, 2009: 5). It argued for a fundamental connection between design and creativity with innovation. On this basis, 35 indicators are grouped under seven categories, of which three measure the 'creative climate' (creative education, self-expression, and openness and tolerance), and four measure 'creativity and design' (creative sector, R&D creativity, design creativity and competitiveness in design). The scoreboard is then used to compare and rank the European countries with each other and with other countries. The results show the importance of a supportive creative climate, but the strongest links are between creative education and innovation, leading to recommendations about strengthening of education attainment and enabling of creative thinking.

The European green paper on creative economies emphasizes the various spillovers from cultural and creative industries (CCIs) in the development of a creative and competitive economy for Europe. First, through their intensive use of information and communication technologies, CCIs provide innovation impulses for technology users: 'these industries provide content to fuel digital devices and networks and so contribute to the acceptance and further development of ICTs' (EC, 2010: 17). Second, they can encourage consumption through their association with the 'experience economy' and 'their ability to shape or amplify social and cultural trends, and – therefore – consumer demand' (ibid). Third, innovative firms seem to use the services from cultural and creative industries more than others, apparently through a more open outlook: 'helping to address behavioural failures, such as risk aversion, status quo bias and myopia' (ibid).

In the discussions on knowledge economy, scientific knowledge seems to be given a higher priority, to be turned into a commodity, around which new relations of production, exchange and consumption can grow. In comparison, the notion of creative economy places a higher emphasis on creative industries and cultural products, which draw on aesthetic experience rather than scientific knowledge, in the realms of arts and cultural practices rather than research or technological development. In this sense, the creative economy refers to the linkage between 'culture' and 'economy', i.e., turning cultural products and practices into economic assets and organizing a web of economic relationships around this nexus. One of its outcomes would be the commodification of cultural practices, in which many new activities are weighed not by their symbolic value in the society, as traditionally applied to many cultural activities, but by their monetary value in economic exchange. Meanwhile, commodification of symbols prioritizes their economic value, but cannot survive if they are devoid of other dimensions. The result is a multi-dimensional symbolic process, in which the monetary exchange considerations may grow to become more prevalent.

Around the world, the importance of creative and cultural industries has been recognized, particularly in terms of freedom of expression, cultural diversity and economic development. However, as UNESCO (2009) argues, 'Although the globalization of exchange and new technologies opens up exciting new prospects, it also creates new types of inequality'. Cultural products from the West have already spread around the world: books that are translated, languages that are learned everywhere, fashion, films and music that are exported to all nations. In this cultural centrality of the West, there is no significant change from the last century and earlier phases of globalization. The economic and military domination of the West since the beginning of the modern age had already turned it into the centre of cultural production in the world. The new global division of labour has changed the location of manufacturing industries, but not the cultural hegemony of the West. A key change has been the expansion of cultural and creative industries as an engine for economic development in the West, filling some of the void left by the relocation of the manufacturing industries, alongside and overlapping with the expansion of science and technology-based activities. The impact on the global consumers of these products, however, could be an erosion of cultural diversity and a widening gap between rich and poor countries. UNESCO argues that the only way to counteract the growing divide is through 'strengthening local capacities and facilitating access to global markets at national level by way of new partnerships, know-how, control of piracy and increased international solidarity of every kind' (UNESCO, 2009). In response, a UNESCO convention in 2005 was set up with the aim of strengthening the five interconnected processes of creation, production, distribution/dissemination, access and enjoyment of cultural expressions, as conveyed by cultural activities, goods and services.

Knowledge-intensive sectors

How is a knowledge economy structured, and which sectors belong to knowledge economy? In other words, which sectors of the economy are knowledge-based? This is partly due to the way data is collected, as large multi-sector and multi-location firms can fall into different categories and statistics. For example, in the US, industry statistics are collected for the firms based inside the country. So if a company designs and markets its products inside the country, but manufactures these products overseas and distributes them inside the country, it is counted as a wholesaler, which is very different from a firm that is solely engaged in wholesale. Or if some activities within a large firm are involved in innovation, they are not necessarily separated from the rest of what the firm, as a whole or that particular branch of the firm, does (Advisory Committee, 2008).

Knowledge-intensive services are at the core of the knowledge-based economy (Simmie and Strambach, 2006). An OECD list of knowledge-intensive industries, which account for 40% of GDP in the UK and France, includes high- and medium-tech manufacturing, finance, insurance, telecommunication, business services, education and health (Brinkley, 2006). The knowledge economy, however, is not limited to these industries; it includes cultural and creative industries, as well as many 'low-tech' industries that create and use practical knowledge. The absence of internal R&D in these industries, it is argued, does not mean that they do not contribute to the knowledge economy. The retail sector, which has particular significance for the urban environment, is not included in the knowledge-intensive industries, while it is a major player in the consumption-driven economic growth. This sector is a big user of ICT, accounting for a major part of improvement in US productivity over the past decade, through its high-performance workplace practices and intensive use of ICT (Brinkley, 2006: 14). The list of knowledge-intensive industries also excludes transport and construction, which are directly involved in the transformation of the urban environment, intensively using ICT, engaged in innovation and centrally involved in the debates about the development of a future low-carbon economy.

If the knowledge economy is driven by innovation in the two sectors of science/technology and arts/design, the question is: where do the other parts of the current service economies fit into this picture? Many activities become part of the knowledge-intensive processes through innovations of various kinds, which in part are helped by the application of ICT. In particular, the role of the finance industry should be noted, which is often included in the statistics of knowledge-intensive industries, and yet it is an industry that cannot be counted as a subcategory of sciences or arts. Alongside, and drawing on, the explosion in the use of ICTs, financial industries have been a driving force in globalization. Through creating an infrastructure that facilitates and speeds up the flow of capital around the world, finance has reconfigured the architecture of global economy. It came to find such a central role that its near collapse triggered a major crisis with far-reaching implications for the lives of many around the world. Knowledge may become a new form of capital, but it still needs to be converted to money if it is to find an economic character. Finance, therefore, is the elephant in the room when discussions of knowledge economy are conducted. It is the underlying framework, both generating the conditions for the production and application of knowledge, and benefiting from the outcome of the commercialization of knowledge (Martin, 1999).

The analysis of knowledge-based economy has often included the financial services as a key component. In the UK, where radical deindustrialization was followed by a considerable growth of financial industries, the 2008 financial crisis appeared to shake the foundations of the country's economy. In response, senior politicians from both sides of the political spectrum talked about the use of knowledge and skills as a remedy for economic problems. The then business secretary Peter Mandelson emphasized the need for policies to develop the creative industries and research intensive, high value-added manufacturing and services, where 'the generation, application and exploitation of knowledge are key to the creation of wealth' (quoted in Hayman, 2008).

In the strategic joint document produced by the new UK government, a coalition of Conservative and Liberal Democratic parties, no mention of knowledge economy was made. The new government promises to 'build a new economy from the rubble of the old' (HM Government, 2010: 7), an economy that is 'competitive' (p. 9), 'low carbon and eco-friendly' (p. 16), 'dynamic and entrepreneurial' (p. 31), and 'strong and innovative' (p. 31).The vision of the new government is that economic growth and innovation are driven by business, and the government's role is 'to take urgent action to boost enterprise, support green growth and build a new and more responsible economic model' (p. 9). The aim is 'to create a fairer and more balanced economy, where we are not so dependent on a narrow range of economic sectors, and where new businesses and economic opportunities are more evenly shared between regions and industries' (p. 9). Before coming to power, faced by the question about the loss of manufacturing industries and the crisis of the financial industries and worries about 'how Britain plc is going to earn its living in the future?' the Conservative Shadow Business Secretary Ken Clarke answered:

> Well you need in the modern world a diversified economy. We can't go back, so although we should have a bigger manufacturing sector and it's a pity that we've allowed it . . . to shrink as it has, you need a diversified economy, you've got to join the knowledge economy, you've got to aim at global markets.
>
> (BBC, 2009a).

In this answer, it seems that knowledge-based economy and global economy are conflated. In the context of the collapse of the financial industry, and the contribution it made to the economy after deindustrialization, the question that needs to be raised is: was it using knowledge or excessive risk, was it an instance of knowledge-based activity or greed? Can this global collapse indicate the end of knowledge economy, or demand a reformulation of the notion of knowledge and its use in the economy? Some policy-makers and commentators recommended strengthening the manufacturing industries as a possible response. However, these industries had already been in decline for a long time, and their revival in competition with the new industrial centres in Asian countries was not going to be easy. A generation ago, the crisis of the manufacturing industries had generated somewhat similar soul-searching questions. The rise of manufacturing industries two centuries ago had facilitated new methods of production and consumption, which in time changed the world in significant ways. With their decline, what was to be done next? How could the industrial economies find new activities for their mass of workers? The partial answer at the time had been the growth of service industries, of which finance was a major player. Now with the near collapse of the financial industry, which was causing a serious global recession, what was to be done next?

The financial crisis that shook the world in 2008 generated many debates about what had caused it and anxieties about the shape of the future after the storm. Was the crisis a sign of the end of capitalism or just a routine market adjustment, 'just another burst bubble' (Jenkins, 2008)? This was, however, the most serious crisis of capitalism since the Great Crash of the 1930s, suggesting a deeper problem; it was branded the end of 'capitalism as we know it' (Buiter, 2008). 'The old model is tarnished', announced the editor of the *Financial Times*, conducting a debate on the future of capitalism (Barber, 2009: 3). The financial industry had come to be the infrastructure of the global economy and the linchpin of some national economies. With its deep crisis, which required astronomical amounts of public funds to save the banks, what was going to be the next key economic activity in such economies?The early indicators do not show any structural change. Following the economic stimulus that saved the banks in many countries, pain seems to have been nationalized in the form of collective austerity, while gains have been privatized and internationalized in the form of new bonuses for bankers and profit for the international producers of consumer goods.

Highly skilled workers

It is equally difficult to define who can be a knowledge worker. Cognitive complexity and relationship to computers may be appropriate bases for identifying knowledge workers, but statistics for this classification are not available at large scale. One definition includes the top three standard occupational classifications: managers, professionals and associate professionals. This accounted for about 42% of all employment in the UK in 2006, up from 31% in 1984 and predicted to reach 45% by 2014, while in this period there was a continuous fall in low-skilled, manual and administrative jobs (Brinkley, 2006: 18). Another, more broadly defined, version of knowledge workers calls them the creative class, i.e., 'professionals whose primary responsibilities include innovating, designing, and problem solving', who make up a third of the US workforce and earn half of all wages and salaries (Florida and Goodnight, 2008: 37). Florida calls this group 'an economic class', which is defined through how its members 'organize themselves into social groupings and common identities based principally on their economic function' (Florida, 2002: 68). However, we may wonder, how far is there any common identity among such a large group of people as a third of the US workforce? How far are their activities 'creative'? Is this a reflection of reality or a way of branding? Many workers in the knowledge economy sectors are indeed clerical staff whose routine work may not require any high-level skills or creativity, while much creativity may go into products that are not considered to be produced by the knowledge workers.

Some have argued that a concentration of creative people would pave the way towards economic regeneration and prosperity, and so a creative class is needed to spearhead prosperity (Florida, 2002). However, the problem of drawing the boundaries between who is creative and who is not, and whose contribution is valued more than the others, would need to be reconsidered. The proliferation of creative industries or activities surrounding science and technology may privilege large cities and particular people, but the rest of the population are not included in the celebration of the new activities. This may be one of the reasons why the emergence of these patterns of activity in the global economy has coincided with the intensification of social inequality. A new elite of professionals, whether creative artists or scientists and technologists, would emerge near the top of a highly stratified society, served by an army of service workers, many of whom are from an immigrant, semi-employed and permanently insecure population.

Even inside the sectors that are considered to be part of the knowledge economy, discrepancies and interdependencies are significant. Services that are offered locally are distinguishable from those that are tradable globally, even if they are both labelled the same. Although these levels are fully interdependent, the economic values of providing advice to a local school or to a rich government are not rewarded equally. A good example of this diversity is the salaries and bonuses of those who work in global investment banks, as compared to those who serve customers in local branches, even of the same bank. Although some salaries in some sectors are set by international standards, the majority of rewards are decided locally, according to the local conditions.

Furthermore, the knowledge economy is also driven by an army of workers with different skills, from health and security to leisure and entertainment, to support this upper tier of managers and professionals, but also to support one another. Police officers, fire fighters, teachers, nurses, restaurant workers, bus drivers, domestic helpers, childminders and many more are needed in an economy, and if they are the support infrastructure of an economy, they are as much part of the knowledge economy as the creative artists and computer scientists. Many of these workers may not technically be counted as knowledge workers, and their sectors may not be included as a knowledge economy sector, but without them the knowledge economy, or any other form of economy, is not possible. Furthermore, many of the factory workers in newly industrializing countrieswho produce the necessary material goods for the consumption of knowledge workers in rich countries, and the farmers who produce the food that travels half the world to feed the knowledge workers, are also part of this economy. The question of knowledge economy's sectors and skills, therefore, is not easily answered; it needs a wider embrace than normally assumed. The sectors and skills that make a knowledge economy are still open to question, although there is a tendency to see the knowledge economy conducted by high-skilled, white-collar workers, as distinguished from the low-skilled, blue-collar ones. But an economy needs a range of skills and services, which is delivered by different types of workers, who are for their part involved in the construction and maintenance of that economy.

Should gambling in the stock market, the making and display of a diamond-studded skull and the discovery of genome all be equally called knowledge activities? The wide range of these activities makes it hard to find a common identity for them. The question would then be whether it is necessary or reasonable to join them together at all, and if so, how can we find a common narrative that would bind these widely different activities together? One answer, which tends to prefer the scientific end of these activities, but is also warming up to its cultural side, is knowledge economy. But the problem of fitting in many types of activity, such as stock market gambling, under this broad banner cannot be easily solved.

Centres and peripheries

Can we be at once inside the knowledge economy and dreaming of entering it? Are these visions of knowledge economy at odds with one another? A solution to this apparent paradox would be that the development of knowledge economy would have to be a historical process, rather than a sudden change. In this historical process, the scale and speed of change would inevitably vary across different agents, activities and places.

The conditions across different sectors, different parts of the world, and even within a locality, vary; while some activities and places are leading the development of a knowledge-based economy, others are yet to enter it. By initiating the knowledge hubs and knowledge-based activities, other places aim at replicating the success of the pioneers in the knowledge economy, aiming to spread innovation inwards and become an active node in the global network of knowledge-based economies. No contradiction, therefore, can be found in the knowledge economy being a reality for some and a dream for others, even within a limited geographical area. So even the local authorities in an active knowledge hub may still see knowledge economy as a dream to realize, as it has not reached many sectors of the economy and spreading it wide and deep within a region would take a long time. The writers who attach a badge of knowledge society to our current age, therefore, appear to be making a generalization on the basis of some examples of a new phase in economic change, which is yet to spread. As it is often the case, the history of artistic styles and scientific paradigms may be written on the basis of the appearance of the pioneers on the horizon, rather than the diffusion of new ideas and practices to all corners of the world, which may never fully happen.

Spatial distribution of new ideas and practices may analytically be distinguished from the phase of innovation and the start of a new paradigm. Geographical spread, within an area and across the areas, nevertheless, is an essential part of the process of innovation itself, through which a phenomenon may be consolidated and new ideas and practices emerge. Spatiality, therefore, is inherent in the emergence and evolution of the knowledge-based economies. The answer to our question, is it reality or a dream, therefore, is that it is both: a reality for some and a dream for others, and many public and private agencies are hard at work to spread it far and wide.

The promotional literature on the subject tends to select some sectors of the economy that are often concentrated in large cities in major economies. The large metropolitan areas, where the head offices of large banks and major multinational corporations as well as a pool of highly skilled workers congregate, are taken to be the living embodiments of knowledge economy. Our broader understanding of the economy, however, would have serious implications for our analysis of the relations between economy and space, between knowledge economy and the city. It suggests that we should not only look for knowledge economy in elite centres, but should also take into account the army of support that make it possible for this economy to work. Knowledge economy should, therefore, be found, and developed, not only in the centres, but also in the peripheries, smaller cities and towns, and in the various parts of the large cities.

In peripheral regions where local resources have been considered too limited to lead to endogenous growth, the strategies for regional development have often focused on capturing resources from elsewhere, in the form of public funds and private investments. In Europe, public funds have for long been mobilized and transferred to these regions from national and European sources, which are used through relocation of public sector employment opportunities, infrastructure provision, social insurance, and provision of leverage to attract private investment. Public funds, however, are not sufficient for a region's economy to grow and become sustainable, so it has been necessary to formulate strategies to mobilize and attract private sector investment.

This has been articulated, consecutively, in two alternative strategies for regional growth and development: attracting mobile capital and attracting innovative people. The first alternative, which was followed in the UK for a long time and came to its culmination in the 1980s, emphasized the need to attract international enterprises that were searching for a pool of labour and a low cost of production in peripheral regions within the European market. For a while, it was thought that developing a branch economy, where mobile capital could energize and engage with the local land and labour, was the answer to the needs of de-industrializing regions. Increasingly, however, these regions are unable to compete in this way in a global marketplace where many places in emerging economies in Asia or Eastern Europe offer far lower costs of production than their Western

European competitors. The top of the global economic production hierarchy is occupied by the world cities, where global headquarters are based as centres of command and control of resources. As the lowest positions in the hierarchy are no longer available to de-industrialized regions, they have been pushed to the middle ground, to aspire to become, like many other medium-sized urban regions, the location of research and development that feed the global economy. This is the second alternative, which seems to be now being pursued by the regional development policies. Rather than, or in addition to, attracting mobile capital, the aspiration now is to nurture a knowledge economy for the region, moving away from a blue-collar to a white-collar economy. With the peripheral regions' limited endogenous capacity for research and development, however, the strategy requires attracting and retaining innovative people and firms who can strengthen the region's human capital and form a critical mass for innovation.

Knowledge economy is a concept that should be analysed against the backdrops of de-industrialization and globalization. As parts of Western economies have de-industrialized, the search is on to find an alternative economic base, and it is promised to be knowing, rather than making, that would form the basis of future economy. In a new global division of labour, it is hoped, the role of the Western economies would be in high-value knowledge-intensive soft products, in comparison to the newly industrializing countries, to which manual labour and manufacturing are now relocated. The term 'knowledge economy', therefore, works as a banner that is waved by politicians to mobilize opinion and show the possible road ahead, used as a promotional and inspirational motto rather than an actual description of current conditions. As such, it invites us to evaluate it critically, rather than accepting it without questioning.

The authors and organizations that have attempted to define the knowledge economy tend to identify its features as the dominance of theoretical knowledge, the spread of information and communication technologies, the significance of knowledge workers and the prevalence of intangible products. However, these are a rather limited range of features, as we will explore in this book. Knowledge economy tends to be defined in terms of the dominance of theoretical knowledge, hence giving priority to science and technology. Meanwhile, other forms of knowledge, from local and historic to practical, creative and cultural also play a significant role in the development of knowledge-based economic activity. Knowledge workers have been regarded as a new type of engine for the economy, without acknowledging the vast range of skills within their ranks and the important contribution made by other workers. A causal role is given to new information and communication technologies, without placing these technologies in the larger context of the emergence of a new international division of labour. The changing nature of products has been used to describe the knowledge economy as a weightless economy, without recognizing how the production of intangible products does not mean that tangible products are knowledge-free or no longer an essential part of the economy. These four themes (the nature of knowledge products, different forms of knowledge, role of technology and social organization of production) emerge as the defining features of knowledge economy, which help us structure the investigation.

Conclusion

Knowledge economy is an economy in which knowledge is used as an economic asset. On the basis of the definitions we have found so far, it is an economy in which knowledge is the driving force in shaping the economic output as well as the relations of production and consumption. For some, it is the label that describes the period after de-industrialization, designating the character of the post-manufacturing phase in capitalist industrial economies. For others, it describes the growing application of information and communication technologies in new areas of activity. For another group, it reflects the advances in scientific knowledge and its applications. For yet another group, it heralds the rise of white-collar professionals who drive the economy forward through creativity and innovation. Overall, knowledge economy is often associated with the spread of information and communication technologies, production of intangible products, the growth and development of new knowledge, and the concentrated presence of highly skilled workers.

These definitions, however, are partial and contested and so they need to be expanded and contextualized. Knowledge economy tends to be associated with the advances in science and technology, but we know that innovation and creativity in arts and culture also play a key role in the economy, as well as other forms of knowledge that are not counted at all. Economically useful knowledge can be scientific or cultural, and so the sectors of the economy and the types of workers engaged in knowledge-based activities are in practice much wider than often assumed. Not only do they include people and activities in complex cognitive and creative processes, but also those who make it possible for these processes to take place, in support infrastructures that provide the necessary goods and services from around the world. Not only do they include sectors that produce intangible goods, but also the tangible goods that are knowledge-rich, or goods that are consumed everyday and whose consumption is an engine for the economy. To explore these inherent but invisible dimensions of the knowledge economy, we need to go further. We need to study the changing nature of knowledge, the products of the knowledge economy, the technology it uses, and the social organization of work in this economy, so as to see what it means and its implications for the city. Before these stages, however, we need to develop a conceptual understanding of the city, economy and urban space.

3 Economy, society and space

If knowledge economy is an intensified application of knowledge in economic activity, and if it becomes so significant with which we identify the economy as a whole, then it is likely to transform the social and spatial dimensions of urban environments in important ways. If a new foundation for the economy is emerging, we should also be able to detect new social and spatial relations: how new concentrations and dispersions would be shaped; how relations of proximity and distance, new hierarchies and identities, new forms of stratification, integration and segregation may emerge; how the notions of here and there, simultaneity and sequence may be transformed. To search for this possible impact on urban space, we need to start by an initial investigation into the relationship between the economy, society and space, as played out in the city. In this chapter, we will look for a general theoretical basis for the analysis of urban space, which would help us engage with the particular relationship between knowledge economy and the city.

One of the first steps is to look for a theoretical framework for analysing space. This search leads us to a number of important questions that require answering. Is space a material object or a set of relationships? Is it fixed or subject to change? Can it be studied as a physical phenomenon on its own or does it have a social dimension? Or, vice versa, is it only a social phenomenon without a physical dimension? Is there a single correct way of understanding it or are there different perspectives into space? When confronting the diversity of perspectives and representations, how do we choose our own analysis? By finding some answers to these questions, in spatial arts and sciences as well as in other disciplines, we will be in a better position to study space. The investigation, therefore, is undertaken through four inter-related themes: the nature of space, its relations with time, its relations with society, and the question of materiality. A study of these themes shows the relational nature of space, its temporal dynamism, its social character, and embedded and embodied diversity of perspectives into its understanding. These provide elements of a theoretical perspective that I have called *dynamic multiplicity*, which could help us on the way.

Knowledge economy is a key theme of interest, and a growing number of books have been published on the subject. It is studied by various disciplines; in particular economists and knowledge management specialists are interested in analysing and managing it, though without much interest in its spatial manifestations (Kahin and Foray, 2006; Mokyr, 2002; Cunningham *et al.*, 2003). There are many studies on the impact of information and communication technologies on cities and societies (Dutton, 2005; Shapiro and Varian, 1999; Castells, 1996). There are different critiques of the subject from various angles, though not necessarily addressing its spatial implications (Barrera, 2007; Walby, 2007; Drahos and Braithwaite, 2002; Sörlin and Vessuri, 2007). Those who do pay attention to the spatial dimensions of knowledge economy are sometimes only interested in national levels or in particular places (Dahlman *et al.*, 2007; Shibata and Takeuchi, 2006; van den Berg, 2005). Spatial analysts of the subject, such as economic geographers, regional economists, and urban and regional planners, tend to keep their spatial focus at the regional scale, not showing much interest in the more detailed levels of urban space (Cooke and Piccaluga, 2006; Corey and Wilson, 2006; Dunning, 2000).

Cities as concentrations in space and time

The complexity of the city appears to be overwhelming, so that an encyclopaedia of the subject starts by asserting that, 'The term "city" means anything and everything' (Caves, 2005: xxi). Lewis Mumford started his classic study of urban history with the difficulty of defining a city: 'No single definition will apply to all its manifestations and no single description will cover all its transformations' (Mumford, 1961: 3). Nevertheless, the literature on the city is vast, indicating that authors and their readers must have a sense of what a city consists of, but while the everyday use of the term suggests a common understanding, technical and legal definitions of the city vary widely across countries and cultures.

The most widely used definition of the city refers to its size. The Oxford Dictionary defines the city as a large town, the same as a more specialist dictionary of human geography, which refers to the city as large urban places (Johnston *et al.*, 2000). The size of population that entitles a settlement with this designation, however, varies widely across different countries, and even between different provinces of a single country. Furthermore, there are variations between official designations and popular attributions. The US census uses the term for any urban place of 2,500 or more that is incorporated as a municipality (Gottdiener and Budd, 2005: 4), although in practice even smaller settlements may be called cities. In some countries a settlement needs to be much larger to be called a city, while in others the distinction between a village, a town and a city may not be held at all.

Inherent in the use of size as an indicator of city definition is its density. Speaking of a large town not only means a sizable population, it also means a concentration of this population in a relatively small area. Urban economists tend to define the city in terms of population density, as frequent contacts between economic activities are made possible in the proximity of many households and firms within a relatively small area. They define the urban, therefore, as a relatively small geographical area in which a large number of people are concentrated (O'Sullivan, 2003: 5–6). Density means a concentration of activities, which is taken to be a hallmark of all cities throughout history: 'All these cities, from the smallest to the largest, the earliest to the latest, have been great points of concentration and increasing density in their time and space' (Southall, 1998: 4). It was this concentration that was felt to be in danger with the advent of new transport and later information and communication technologies. 'The age of the city seems to be at an end,' wrote a commentator half a century ago (Martindale, 1966: 62). However, the continuing rates of urbanization, by the turn of the millennium, have changed the balance of global population in favour of cities, showing that the trend of concentrating people and objects in cities is by no means disappearing.

To size and density, Louis Wirth added a long recognized feature of cities: their heterogeneity. For him, cities are identified by size of population, density of settlement, and heterogeneity of inhabitants, and so cities are defined as 'relatively permanent, compact settlements of large numbers of heterogeneous individuals' (Wirth, 1964: 68). The diversity of urban population has always been a key feature of the city, going back to the very beginning of urban civilization ten millennia ago, when the division of labour made the emergence of cities possible. This was a feature well known in the ancient world, seeing cities as sites of a wide range of people with different skills and roles necessary for a community to live together (Aristotle, 1992). In our own time, with the intensified movement of people and the recognition of cultural and individual differences, diversity is no longer viewed only in functional terms, but nevertheless still a primary feature of urban life. It is now more common to acknowledge that one individual is different from another, and a concentration of people would inherently mean a concentration of different people.

The criteria of size, density and diversity would describe cities, but they would also describe ant hills and beehives, where a large number of ants or bees live in a relatively small area and are involved in different activities. We need, therefore, to go beyond these three indicators and search for other dimensions that may be used in defining the city as a human settlement. Economic activity is used by many urbanists to characterize the city: the medieval city was seen as a marketplace, where all of its spaces, from houses to streets as well as the marketplace, functioned as the places of trade (Saalman, 1968). The modern city was interpreted for its economic role as a location for manufacturing industries, or a mechanism for capital accumulation (Bater, 1980).

Urban economists relate the concentration of population in the city to the economies of scale. Some even insist that, 'if there were no economies of scale, there would be no cities' (O'Sullivan, 2003: 19). Concentration of economic production would reduce the costs and make it more efficient to produce goods and services. If the population were evenly spread, as Frank Lloyd Wright had advocated in his Broadacre city (Fishman, 1977), and if they lived with self-sufficiency, which Rousseau had praised in the life of villages (Cranston, 1968), there would be no need for cities. Indeed the radical critics of capitalism have seen the city as a concentration of privilege and therefore best to be dispersed, by force, as in the Soviet Union and China, and even by mass extermination, as practised by the Khmer Rouge in Cambodia. According to an economic interpretation, therefore, cities are concentrations that reflect the economies of scale, the sites of production around which workers cluster to minimize their travel costs, and related services emerge to support them. However, reducing the complex world of the city to its economic rationale would not be enough.

In defining the city, Max Weber (1966) added an organizational dimension to economic functions. For him the medieval city was a fusion between garrison and market, as reflected in the city wall and the marketplace, combining defensive and economic roles, within the context of corporate institutions and political and legal autonomy. The political organization of the city is one of its oldest features. Aristotle defined the city as an association (1992), where the term politics referred to the affairs of the city, the *polis*. In the Roman world the word *civitas* primarily referred to the body of citizens, and the term city mainly indicated citizenship and the membership of a political community. It was only later that the city was equated with *urbs*, i.e., the place occupied by the community. The political significance of the city, however, has radically declined, as the rise of the nation-state moved the level of political authority to a higher level, even if some of that significance has been reclaimed after the advent of globalization and some decline in the powers of the nation-state.

The distinction between *civitas* and *urbs* refers to a distinction between the social and physical dimensions of the city, as we will see later in this chapter. A concentration of people would require a range of physical objects and structures to support and shelter them. The city therefore is an agglomeration of people as well as of the objects that should make the life of the urban society possible and comfortable. Houses and roads are distinguishable in the remains of the earliest cities, and later cities show economic, political and cultural institutions housed in palaces, temples, markets, offices, factories, restaurants, theatres,meeting places, etc., all filled with smaller objects used for various purposes.

Beyond political and economic dimensions, we can also see a cultural dimension, which is reflected in many aspects of urban life. In the ancient Greek world, cities were taken to be 'the symbol and the outward evidence of a superior civilization', as compared with those civilizations that did not produce cities (De la Blache, 1926: 472). A symbolic value is still held in many countries, including the UK, where a city status is conditional upon acquiring a royal charter, which comes with a prestige to which many towns aspire. Historically this status was marked by a cathedral, but this is no longer a necessary basis for being granted this status. According to the Department for Constitutional Affairs (2002):

> City status is a rare mark of distinction granted by the Sovereign and conferred by Letters Patent. It is granted by personal Command of the Queen, on the advice of Her Ministers. The grant of city status is purely honorific; it confers no additional powers or functions on the town.

There are no set criteria that would automatically turn a UK town into a city, as this is considered to be negative and downgrading: 'City status is not, and never has been, a right which can be claimed by a town fulfilling certain conditions' (ibid).

Becoming a city is a competitive process, in which 'applications are considered on their individual merits', and if specific criteria were set that would enable a town claiming city status as of right, the fear is that it 'might devalue the honour' (ibid). However, the main factors in a town that the ministers take into account when advising the monarch include 'notable features', which would include regional and national significance; 'historical (including Royal) considerations'; and 'a forward-looking attitude' (Department for Constitutional Affairs, 2002).

Defining the city by what people do within it needs to be supplemented by the role it plays in relation to its surroundings, or to the wider world. The city then becomes a bridge between different places and activities, between different periods of time. Its location and permanence give it a spatial and temporal context, without which its meaning would be lost. It is a singularity that bends space and time. According to one urbanist:

> A study of the growth of cities in the past shows that what made the seed spring to life and guaranteed its growth, was usually an obstacle. At borders of mountain-barriers, at river-crossings, on the edge of deserts, on the seacoast, in short, wherever it is necessary to halt and to find new methods of transportation, there is opportunity for city growth.
>
> (De la Blache, 1926: 473)

This may indicate the location of the city on the edges of territories, but cities also grew at crossroads. Medieval cities grew around crossroads, as places where important roads met, facilitating transport, communication and trade (Platt, 1976; 1990). The cities' major spaces had grown, since ancient times, out of the crossroads inside the city. As the Renaissance architectural theorist Alberti puts it, 'a forum is but an enlarged crossroad, and a show ground [which included theatre, circus, and gladiatorium] nothing but a forum surrounded with steps' (Alberti, 1988, IIX, 6, p. 262).

This may be interpreted by economists as the significance of a location in which economies of scale with regards to transportation would entail the establishment and growth of a trade city. Similarly, manufacturing cities are interpreted as having developed as a result of scale economies in manufacturing production (O'Sullivan, 2003). Many successful cities have combined both these scale economies of transportation and production, combining trade and production, and consolidating a diverse economy that can be resilient in the face of various threats to its economic foundations.

As relationships between different parts of the world have intensified, especially in the period of globalization, the nodal role of the city has become stronger. The city is not a self-contained entity that is cut off from the rest of the world, but one that can only make sense in relation to other places and activities. Cities are permanent but dynamic concentrations of diverse people, life forms and objects that draw on and relate to one another within the city, and others beyond its boundaries, as well as relating to the past and future. Cities are embedded concentrations in space and time, of wealth and power, which now house the majority of the world's population, related to one another through multiple linkages, while internally fragmented and stratified along the lines of division of labour and its subsequent social and economic diversity.

Space of material objects and relationships

If cities are concentrations in space and time, a key question to ask is about the nature of space: does it exist as a separate entity? The primary debate about the nature of time and space is whether they exist as independent substances or whether they are merely relations between objects and events. This is a debate that goes back to the ancient world and has consistently been a key theme in philosophy (Blackburn, 1996). The attempts to define space can be split into three periods: common sense, Euclidean abstraction, and post-Euclidean relativity (Cornford, 1976). At an early period of common sense, which prevailed in most ancient civilizations, space was the place that bodies occupied in the world; space was therefore finite and relative. With the development of abstract methods of thought in ancient Greece, space was turned into an abstract construct. As consolidated by Euclid, the universe was a limitless void and space was infinite, without any centre or circumference. This abstract space was 'an immeasurable blank field, on which the mind could describe all the perfect figures of geometry, but which had no inherent shape of its own' (Cornford, 1976: 5). The scientists of the modern age embraced this conceptualization of space, using it as a basis for modern physics. For modern philosophy, a new ontological problem emerged, which revolved around the existence of Euclidean space (Torretti, 1984: 25).

The famous formulation of abstract space in modern philosophy (Smart, 1979: 5) was by Descartes, who was also an accomplished mathematician. According to Descartes (1968: 56), space was 'a continuous body, or a space extended indefinitely in length, width and height or depth, divisible into various parts, which could have various figures and sizes and be moved or transposed in all sorts of ways'. Newton used this abstract concept of space in the development of his physics, according to which fixed mechanical rules governed the universe. The dominant formulation of space between the seventeenth and nineteenth centuries came to be 'continuous, infinite, three-dimensional, homogeneous and isotropic', as any of its points resembled any other and it had no preferred direction (Poincare, quoted in Torretti, 1984: 25). This space was imagined as 'an enormous stage, across which pass the events that make up the universe: the enduring stars, the brief particles, ourselves. Inside this box everything has its position, its path, and its time, and the business of the scientist is to give a rational account of it all' (Gray, 1989: 176).

A parallel notion of absolute time also emerged with the advent of the modern scientific revolution. The invention of mechanical clocks made more detailed measurement of time possible, hence changing the concept of time altogether. Time changed from being discontinuous and cyclical to being uniform, continuous and linear. Galileo represented time as a geometrical straight line, while Newton thought of absolute time as an independent entity flowing at a consistent rate. Newton wrote in 1687, 'Absolute, true and mathematical time, of itself and from its own nature, flows equably without relation to anything external' (Whitrow, 1972: 100).

An early objection to this interpretation was made by Leibniz, who believed absolute space and time to be merely imaginary:

> I hold space to be something merely relative, as time is; that I hold it to be an order of coexistences, as time is an order of successions. For space denotes, in terms of possibility, an order of things which exist at the same time, considered as existing together, without enquiring into their manner of existing. And when many things are seen together, one perceives that order of things among themselves.
>
> (Leibniz, 1979: 89)

Space and time, therefore, did not exist in themselves; they were merely relationships. Although disagreeing with Leibniz, Kant went further in relativizing time and space, interpreting them as aspects of our perception. Space and time were not substances or relationships; they were merely representations of appearances, which 'cannot exist in themselves, but only in us' (Kant, 1993: 61). Space and time were 'the necessary conditions of all our external and internal experience'; they were 'merely subjective conditions of all appearances, and not things in themselves' (Kant, 1993: 64).

The paradigms of absolute space and time were fundamentally changed by the nineteenth century non-Euclidean geometry and early twentieth century relativist physics; they were finally dethroned by Einstein's theory of relativity, which showed the dependence of space on mass and its motion, and how length and duration are relative to the motion of the observer (Nerlich, 1994: 267–8; Jammer, 1954). Challenges to the metaphysical interpretation of space and time have heralded two new developments that dominated the twentieth century: emergence of observer-dependent interpretations of space and time, and attempts at integrating time and space.The abstract paradigms have, nevertheless, survived, to the extent that Albert Einstein, while promoting his theory of relativity, believed that both concepts of space are 'free creations of the human imagination, means devised for easier comprehension of our sense experiences' (Einstein, 1954: xiv).

In our analysis of the urban space, however, we need to go beyond this historic dichotomy. A metaphysical concept of space as an invisible substance is not tenable, but neither is the notion of relations on their own. These relations are embedded in particular contexts, and it would be impossible to imagine them to be decontextualized as if existing outside a material and social dimension. The focus on space as pure relations could be as metaphysical as the focus on the space as a substance, and many analysts of space seem to fall into this trap, appearing to deny the materiality and sociality that are inherent in this relationship. The relational interpretation needs to be analysed and broadened, as we need to be clear about what these relations are. They are not relations *per se* and existing independently, but relations between objects (animate and inanimate), and so any conceptualization of urban space needs to include both these objects and their relations. To understand space, we cannot see it only as relations, but we should see it as a collection of objects and their relations. In this sense, the urban space is a collection of people, life forms and inanimate objects and the variety of relations that can be identified between them, relations that can range from events and processes to perceptions and feelings, which can lead to the generation of new objects and relations. This collection of objects and relations, however, is not fixed and unchanging, which is why the dimension of time also needs to be taken into account.

Temporal change and transformation

As we have seen, space and time have both been envisaged as abstract or relational. However, space and time have only limited parallels: it is possible to move from one location to another in space, but not from one time to another; the distinction between two directions in space, like left and right, appears trivial, while the distinction between past and future is not; we are surrounded by space, but can only experience time piece by piece (Coveney and Highfield, 1991: 24). Each has its own facilitating and limiting features: in space, we can change our location and potentially be anywhere else, but in time we cannot change our time and be anytime else. In time, we can occupy exactly the same time as anyone else, while in space two objects cannot occupy the same place; so ownership and control of space can exclude others from using that space. Ownership of time, however, is not as straightforward: paid employees who sell their time in exchange for money have some control over their time, but if they sell their home, they no longer have any control over its space.

As we shall see in later chapters, attempts to overcome these spatial and temporal limitations are a major engine of economic transformation. As time is limited but space more plentiful, technological innovations are promoted that would speed up the pace of activities, while economic activities are spread to new locations to facilitate simultaneity, and hence new ways of using the time available. By changing the social organization of work, transforming spatial relations and intensifying temporal beats, what we know as cities, how they are organized and run, would consequently change. Globalized economy transforms space and time, using space to overcome the limitations of time; this is made possible through the use of new technologies that help create a new global division of labour. But the ultimate asset is still time, hence the accelerated speed of life to intensify how it is used.

While space and time have always been analysed separately, the language that has been used to describe them has built bridges between the two, spatializing time or temporalizing space, as exemplified by using 'long' or 'short', and 'behind' or 'ahead' to describe both time and space, which can be found even in more systematic attempts, such as John Locke's definition of time: 'Duration is fleeting extension' (Locke, 1979: 103).From the beginning of the twentieth century, this fusion of time and space found both a scientific and an artistic character (Madanipour, 2007a).

Around the beginning of the twentieth century, the new artistic movements of cubism and futurism integrated time and space into one another by depicting people and objects from several angles and in movement. The traditional, static methods of depiction, which since the Renaissance were based on perspective, were shattered and space and time were integrated through motion. The modernist movement in architecture that followed was inspired by the new technologies of ships, trains and cars; it helped change the urban space, and with it the conception and experience of space, which changed from slow movement of pedestrians to fast vehicular movement. The modernist art and architecture detached objects and buildings from their contexts, allowing the observers to move around them and see them from different perspectives, heralding the arrival of multiple and complex geometries (Giedion, 1967; Madanipour, 1996; 2007a).

This artistic movement coincided with the attempts in science to integrate space and time. Einstein's special theory of relativity related time and space together, with the consequence that the notion of space-time would be needed (Smart, 1979: 10). In 1908, Minkowski argued that 'No-one has yet observed a place except at a time, nor yet a time except at a place,' and so it was necessary to have a complete integration of space and time, to see a four-dimensional world, where 'three dimensional geometry becomes a chapter in four dimensional physics' (quoted in Gray, 1989: 185–86). As he put it, 'Henceforth space by itself, and time by itself, are doomed to fade away into mere shadows, and only a kind of union of the two will preserve an independent reality' (Minkowski, 1979: 297).

This attempt at integration generated some controversies about conceptualizing the world as three-dimensional or four-dimensional. The 4D view held that everything exists in time and no understanding would be complete if this temporal dimension was not included. But this meant that everything was continuously unfolding and never complete: human beings could never become wholes, as they were living their lives, while cities could never be understood in their totality, as they would continue to change and unfold. At best, we can grasp a snapshot of this continuum, knowing that it is a mere slice of a process, seen from an angle and from a particular vantage point. We can look forward and backward in time to see what it was like before or what it is likely to be in the future. The problem of identity, however, emerges, as to whether what we are observing now is the same thing as it was yesterday, a year ago, or a generation ago (Madanipour, 2009; Markosian, 2002).

Some critics of modernity have tended to emphasize simultaneity and spatiality to counter the temporality of historical processes that dominated social analysis. For example, to spot gaps and discontinuities, Foucault (1989) focused on depicting a landscape of diversity and dispersion, identifying rules that governed discourse, rather than telling a historical story of how one thing led to another. This was a critique of the privilege that was given to time since the nineteenth century, arguing for a shift of paradigm from time to space (Flynn, 1994: 40ff). Simultaneity on its own, however, appears to be static, only showing a picture of a co-presence at a particular moment in time, unable to account for the process of change that each undergoes. It is necessary, therefore, to include a temporal dimension in the analysis of space, as spatial objects and relations are subject to continual change. To understand a phenomenon, as Aristotle had stressed, there is a need to find out how it emerged, developed and changed to become what it is now (Aristotle, 1992; Bottéro *et al.*, 2000); in other words, finding out about how it was made, exchanged and used (Lefebvre, 1991).

Furthermore, we now know that, as will be discussed later, the late capitalist economy has used spatial dispersion, as combined with organizational and technological innovation, to expand the global workforce and facilitate a more condensed use of time. Transition to space has not avoided the tyranny of time, which always feels to be the more limited of the two, while both are ultimately limited in availability and reach. Here too, therefore, we need to go beyond an opposition between space and time, and beyond a perspective that privileges one over the other. Without taking time into account, our understanding of space would be severely limited, as indeed the understanding of time would be limited without a spatial dimension. As the focus of our investigation is spatial change, this would suggest investigating space through its temporal dynamics, taking into account from daily routines to historic periods. Looking at a snapshot is not enough and we need to see the phenomena in their temporal context.Dynamic multiplicity combines the dynamism of time and spatiality of the material world, but it also needs to address the social world.

The material and the social

Studying a city's economy investigates the production, distribution and consumption of goods and services in that city, which cannot be separated from studying where these activities take place and how they relate to one another. The notion of separating the economic and social dimensions of cities from one another may be appealing to analysts, who can then focus on particular aspects of the urban life, but in practice these dimensions are closely intertwined. How people earn a living and how they live are not fully unrelated issues. In the same way, the question of where they live and work is closely related to these questions of how they earn a living and how they live. In other words, the social, economic and spatial dimensions of cities are intimately linked. The urban economy shapes the urban space, and in return is shaped by it. This suggests that if we witness a major change in the economy, it is likely that we see a corresponding change in society and space. What are the ways in which the relationship between space, society and economy are manifested and how should they be analysed?

The answer to the question '*what* is knowledge economy?', therefore, cannot be separated from the answer to the question '*where* is knowledge economy?' The location of and relations between various activities that make up the knowledge economy are significant features of the knowledge economy. Even though it is called an economy that produces intangible products and is located in cyberspace and in the interstices of physical objects, it is ultimately an economy based on the production and consumption of material wealth, conducted by embodied human beings living in physical spaces, consuming material products even if produced elsewhere and exchanging material signs.

The collection of objects, their relations and their temporal change are all situated in, and help constitute, a social space. Rather than a thing, Lefebvre (1991: 83) writes, space is 'a set of relations between things (objects and products)', as 'The Thing . . . never quite becomes absolute, never quite emancipates itself from activity, from use, from need, from "social being".' In other words, the meaning of objects and their relationships can only make sense in a social context, in which we assign this meaning through collective symbolization. A physical object such as a chair, or an institutional phenomenon such as marriage, can only have meaning when we agree to accept them as such (Searle, 1995).

Space, therefore, is a collection of people, objects and their relationships. As these objects only find meaning through social relationships, their materiality cannot be separated from their sociality. It is important to keep coming back to this integration of the physical and the social, avoiding the mistake of seeing only one or the other as the sole feature of space. Some commentators insist that space is not physical; they appear to equate the spatial with the social. They appear to think of spatial relations as being the sphere of activities but not of physical objects, as if devoid of physicality. This point of view, however, is in danger of being an idealist interpretation of social relations with an inherent Cartesian dualism.

There is an old criticism that keeps being repeated against architects and some planners and geographers that they are interested in the physical dimensions of the spatial world, as if this is a reductionism through which reality is undermined. This is a manifestation of Cartesian dualism, through which physical and the mental are separated, privileging the former over the latter, a dualism that has been criticized ever since Descartes but one that appears to be knowingly or unknowingly adopted by these critics. The ability to combine the spatial and the social would avoid the urban version of the problem of mind–body dualism. In philosophy, the problem of a full separation between the body and mind, an ancient distinction often described as Cartesian dualism, has continuously created the problem of deciding on the nature of the relationship between the body and mind, between the material and the immaterial (Descartes, 1968; Cottingham, 1992; Searle, 1999). In urban studies, this is reflected in the distinction between the social and the spatial, seeing a split between the people and the objects. The problem then becomes deciding on their relationship, resulting either in an idealist interpretation of spatial relations, in which physical objects do not count, or in a naïve materialist interpretation of spatial relation, in which people are the same as objects, all material bodies with similar levels of agency. To go beyond this trap, dynamic multiplicity would allow a socio-spatial understanding to emerge, in which the agency of human beings only makes sense in the context of their own materiality and that of the context in which they live.

An analysis of the city cannot separate action from object. Actions are themselves material processes played out in space and time, as human beings cannot live in the absence of materiality. Material objects are also the target and vehicle of many of our actions: we create them, transform them, find meaning in them, inhabit in them, use them, and exchange them. The idea of a city, and an economy, that lacks materiality is merely an idealist notion. The spatial includes a material dimension, both in the bodies of the social agents and in the physical environment in which they live and relate to one another. If the spatial and the social are one and the same, what is the need for using the term spatial? By imagining the social to be non-physical, the analysis would risk denying the materiality of the social and psychological processes.

The ontology of the social

A question that needs addressing is the relationship between knowledge economy and social ontology. Depending on how we analyse society, we can then investigate social change with the rise of the knowledge economy. The ways that the social structure and relationships are likely to change in a new economy would be closely intertwined with how the spatial structure and relations change. If social change coincides with economic change, which is highly likely, then spatial change would be expected to be an integral part of this change. The first task, however, is to see how the society is structured and how it changes. Since the emergence of large cities in the modern period, a number of theories have been advanced that try to describe the way society is organized: is it formed of individuals, households, social groups, networks, tribes and communities, or classes? Depending on the way we analyse society, our analytical and normative notions of social and spatial change would be different.

A long-lasting analysis of society sees it as made of distinctive social classes, originated in the historic systems of slavery, serfdom and caste that subdivided the society into a hierarchical and fixed order. Compared with these ancient and rigid systems of stratification, the notion of social class is a more flexible subdivision of society, but one that lingers and is difficult to change, for some only through violent revolutions. On the basis of this thinking, if knowledge production is to replace manufacturing of physical objects as a new basis for the economy, it would be expected to have its own social class system, in the same way that the middle and the working classes defined the nineteenth- and twentieth-century industrial societies. If industrial capitalism created the bourgeoisie and the proletariat, what would be the social classes associated with knowledge capitalism, if such a system is coming to be born?

Inherent in the notion of social class has been the concept of conflict, which some have thought would solve social problems through binary dynamics. Marxian analysis also projected a new phase in history, in which the industrial working class would take over from the middle class through revolutions, a scenario that was induced in the communist regimes that emerged in the twentieth century. The demise of these regimes and the de-industrialization of major parts of the Western capitalist economies, however, appear to have diminished the size and strength of the industrial working class, no longer considered to be a force for revolution.

The predominant interpretation of history, influenced by Marx, has argued that the nineteenth century was marked by two revolutions: the French Revolution and the Industrial Revolution, bringing the middle class to the centre in Europe as liberal revolutionaries that became the driving forces of change. In this change, the aristocracy that was associated with the feudal mode of production was being replaced by a new class linked with industrial capitalism. This version of history, however, has been doubted by historians who have rewritten the history of the century as a more gradual change. According to these historians, the French Revolution was a political revolution against rather than for capitalism; and the Industrial Revolution was a more gradual process rather than a sudden move. As a result, these revisionist historians either interpret class as a linguistic category or an ethnographic one (Harrison, 2005). The concept of class is widely used in everyday language, especially in class-conscious societies such as the UK. The labels of middle class and working class are continually used, but the lines of distinction are more blurred than ever before. In this context, it becomes increasingly difficult to accept the rise of a new 'creative class' that is markedly distinctive from the industrial society's middle-class white-collar workers. If we compare the so-called creative class with the earlier notions of the middle class, we may have serious difficulty distinguishing them, and so we cannot argue for the emergence of a new social class as compared with the old. If anything, more distinctions may be found between the old and new working classes, whereby continuity and self-organization are replaced with precarious and fragmented conditions.

An integral part of the social class analysis has been the analysis of the family. The shape of the modern family is closely related to its economic role, which is why it has been a battleground of conflicting social forces for more than two centuries.As the rise of industrial capitalism uprooted people from their historic contexts and brought them together in large modern cities, it brought about a degree of social fluidity and unpredictability that was hitherto unknown. Combined with poverty and misery, these new social conditions occasionally erupted in urban revolutions, causing fear and anxiety among the elite. Away from the historically evolved social contexts and with the disappearance of the agrarian extended family, the nuclear family became the key institution in the new industrial capitalist society. While family had lost its role as a unit involved in economic production, it was now the centre of social reproduction.

A battleground was formed around the idea of the family. For Marx and Engels, the bourgeois family was the source of all evil, the original place in which the desire for private property took shape and where unfair gender relations were set up. For them, the best solution was to abolish the family, abolish social classes and reshape the society in utopian communes. Meanwhile, the household continues to be one of the cornerstones of middle-class thinking about society. Conservative political parties and governments have always placed a special emphasis on the family as a safe location for the reproduction of traditional values. The nuclear family, however, has been changing in reality.

During the past century, the average size of the household in the US has almost halved (from 4.60 in 1900 to 2.59 in 2000). The shape of the household has also changed considerably, as indicated by the proportion of married couples to the total number of households (from 80% in 1910 to 52% in 2002), showing a stronger downward trend, especially after the Second World War (when it was still 78% in 1950) (US Census Bureau, 2010a). In parallel, these households have become more urbanized (from 40 percent of the population in 1900 to 79 percent in 2000), and more mobile (where in 2000, 55.5 percent of occupied housing units had two or more cars, as compared to 21.5 percent in 1960) (US Census Bureau, 2010b), which runs in parallel with the growth of suburbanization in the post-war US.

The decline of the manufacturing industries and the transformation of the family have both created unease about conceptualizing society as being made of classes or families. In their place, social analysts have envisaged society to be formed of groups, structures, subcultures or networks. In many social studies, different features are used to classify social groups, such as gender, ethnicity and age, as well as income, employment, immigration, education, crime, housing and lifestyle, which may become the key indicators of the social structure and conditions. These features are used as a basis for data collection and classification that can be measured through statistics (e.g., Hughes, 2009). Classifying the members of a society into groups tends to be a functional analysis, enabling researchers to quantify and compare these features and functions. Most people, however, have a combination of different features and so they will fall into more than one group. This functional description of the society, however valuable, remains limited in its ability to explain these features or their relationship with other features.

There are some similarities between analysing society as a collection of overlapping social groups or a collection of communities and tribes, although they may be different in their methodological outlooks, in many instances they do overlap, as exemplified in the work of Pierre Bourdieu (2000; 2004). Bourdieu's concept of field appears to be a reworking of the concept of community (Tönnies, 1957), of the Hegelian notion of social context that challenged the Kantian idea of individual autonomy. The development of multiple links between individuals and groups leads to the formation of tribes, which may be useful in analysing subcultures and communities of interest or practice, who may be coherent in some respects but divergent in others (Maffesoli, 1996). Some have tried to overcome the dichotomy by focusing on the interplay of the context and the individual actor, linking the structure and agency, to avoid the methodological problems that this distinction may cause (Hollis, 2002). So social processes are seen as an interaction between agency and structure (Giddens, 1984), an interface between habitus and field (Bourdieu, 2000), between actors and networks (Latour, 2005).The idea of society as a collection of overlapping subcultures may explain some social phenomena that have the resemblance of a distinctive identity, such as professions, academic disciplines or even cultural tastes, but how far is it useful when analysing widespread phenomena such as the emergence of a new economy?

The analysis of society as a network of actors is also limited in its explanatory strength. It tends to spatialize social relations, as if merely mapping the way people and objects relate to one another in an interpretive framework. This morphological approach may describe these relationships, but is not capable of differentiating between them, or explaining their behaviour, as it avoids engaging in a discussion of causality. The network analysis is inspired by technological metaphors and market operations, but it can at best show that members of a society are related to one another, and to the physical world around them. As such, its theoretical power may not go beyond stating the obvious links between the different constituent parts of society. Many have used the notion of network society, which has been inspired by the phenomenal growth of the information and communication technologies (Castells, 1996). But describing the spread of these technologically mediated relationships would not be able to explain or understand the dynamics of these relationships and what they mean for human beings involved in them. In particular, it appears to assume the disappearance of hierarchies and inequalities by ignoring them. In its desire to avoid binary and conflictual explanations, it loses its capacity for explanation by denying the power imbalances in the network.

All these forms of social analysis are attempts at pattern finding, aiming towards a way of understanding the patterns of differentiation that goes beyond family and class. Groups, tribes, structures and networks all try to say something about the social relations that link people to one another, attributing them with the membership of larger social patterns. The empirical categories of individual and family are superimposed by a series of interpretive categories that try to describe the way society is organized and how it might change. The category of class may be too crude as a tool to describe the social scene, with its increased diversity of cultural forms. The categories of function, group and subculture may also remain limited in their coverage and explanation, but each in its way is useful in finding distinctive patterns that would link individuals and make sense of the patterns they form in society. What remains in all these different economic formations, however, is the problem of hierarchy and inequality, which is a result of the widening gap between the different parts of diverse societies. Is this growth in social inequality and differentiation in lifestyles and consumption patterns the change that can be associated with knowledge-based economies?

Embedded and embodied perspectives in social space

A social phenomenon such as a city is a complex world. The nature of discipline-based rationalist analysis, however, is often reductive, so that we tend to view this complexity only through a particular, but anonymous and generalized, perspective. We may analyse matters to represent a particular interest, or are only using the language and techniques of a particular discipline. Examples of such analysis include those in the urban development process that represent the concerns of regulators or producers or users of the built environment, without reference to others, e.g., studying from the viewpoint of authorities without those of developers, residents of neighbourhoods and community organizations. In reality, however, a city, or any other complex social phenomenon, goes beyond such simplicity: it is a world of multiplicity of agencies and contexts, and it is important to capture this multiplicity in any study of the phenomenon.

We are warned by Nietzsche that any rational analysis is an interpretation from a viewpoint, and so some analysts have concluded that we cannot go beyond perspectivism. To counter the effects of entrapment in a single perspective, however, Nietzsche invites us to 'employ a *variety* of perspectives and effective interpretations in the service of knowledge' (quoted in Schacht, 1996: 159). As he puts it, 'the *more* affects we allow to speak about one thing, the *more* eyes, different eyes, we can use to observe one thing, the more complete will our "concept" of this thing, our "objectivity", be' (ibid).

Phenomenology, following Descartes, emphasized the significance of the first person view of the world (Schutz, 1962; Descartes, 1968). While individuals are bound by their own perspective, they have always been able to see things from another person's perspective, which is the foundation of their ability to sympathize and communicate with others. At the same time, many inquiries have depended on a third-person view of the world, in which a knowledge of phenomena can be acquired (Searle, 1995). Dynamic multiplicity is the attempt to go beyond our limited perspectives, appreciate the multiplicity and complexity of views into any social phenomenon, and try to understand as many perspectives as possible. We may wish to support one viewpoint against others, but we need to do so knowingly and understand the viewpoints of others.

Social fields tend to develop limited perspectives of their own, and it is through the agency's interaction with this context that social phenomena are shaped and transformed (Bourdieu, 2000; Giddens, 1984). Disciplinary focus has imposed limitations on how to analyse social phenomena, for example whether phenomena should be considered primarily as social or spatial; whether it is economics or culture that should be the target of analysis, whether it is the struggle for recognition or redistribution that help its development (Fraser and Honneth, 2003). A better understanding of social phenomena, however, can be built at the intersection of these fields, where political economy and cultural analysis meet (Lefebvre, 1991; Madanipour, 1996).

We need to go beyond merely capturing the range of voices; we need to make distinctions between them and acknowledge how some are more powerful than the others. Network theories that appear to insist on spatial interpretation of social relations, therefore, can map out the relations, but not be able to show the underlying stratification or the position of the narrator in the stories told about this landscape. In an analysis of space, it is necessary to find out what stories remain hidden, untold and unheard. Seeing the visible is essential, but so is acknowledging the unseen and the invisible. Capturing the voices and surveying the landscape are needed, but searching for the excluded and the marginal would also be equally essential. Indeed, it is through the untold stories that the narrated ones can be judged. Understanding the dispersion and multiplicity of the phenomena, and the conditions that made them possible, is necessary. We have to see the conditions for the existence of these perspectives, and how they are set within, and made possible through, particular circumstances (Foucault, 1989). But we cannot wish away the hierarchies and stratifications by searching for the horizontal and forgetting the vertical relations of power.

Dynamic multiplicity, therefore, is the ability to see things in their place, through their change, and from more than one perspective, either that of individuals and agencies, or of the fields and disciplines involved in the inquiry, or of the interaction between the agencies and contexts. Each of these multiple agencies and contexts, as well as the social space in which they interact, will have their own dynamics of change and are subject to individual as well as shared spatial and temporal conditions. Dynamic multiplicity looks for understanding the phenomenon as embodied and embedded in its material and social context, as evolving through its temporal transformation, and as seen from a variety of perspectives set within a social space. Investigating the urban space would multiply the number and range of these perspectives and the complexity of the context.

The point of paying attention to this plurality of perspectives is not merely to depict a landscape of ideas and voices, but to make visible that which remains invisible. Powerful voices are often heard loud and clear, as they are able to articulate their interests and claims over space. It is the voice of those unable to do so that needs to be also heard and taken into account. Dynamic multiplicity, therefore, means paying particular attention to those aspects of the phenomenon that are not visible, those voices that are not heard and the temporal dynamism through which change unfolds in time. To find out about the spatial implications of the knowledge economy, we need to see in what ways it changes the location and movement of activities and physical objects.

Location, distance and context

The notions of space and place have long been discussed in spatial arts and sciences such as geography, planning and architecture. The humanistic interpretations of space have associated the relational space with the concept of place, using cultural and emotional dimensions of spatial experience to attach meaning to space. The positive science interpretations, however, have looked for aspects of space that can be measured, hence using the notions of distance and location.

According to the philosopher John Locke, space is 'the relation of distance between any two bodies or points', while place is the 'relative position of anything' (Locke, 1979: 101), definitions that are somewhat similar to those by his contemporary Leibniz, which were mentioned earlier. In the economic interpretations of space, these two concepts may not be explicit, but if we see how economic geography and urban economics use the concepts of distance and location, we can clearly see the presence of space and place in these disciplines in the forms that can be measured. This measurement is closely related to their exchange value. The translation of relations to the monetary value of distance and location enables the economic analysis to establish a spatial understanding of activities. There is, however, a problem, somewhat similar to the absolute concept of space: it reduces the complicated set of relationships among multi-dimensional agents acting within complex contexts to a bare minimum, which can be expressed by numbers. The language of mathematics is the language of science, used here to provide accuracy and give the impression that its use guarantees objectivity and precision. Such calculations, however, are about human behaviour, which cannot be easily reduced to numbers, despite the best efforts of social sciences.

In economic terms, the city is an agglomeration associated with economies of scale. Economists, however, have generally been uninterested in the location of economic activity; their main interests have been the production, distribution and consumption of goods and services; but where these activities took place and why were thought to be of little relevance. The processes of globalization and European integration, regional decline and emergence, nevertheless, have brought about a new awareness among some economists who have witnessed the significance of the new spatial pattern of economic activity across the world (Fujita *et al.*, 1999; Vertova, 2006). A branch of economics – urban economics – has undertaken extensive research into the 'where' of economic activity, studying the location choices of firms and households (O'Sullivan, 2003). Economic geographers, meanwhile, have long been interested in the spatial organization of economic activity: where the component parts of the economic system are located, how they are related to one another in space, and the spatial impact of economic processes. They have been concerned with the ways that economic activities are spatially organized, why they are organized as such, how they change and how this spatial organization and transformation influences the economic and other social processes (Dicken and Lloyd, 1990: 7–8). Studying households' decision on where to live and where to work, and firms' decisions on where to locate their factory, office or shop would make it possible to explore the relationship between the city and the economy. It would help examine why cities exist and grow, how and why different activities are arranged within them, and how urban problems such as decay, pollution, congestion, crime and poverty find spatial manifestation (O'Sullivan, 2003: 2).

The analysis of the relationship between space and economy has largely focused on location and distance, which are given economic dimension through the cost of land and transportation. For a household or a firm to decide on where to locate, the primary economic consideration is the cost of land, which is mainly determined through the land market, which in turn shapes the social geography of a city. Furthermore, movement between locations is the primary form of their relationship with one another; movement is an essential feature of urban activities, which in economic terms is conditioned through the cost of transport. The cost of land and transport are therefore the classic economic indicators of dealing with space through location and distance. A large body of elaborate theories has evolved to address these dimensions and the spatial organization that they generate.

An early articulation of location-distance relations was developed by von Thünen in the early nineteenth century (Dicken and Lloyd, 1990; Fujita *et al.*, 1999). His model was based on an isolated town in the middle of countryside, where farmers produced different crops with different yields and costs of transportation. Those who were located nearer to the town had lower transportation costs and were willing to pay higher rent for their land, while those further away from the town had higher transportation costs and therefore paid lower rent. It showed that farmers were faced by a trade-off between transportation costs and land rents, generating a model of concentric rings around the town, representing where different crops may be more economical to produce. Von Thünen presented a simple but powerful economic model of land use, whereby the allocation of land around the town minimized the total cost of production and transportation of food to the town.

This desirability of the centre as the place in which transportation costs are minimized is used by the central place theory, developed by Christaller (1966) and Lösch (1954), to explain a network of urban centres and sub-centres that reflect the intersection between economies of scale and costs of transportation. The starting point of this theory is the assumption that if we had a population of similar people who are evenly distributed in a homogeneous and unbounded plain, the services that they need cannot be thinly and evenly spread and would be subject to economies of scale. These services (administrative, commercial, industrial, etc.) would cluster in the most accessible locations, which together form a lattice of central places, hierarchically organized to account for the economies of scale applied to different services.

These models of central places and land rent/use relations, which were developed for market towns and agricultural lands, were later used to explain the relationship between location and distance in urban areas (Alonso, 1971). The centre of a city is geographically the most accessible location, and therefore the most desirable place for the firms to locate, which is translated into the highest land prices, and subsequently to the highest densities. Concentric rings of commercial, industrial, residential and agricultural land use would then construct the spatial structure of the city, in trade-offs between land rent and transportation cost as applied to each activity. With distance from the centre, the cost of transportation to the centre grows, but the price of land falls, hence the trade-off between availability of land and nearness to the centre, between larger houses and more spacious offices and shops built on cheaper suburban land, or smaller apartments and more expensive offices in the centre. Within the city, smaller centres at district or neighbourhood levels emerge that cater for local needs, in a similar way to how market towns served their catchment area, benefiting from the economies of scale at the intersection with transportation costs. The relations of distance and location, and the trade-off between transport cost and land rent, would also apply to the local centres that make up the modern polycentric city.

While the dynamics of location and distance would explain some of the features of the city, their explanatory reach is limited. The underlying assumption appears to be that they are expressions of choices made by free agents, fully informed of the circumstances, in a level playing field, motivated only by economic considerations. However, the choices made by individuals, households and firms are not completely free; they take place in particular contexts, in which the amount of information about the choices and the ability to choose are both limited. The in-built limitations of the context influence the choices they make, whether inscribed on individuals such as their position in social space, or in the society in general, such as the values and norms that are acceptable or abhorred. Different actors have different economic and political powers, hence making decisions for different reasons. Furthermore, the actions of individuals and groups are not always based on rational calculation, but also on expression of emotions, the desire to assert status, the reflection of biological urges, etc. Location and distance may still exist as spatial relationships, but they are subject to a more complex web of beliefs and practices than often assumed.

Production of space

Space is the embodiment of social processes: as a commodity that can be traded in the marketplace, and an indicator of social position, giving individuals and organizations a means to social recognition. The relations between space and economy can be analysed in two senses: how space is transformed to cater for economic needs, and how space itself becomes a commodity. In the first sense, we may look for the different functions that a changing economy needs, and observe how the processes of obsolescence and creative destruction transform cities to be adjusted to new social and economic conditions. In the second sense, however, space finds dynamics of its own; producing space can be undertaken speculatively for financial rewards, which may or may not cater for a deeper level of social and economic change.

The connections between society and space are not necessarily direct, causal or permanent. Many of the spaces that we inhabit have been produced in the past, where society, economy and culture were very different. In European cities, buildings and public spaces built centuries ago under the absolute rule of monarchs with a completely different sense of aesthetics and spatial practices have continually been used under the different economic and social conditions that have followed. Many adjustments have been made to these spaces to make them fit for contemporary purposes, but the basic structures have remained the same. What has changed, however, and to varying degrees, are the representations and interpretations of space, and how we use and inhabit space, which would mean that the same physical space can incorporate another social space.

An example of the rupture between the physical and the social dimensions of space is the different paces of change in the ingredients of urban space. The use of a place may be changed from one day to the next, and so its social significance may be open to frequent change. A building, however, has a longer life, and it could be used for different functions for several centuries. More long-lasting, however, are the streets, as some streets may remain in use for millennia, as exemplified by many European streets that have Roman origins. The different paces of change, therefore, create a multi-layered socio-spatial environment with multi-speed dynamics, suggesting the absence of a coherent and permanent relationship between the physical and the social dimensions of the urban space. If there is any coherence, it would be in the reinterpretation and reuse of old buildings, roads, monuments and other urban elements. Every new person and every new generation may transpose their patterns of interpretation and use on the built and natural environment that they find. It is a recreation of history and geography, which always carries with it some of the meanings of the past.

Understanding the relationship between economy and space needs to investigate what demands the economy may have, so that space is produced in response. We might assume that if the economy needs more roads or schools, for example, the relevant spaces would be produced to meet those needs. Investigating the relationship between knowledge economy and space would then be searching for the specific needs of knowledge economy and see whether the necessary spaces are being produced. These specific needs would distinguish the knowledge economy from other types of economy; what makes it different from agrarian, mercantile, or manufacturing economies. Understanding the relationship between economy and space would also need to investigate the process of making space. The construction sector is a major part of many economies and, together with the financial system that feeds it and the public sector that facilitates and frames it, the processes that produce the built environment play a considerable role in the economic structure of any society (Harvey, 1985; Lefebvre, 1991). As such, owing to its size and significance, it finds an internal logic of its own, which drives its activities.

Around the turn of the century, the contribution of construction industry to the national economy in the UK, US, France and Germany have all been around 5% of the GDP (Blake *et al.*, 2004). In the UK in 2005, 6.3% of the national Gross Added Value was attributed to construction (Dye and Sosimi, 2009: 20). In the US construction industry in 2002, there were 710,000 establishments employing 7.1 million workers. The number of these establishments had grown by 8% from 1997, which was not as much as some booming sectors such as information (by 20%), professional, scientific and technical services (by 19%), and educational services (by 20%), but compared favourably with declining sectors such as manufacturing (−3%) or mining (−2.9%). Furthermore, construction industry was not the only sector involved in the production of space, which would also include utilities (10% growth), real estate, rental and leasing (12%), and transportation and warehousing (12%), all showing strong growth (US Census Bureau, 2010c). From 2002 onwards, the annual value of construction put in place grew by more than a third to reach a peak of US$1.1 trillion in 2006, before starting to decline after 2007 (US Census Bureau, 2010d). However, the share of space production in the national and international economies was even much more significant than these substantial figures suggest. National economies, from the US and UK to Ireland and Spain, suffered from the overproduction of space in the boom years as accompanied by the oversupply of money, which led to a national and personal debt crisis. The global financial crisis in 2008 was triggered by the so-called subprime mortgages, showing how the finance industry and the development industry were involved in what nearly led to the collapse of the financial architecture of the global economy.

The production of space, therefore, is a major part of urban and national economies, with its own internal dynamics that are bound closely to the other parts of the economy. Its major productive capacities encourage its members to search for opportunities to employ these capacities, or try to expand these capacities and financial rewards through speculation. So the logic of production may drive the agenda of urban development, rather than the logic of particular needs. The ability to make may suggest transforming cities in new ways, as when new productive capacities and technologies would allow large development companies to change large parts of cities in short periods of time, at unprecedented speeds and scales. Making space then follows the logic of making, rather than what a society needs. The development industry does not necessarily follow a causal line with functional needs; it generates need and it has an internal logic of its own.

Social space, Lefebvre (1991) argued, could only be understood when it was analysed through the process of its production. Objects could only make sense in this social context, which included how they were made, exchanged and used. Space had an additional significance: it was 'a product to be used, to be consumed', but it was 'also a means of production; networks of exchange and flows of raw materials and energy fashion space and are determined by it' (Lefebvre, 1991: 85). It was necessary, he argued, that space should be analysed in connection with the processes of production, hence making a close connection between space and political economy. Analysing space as a commodity and spatial relations as commodity relations that are essential to the economy (Harvey, 1985) would help a better understanding of the knowledge economy. A functionalist interpretation of the notion of production and limiting the value of space to commodity, however, would have their shortcomings.

The notion of production entails purposeful transformation, while significant spatial transformation could take place through accidents and events such as natural disasters over which no one has overall control. The passage of time may render a purposeful object devoid of its original meaning, hence we may use an ancient object in a new way: an ancient object that once had a sacred meaning can now be used as a mere ornament, or a building built as a church may now be used as a house, or the stones of an ancient castle may have been used as the building blocks of a wall surrounding a farmyard. The producers of these objects may have had some ideas in mind about their value and use, but these meanings have been lost or fully transformed by others.

How far does space matter? By the virtue of their interests, the students of spatial arts and sciences may sometimes be accused of exaggerating the significance of space. Some can actually be blamed for physical or spatial determinism, the idea that the physical arrangements and spatial relations determine the social and economic conditions. While the 'where' of economic and social activity does matter, it is not the only factor at work, and any analyst who gives it undue significance has risked being accused of physical or environmental determinism. In the same sense, economic determinism should be avoided, refraining from the notion that exchange value is the only driving force for human individuals and societies.

For Pierre Bourdieu, following Max Weber, social agents' main motive is a struggle for status. Bourdieu (2000: 134) places 'the quest for distinction' to be 'the principle of all human behaviour'; and so social space becomes a map of these distinctions, 'a structure of juxtaposition of social positions'. The urban physical landscape is a translation of this landscape of status, this social space that finds expression in 'a certain arrangement of agents and properties', through which 'all the divisions and distinctions of social space (high/low, left/right, etc.) are really and symbolically expressed in physical space appropriated as reified social space (with, for example, the opposition between smart areas . . . and the working-class areas or the suburbs)' (Bourdieu, 2000: 134). In this way, Bourdieu (2000: 135) takes us back to Leibnitz's relational idea of space, in a version in which the physical and the social are intertwined, whereby 'a certain order of coexistence (or distribution) of agents' corresponds to 'a certain order of coexistence (or distribution) of properties' to define social space.

As reflected in the dynamics of space production, space and economy, therefore, are related in a number of ways: creating new spaces or transforming existing ones as a response to new functions, meeting needs, maximizing financial rewards, or feeding consumption and satisfying a desire for status and recognition. While some of these ways may correspond to the emergence of a new type of economy, others would inevitably relate to a continuation of longstanding trends.

Conclusion

In search of mutual support, people congregate in cities, creating concentrations in space and time in which the relations of distance and location act as spatial indicators of economic relationships. This permanent concentration, in connection with other forms of dispersion and concentration, forms a social context in which the beliefs and actions of individuals, households, firms and other organizations and groups can be understood. The space that is produced is a collection of animate living beings and inanimate material objects and their relationships, constituting a multiplicity of overlapping contexts in which these beings, objects and relationships find meaning, where temporal change and social diversity are defining features. Understanding space would only be possible through understanding a variety of perspectives into this collection, drawing together a range of stories told from different perspectives, but done so from a critical angle, to find out what stories remain untold and who gets marginalized in this presentation of narratives. Understanding the spatial implications of knowledge economy then becomes investigating how this context is being transformed; how the processes of production, distribution and consumption of goods and services are changing; their implications for the disappearance of the old clusters and the emergence of new ones; and the development of new spatial forms and the decline of some of the older patterns.

Part II

Changing nature of production

Part I addressed some of the basic ideas that were needed to embark on a journey of investigation. Part II now takes us into the knowledge economy proper by examining the changing nature of its products (Chapter 4), and the ingredients of production involved: knowledge (Chapter 5), technology (Chapter 6) and the organization of production (Chapter 7).

4 Intangible products, tangible places

In the classification of economies, the nature of their products has played a major role; so we speak of agrarian and industrial economies, distinguishable by agricultural and manufacturing products. Foodstuff and manufactured goods have come to be symbols of entirely different ways of life, creating different types of cities. Has the nature of the product changed now to the extent that we can call it a knowledge economy, characterized by producing knowledge and information and creating knowledge spaces and cities?

Weightless and immaterial?

A knowledge economy is where the economic output is primarily in the shape of knowledge products. According to the OECD (1996: 8), knowledge-based economies are 'economies which are directly based on the production, distribution and use of knowledge and information'. Joseph Stiglitz (1999: 15) suggests that knowledge economy is a phase in which 'industry in the developed countries is moving from metal-bashing to knowledge generation'. The process is gradual but brings about significant change, to the extent that 'knowledge and information is being produced today like cars and steel were produced a hundred years ago' (Stiglitz, 1999: 1). Knowledge economy is seen as a phase in capitalist development that is driven by knowledge, which succeeds the phase marked by accumulation of physical capital (UNESCO, 2005: 46).

A way of defining the knowledge economy, therefore, would focus on the changing nature of economic products: from material goods to the so-called immaterial and weightless goods and services, from physical and tangible products to intangible ones. The digital streams that constitute computer programs and games, which go through global networks of communication, cannot be seen or touched. Owing to this changing nature of its products, the knowledge economy is also called immaterial economy, intangible economy or weightless economy (Quah, 2002).

The idea of immateriality is also stretched to labour (Lazzarato, 1996), which has been seen as apathway to some form of emancipation (Hardt and Negri, 2000). It has been used in analysing culture (Thomas, 2008), society (Diani, 1992), and architecture (Hill, 2006), among others. The prevalence of a visual culture and the rise of a society of spectacle, where the image rather than substance rules (Debord, 1994), feeds the sense of living in a realm of immateriality. The meaning of the immaterial culture lies in symbolic production, in its contrast with the material culture: if the latter was expressed through the production and use of various objects and artefacts, the immaterial culture is the realm of beliefs, performance and communication. With the arrival of digital media and communication, cyberspace is imagined as an immaterial world, in which physical objects are replaced by images and ideas, a parallel realm in which the norms and conditions of the material world seem to desist (Nayar, 2010). A virtual weightless world is imagined in which expression and communication are made through electromagnetic processes.

Some have equated this weightlessness with aspatiality. 'A good,' Quah (2002: 383) argues, 'is *aspatial* when its extent is not localized to a physical spatial neighbourhood.' Sounds and images that flow through the Internet are, therefore, imagined to be aspatial. They exist in the global electromagnetic domain that is called cyberspace. It becomes tempting to think of an alternative reality that does not fall within the spatial and temporal limits that frame the existence of human beings.

The notions of immateriality and aspatiality are metaphors that many find exciting. However, if we analyse the concept of immateriality, as used in the context of knowledge economy, we find it wanting. If we cannot hold something in hand, should we think of it as immaterial? Should we call the atomic and subatomic world an immaterial world that exists with no spatial or temporal dimensions, because we cannot see it with our eyes, while its constituent parts are the basic blocks of material reality? Indeed, the production, processing, transmission and display of data are all material processes formed of energy and matter. The people, machines and networks that undertake these processes are all material beings, all with spatial features of mass, location and distance from others. These products are all produced, distributed and consumed under particular material conditions. Judging by the sheer number of material objects that people possess, the extent of consumption of material goods and the sea of waste that is produced as a result, it would be hard to call this an immaterial economy.

Another dimension of scientific-technological and cultural products is their non-rival character, which gives the impression of immateriality and non-spatiality. Historically, economic products such as items of food, clothing or transport are often physical objects that are finite. Food items are eaten, clothes worn out and cars rot and become obsolete; they can be used and consumed by a limited number of people. If others wish to consume similar products, there will be need for fresh supplies. Their key feature is their materiality and spatiality, which may be transformed through the process of production and consumption, but remains an essential part of these products. Now, knowledge products, as presented in the digital form, can be simultaneously available to as many people as there are network connections. The non-rival and non-finite qualities of knowledge and information, as we will see in Chapter 5, have always been known. What is new in knowledge economy, armed with the information and communication technologies, is the ability to process and share this knowledge at completely different speeds and scales. It is this ease of distribution that helps imagining a weightless and immaterial economy. However, if we see how the production and transmission of these products are closely related to the production and consumption of material goods, we see how they are parts of an overall economic process, in which the intellectual labour and the physical labour contribute to the production and consumption of a range of various goods and services across the globe. Separating one part of this process and giving it a label that would exclude other parts would only be a limited analysis.

Knowledge products are not mental events, but they are material processes directed towards the outside world. If we may borrow a term from the philosophy of mind, we might speak of the intentionality of knowledge products, which means that they are not necessarily the end in themselves and that they are representations of the world. The knowledge economy producers provide knowledge and information *about* the world and they are not the end in themselves. Various forms of knowledge and information, in science and technology as well as in arts and culture, may appear to be merely an exchange of representations, hence the notion that they are immaterial. But in fact they are much more than this exchange of representations; they are representations of the world, including the non-representational artworks, and are used to relate to, interpret and transform the social and material world. The notion of an immaterial product that comes from and remains within an immaterial mental domain is no more than a pure fallacy.

A feature of knowledge-based economic products is that they are symbolic representations, such as ideas, images and words, which find economic value. By selling an idea or software, the economic process appears to be involved not in the creation and transportation of physical objects, but intangible ones. Immateriality, however, is not an accurate way of describing such products. The idea that they are immaterial and hence distinctive from other material phenomena is partly rooted in the historic dualism between mind and body, upon which we touched in Chapter 3. If we envisage an entirely immaterial world, which is distinctive from, and parallel with, the material world, then we have come close to an idealist interpretation of the cyberspace. Some commentators on the cyberspace seem to embrace this interpretation, seeing its economic dimension as a material intrusion into an immaterial world.

When it comes to the economic value of the intangible products, we are strictly within the material world of trade, where money is the medium of exchange and generator of access to material resources. But it is important to recognize that, even in their capacity as items of expression and communication, and not necessarily as items of economic exchange, the so-called intangible products remain material representations, made by material processes. The nature of these knowledge products is different, but they too are subject to the dynamics of obsolescence, even more so than the traditional physical objects. As their consumption becomes more easily possible by a larger number of people, the producers are urged to renew their products, so as to create new economic value. So the notion that tangible products perish while intangible ones persist may not ring true. They are both subject to the logic of production and consumption, which is creating faster cycles in the hope of larger returns.

What the commentators seem to mean by referring to the intangible nature of products is that knowledge products are not bulky objects in the same way that manufactured objects are, and that they exist in the exchange of symbols rather than exchange of goods; this is particularly reflected in their transaction costs. Knowledge products can be sent around the world at very large scales and phenomenal speeds, with a much smaller transaction cost than sending objects, which require packaging, handling and transportation. But new knowledge is also embedded in many physical goods that are produced through manufacturing processes and transported through traditional channels of sea, land and air. Knowledge products may be intangible as well as tangible, in the sense that they are embedded in people, artefacts and practices. So what characterizes knowledge economy's products is not their immateriality but their symbolic and relational character, their knowledge intensity and, for some products, ease of transportation.

Post-industrial economy?

As a result of this change in the nature of economic output, therefore, some have equated the knowledge economy with post-industrial economy (Bannock *et al.*, 2003). It draws on the observation that in the advanced economies there has been a transition from manufacturing industries to services as the primary form of economic activity, heralding a significant transition in society, leading to fundamentally different conditions.

In his famous book, Daniel Bell analysed the post-industrial society to have three components: a shift from manufacturing to services in the economy, the prominence of new science-based industries, and the rise of new technical elites and a new principle of social stratification. For him, this indicated 'a changeover from a goods-producing society to an information or knowledge society' (Bell, 1973: 487). Through the use of new machinery, industrialization had increased productivity in agriculture and reduced the number of people employed in that sector. In the same way, automation and mechanization was now increasing productivity in the industrial sector, reducing the reliance on manual workers, and swelling the services. As wealth grew through gains in productivity, services would grow to create new activities to cater for existing and new needs. This society's approach to knowledge was changing: 'from empiricism or trial-and-error tinkering to theory and the codification of theoretical knowledge', which would be used to direct innovation and formulate policy (Bell, 1973: 487). This society was, therefore, becoming more rationalist, as it focused on developing its theoretical knowledge and using it to decide its future path.

Since its early appearance a generation ago, the term post-industrial has been widely used, but has also come under sustained attack for its theoretical, empirical and methodological shortcomings (Webster, 2006; Kumar, 2005), not quite satisfying even those who use it (e.g., Touraine, 1995: 244; Esping-Andersen, 1999: 4). For example, while Touraine has been widely associated with the concept of post-industrial society (Clark and Diani, 1996), he later used the term 'programmed society', where 'the production and mass distribution of cultural commodities plays the central role that belonged to material commodities in industrial society' (Touraine, 1995: 244).

Alvin Toffler's *Third Wave* is a similar attempt, defining a phenomenon by what had gone before, rather than its own qualities (Toffler, 1981). The first wave started with the growth of agriculture 10 millennia ago, followed by a second wave of industrial revolution. The third wave, which started in the 1950s in the United States and spread to other advanced industrial countries, was a major change from the second. Toffler called it a 'super-industrial society' (Toffler, 1970), but he found this term, as well as Bell's post-industrial society and what the Soviet futurists called 'scientific-technological revolution', unsatisfactory (Toffler, 1981: 23). Ultimately, however, his third wave 'describes a dying industrial civilization' in its various spheres and the changes that these spheres are going through (Toffler, 1981: 19).

The decline of manufacturing and the rise of services as the main form of economic activity in the advanced industrial countries is a widely observed phenomenon, but the interpretation and the historical framework into which this phenomenon is placed are open to question. It is difficult to determine exactly what services are, as the three-sector typology (agriculture, manufacturing, services) is primarily drawn on the basis of the first and second sectors, and leaving everything else in the tertiary sector. Industrial classification lists the service industries as the institutions that are involved in the production of 'impermanent and immaterial' products, as distinctive from permanent and material goods produced by the primary and tertiary sectors (Gershuny and Miles, 1983: 23). It is the rise in these so-called immaterial products from the service industries that has been used as the defining feature of a new service-based, post-industrial economy.

Close scrutiny, however, shows the interdependence between services and industry, displaying a division of labour, rather than displacement of one by the other. For example, the demand for household services, coupled with the high cost of labour, led to technological innovation in providing new household gadgets (Gershuny, 1978). Growth in services could be explained by increasing demand from the producers of goods and services, where the division of labour requires new support services; it could grow in response to the growing wealth of the society and demand for more consumption services; or it could grow due to the lower rate of increase in labour productivity in services as compared to manufacturing (Gershuny and Miles, 1983).

The interdependence between production and consumption has now been globalized, owing to the new information and communication technologies. A key dimension in the rise of services is that the presence and significance of material goods has not declined; if anything, after the 1980s' exaggerated adoration of wealth and success, the possession of material goods has become even more significant. The crucial change is that these goods are now increasingly produced elsewhere. Hence there has been much talk of the rise of consumer society, which consumes but not necessarily produces its goods. Nevertheless, as shown in the context of national economies, the demand for consumption activities provided impetus for new products and employment, showing interdependence between the production and consumption (Gershuny, 2000).

The notion of post-industrialism displays a linear historic process from pre-industrial to industrial and post-industrial, implicitly assuming a growing degree of sophistication and complexity along the way. Inherently, this progression is a historicist periodization, through which history advances towards better, more advanced stations, whereas the course of events may not support this assumption. An example is the global financial crisis of 2008, which showed how the balance of power shifted towards those industrializing goods-producing countries such as China, which enjoyed a huge trade surplus with the service-producing countries of the West. The depiction of history by post-industrial paradigm showed structural shifts in the basis of the economy: from agriculture to industry, which was now being replaced by services. The changing nature of economic output, however, can be considered a consequence of rather than a driver for change.

De-industrialization has been a partial, gradual and local process rather than a universal and global one, as the new global division of labour has redistributed the location of manufacturing activities. The change in the nature of economic output could not have taken place in a void. Replacing manufacturing with services was not automatic and in the absence of decisions by industrialists. Relocation to low-cost areas or the development of new automated production technologies could be seen as a conscious response to the ideological cold war between markets and planned economies. It was a response to post-war Keynesian economics, which was rewriting the social contract, developing a welfare state that provided unprecedented privileges for workers, the cost of which the employers now wished to avoid. Relocation and automation of manufacturing, therefore, was a trend in which Western industrialists played an active part, changing the shape of economic output and industrial relations at home. Bell (1973: 485) himself hints at this change: 'American management and capital find their most efficient use abroad, and the employment of foreign labour for manufacturing.'

Rather than the death of the industrial civilization, automation at home and relocation of manufacturing industries to low-cost regions was not being disconnected from the structure of production or their command centres in the West. This relocation could take place even within the Western countries, therefore instigating a transfer within national space to regions with lower costs of land and labour, rather than complete disappearance from the scene. Globalization of the industries, therefore, shows a growing interdependence in industrial production and consumption across the world and its local effects in different regions. The local effects are at times substantial, and the impact of these large-scale processes on the way people in different localities cope with the rise and fall of industrial production may be the main story for a generation. While some parts of the world are de-industrializing, others are industrializing, and yet others are not industrial at all, even though they all play a part in the global processes of production and consumption of goods and services. They are increasingly integrated through political and economic bridges, in global markets run by fast-moving capital, supported by networks of communication and deployment of military power.

Looking at the conditions of industrial cities and societies, it is possible to distinguish the discussions about the post-industrial from those about the knowledge-based economy. The term post-industrial may describe a city or a region that used to be dominated by manufacturing industries and is now losing population and wealth due to the decline of these industries. It is, however, inaccurate to use it for societies and nations as a whole, as they are more complex phenomena than single-sector economies. Even now, when the leaders of the eight most powerful countries gather together (G8), they are called by the media as industrial nations: 'The G8 comprises seven of the world's leading industrialised nations, and Russia' (BBC, 2010). The term post-industrial is also unable to describe the broader conditions of the global economy, in which manufacturing has been partly relocated to new cities and regions.

While the post-industrial discourse described the local economies' transition out of being dominated by manufacturing industries, it had no clear vision of where these places were heading. This was a phase of social and economic decline and could only be characterized with what went before. However, as the contours of the new economic conditions have become clearer, as one in which knowledge plays a key role, the label knowledge economy has found a rather positive meaning, describing a condition and a future destination. It provides a basis for local authorities to plan around, and display their intentions for achieving, a vision in which particular types of activities are given priority.

Knowledge products and innovation

Knowledge products are the outcome of innovation, but while innovation is one of the most important drivers for the economy, it has proven elusive to understand and measure. By 2008, before the advent of the global financial crisis, the GDP per capita in the US had in real terms become 75% larger than 30 years previously, mainly attributed to productivity gains largely driven by innovation. This was changing the shape of the economy, but in ways that could not be clearly explained or measured. Innovation is thought to result in the creation of intangible knowledge assets (Advisory Committee, 2008: 18). As the importance of intangibles grows, the task of measuring the key drivers of knowledge economy becomes more challenging for the analysts and policy-makers (Bureau of Economic Analysis, 2008). Therefore, to improve the analysis and measurement of innovation and its role in the economy, in 2006 the US Department of Commerce established the Advisory Committee on Measuring Innovation in the 21st Century Economy. According to its chairman, Carl Schramm, 'While we recognize that the American economy is changing in profound ways – mostly due to innovation – our understanding is minimal' (US Department of Commerce, 2008). The relationship between innovation and growth was a crucial one; indeed the way that innovation emerges and leads to economic growth is considered to be 'the most important story of economics' (Advisory Committee, 2008: x). In this era, 'the axiom of innovation, and the vocabulary of growth' are summarized as 'the simple expectation that things will be "better, faster, cheaper" '(Advisory Committee, 2008: ix).

The committee defined innovation as 'the design, invention, development and/or implementation of new or altered products, services, processes, systems, organizational structures, or business models for the purpose of creating new value for customers and financial returns for the firm' (Advisory Committee, 2008: i). Rather than something new that can be measured by input (such as spending on research and development), this definition was an attempt to include also the added value of innovation for both customers and firms, and so include the outcome as well as input. This required an emphasis on measuring growth in 'total factor productivity', which is the change in productivity after taking account of the growth of capital and labour, pointing to the contribution made by innovation. In an optimistic note on the eve of a global financial meltdown, the chairman's message was that 'In an era where capital and labor seem abundant for at least the foreseeable future, we have come to see innovation as the most important avenue to growth' (Advisory Committee, 2008: ix).

A single 'innovation index' appeared a desirable measurement of the role of innovation in the economy, but it was difficult to create or to defend, owing to the diversity and incomparability of different data sets, difficulty in measuring some phenomena at all, difference in the performance of different sectors, and the continual change in what constitutes innovation at any moment in time. Innovation draws on collaboration among firms, universities, research organizations and governments. It also draws on a series of drivers, such as R&D tax credits, education policy, immigration policy, availability of venture capital, level of education and skills, market conditions, organizational culture, investment in research and development, etc. Data about some aspects of innovation are collected, such as expenditure on R&D, the number of scientists, engineers and technicians employed, expenditures on information technology equipment, and the number of newly issued patents.

Data on other aspects of innovation, however, are scarce. While data on physical capital investment is collected, data on intangible assets are not extended to firms' investment in human and organizational capital or in marketing and brand equity. While data on patent and trademark applications and assignments are collected, it is not easily matched with data on their applicants. Data on the income from intellectual property, and the wealth created through investment in intangible assets, are also scarce. Overall, therefore, while innovation is a key driver in the knowledge-based economy, its contribution to the economy is not well understood and measured. To compensate for this shortcoming, the committee proposed that the national accounts should have a supplement on intangible assets, which included intangible asset capital stocks and service flows. Intangible assets include investment in R&D, conducted by scientists, engineers and other occupations (which so far had been considered as expenses rather than accumulated capital), human capital and intellectual property (such as patents and trade secrets, copyrights, trademarks and brands) (Advisory Committee, 2008: 8).

The European innovation scoreboard, which has been published since 2001, identifies seven dimensions in measuring innovation performance, grouped into three blocks: enablers, firm activities and outputs (European Commission, 2009a: 8). Enablers are the drivers of innovation that are external to firms, including human resources (the availability of highly educated and skilled people), and finance and support (the availability of financial and government support for innovative activities). Firm activities in innovation include investments (different investments to generate innovation), linkages and entrepreneurship (entrepreneurial efforts and collaboration with other firms and the public sector), and throughputs (intellectual property rights and technology balance of payment flows). Outputs are the outcome of firm activities, including innovators (the number of firms that introduce technological and non-technological innovation in the market or in their own organization) and economic effects (the levels of employment, sales and exports attributable to innovative activities).

The firms and sectors that figure explicitly in the scoreboard are the SMEs, medium to high-tech manufacturing firms and knowledge-intensive services. The European innovation scoreboard shows that, despite improvements in graduate numbers, broadband connections, venture capital provision and stronger public–private linkages (measured by joint scientific publications), the EU is still lagging behind the US and Japan but ahead of the emerging economies. The gap with the US and Japan is concentrated in four areas of international patenting, public–private linkages, numbers of researchers and business R&D expenditures (European Commission, 2009a: 6–7).

A global innovation scoreboard is also devised for international comparison, with dimensions that heavily focus on science and technology. Its indicators are grouped in three blocks: firm activities and outputs (measured by triadic patents and business R&D), human resources (measured by science and technology tertiary enrolment, labour force with tertiary education, R&D personnel and scientific articles), and infrastructure and absorptive capacity (measured by ICT expenditure, broadband penetration and public R&D) (European Commission, 2009a: 24).

A closer look at the various measurement and comparison tools by the governments and international organizations shows an overall pattern. If government support, financial capital, and educated and skilled workforce are available, and the infrastructure of information and communication technologies is in place, a country has the potential to enter the knowledge economy and become innovative and subsequently prosperous. The discussion of knowledge-based economy often privileges high-tech industries and science-based activities, and the emphasis on science and technology can be seen in labour, infrastructure and assets. Nevertheless, the indicators do not seem to favour any particular sector. Judging by these measures, knowledge economy is the economy in which the availability of ICT infrastructure, a pool of skilled labour and the production of intangible assets are the key, features that can potentially be found in any traditional or new sector, or in any country.

The EU includes manufacturing industries in its account of information society and knowledge economy, as its primary indicator is the use of ICT (European Commission, 2009b). Therefore, the intangible assets may include the more traditional outputs. In some formulations, the listing of intangible assets has given priority to science and technology, hence the World Bank listing them as R&D, software and education (World Bank, 2008a). But as we see from the measurement of innovation in the US, brands and trademarks are also included in intangible assets, hence not limiting them to science and technology activities (Advisory Committee, 2008).Furthermore, the global division of labour is not a fixed arrangement or the final word in how things are done. As people in different parts of the world struggle to improve their position in this division of labour through innovation and competition, new arrangements emerge, keeping almost all parties continually on their toes. This is evident in the literature that is produced in different countries, creating league tables and comparative indicators (e.g., European Commission, 2009a; Advisory Committee, 2008; World Bank, 2008a). The development of the knowledge economy, therefore, is not necessarily limited to particular places, sectors or activities. Alongside science and technology, culture and creativity also figure highly in the contribution to intangible assets, a point that is not always appreciated by the promoters of the knowledge economy, who tend to be within business or science departments. An example is the EU directorate on the subject of knowledge economy, which is Directorate C – European Research Area: Knowledge-based economy. The creative and cultural economy, however, needs particular attention.

We now know that knowledge products are both scientific-technical and cultural-creative. Differences between scientific and cultural products are widely held and stereotyped, as produced by different groups, according to different procedures, values, expectations and forms of consumption. Scientific investigations are expected to produce reliable and replicable outcomes with objective value, expressed in the language of mathematics, which is the language of science. Cultural production, however, is not expected to go through a replicable and rational process; it is instead expected to engage in emotional articulation, leading to products that could contribute to the consumers' well-being, but not necessarily considered as utilitarian objects. One appears to be an instrumental process, generating objective knowledge for problem-solving and, in the past, explicitly aiming to have control over nature; the other an expressive one that would communicate feelings and personal judgements. They represent different cultures, which have been growing apart since the rise of the modern scientific age, and their practitioners are stereotyped in completely different ways. On the surface, therefore, their differences could not be more. For many, the term knowledge economy would only indicate products associated with science and technology, and the inclusion of cultural products would appear to be a contradiction in terms. However, the information and communication technologies have facilitated the possibility of producing cultural and scientific-technical products that can be handled through data processing and transmission, and converted to economic asset.

Intellectual property: intangible products, tangible commodities

The economic application of knowledge is the turning point at which the intangible and the weightless become tangible through economic value. This is, however, far more difficult than assigning monetary value to physical objects, posing challenges for the creators and distributors of knowledge products, for the authorities who look for taxation mechanisms and for the consumers. Digitized forms of scientific and cultural products are increasingly easy to share and transmit, and the publication of personal images, text or sound without any expectation for monetary reward is one of the major applications of information and communication technologies. Meanwhile, there are pressures to monetize some forms of expression and communication, which is why the question of intellectual property rights has emerged as a cornerstone of the knowledge economy.

Private property rights allow the owner to exclude others from the use of that property (Epstein, 1998). Knowledge products are essentially public goods, in the sense that they are non-rival and can be used by many people simultaneously. However, while some products are personal expressions that are made to be freely available to others, other products are the means for some people to earn a living, and the consumption of those goods is expected to lead to financial returns. Intellectual property rights are 'means of permitting exclusive use to knowledge in order to encourage its further development' (Drahos, 2004: 322). To ensure that their creators would benefit from their work, therefore, their exclusive rights over their work have been recognized by law. If the works of music and literature as well as scientific inventions and technological developments could be used without permission and due financial reward, it is argued, the production of these works would not be possible. The laws of intellectual property are therefore adopted by the states for the two reasons of protecting the economic and moral rights of creators and inventors, as well as promoting creativity and encouraging fair trade (WIPO, 2010).

As knowledge products have become more central in economic development, governments have placed a stronger emphasis on developing a system of intellectual property rights and institutions that would protect and regulate these rights. The UK government's Intellectual Property Office, for example, offers help to 'get the right type of protection for your creation or invention', as intellectual property 'lets people own the work they create' (IPO, 2010). Intellectual property can be a brand, an invention, a design, a song or another intellectual creation, which can be 'owned, bought and sold' (ibid), reflecting the economic dimensions of intangible products. Intellectual property can take various forms: patents, which 'protect what makes things work'; designs, which are 'what something looks like'; trademarks, which are 'symbols that distinguish goods and services in the marketplace'; and copyright, which is 'an automatic right which applies when the work is fixed, that is written or recorded in some way' (IPO, 2010). When these rights are violated, the law may consider a crime to have taken place, e.g., in counterfeiting of trademarked products, or piracy of copyrighted goods and services. Items of clothing, footwear, handbags, perfume, automotive parts and pharmaceuticals may be counterfeited; and products such as DVDs, CDs, music or software may be subject to piracy.

It has been argued that market economies are driven by innovation rather than price mechanism, and at the core of innovation lies intellectual property. It is 'not a marginal feature of the property-rights regime of a modern market economy, but its core . . . the most important example of property that only a powerful state can protect' (Wolf, 2005: 51). The recognition of intellectual property is long established, as consolidated by the Paris Convention for the Protection of Industrial Property in 1883 and Berne Convention for the Protection of Literary and Artistic Works in 1886 to encourage and enable cooperation among the states for the protection of intellectual property rights. These two distinctive groups of scientific-technological and artistic-cultural products were brought together in a new convention in 1967 by the United Nations: Convention Establishing the World Intellectual Property Organization (WIPO), which administers these two treaties. WIPO defines intellectual property as 'creations of the human mind', which include literary and artistic works, and symbols, names, images and designs used in commerce, all grouped under two categories of industrial property and copyright (WIPO, 2010: 5). Intellectual property is related to knowledge and information that may be used as intangible products, as well as incorporated in tangible objects that may be copied in large numbers in different parts of the world. The property, WIPO (2010: 6) insists, is 'not in those copies but in the information or knowledge reflected in them'.

The two branches of intellectual property have different contents and are given different forms of legal protection for different lengths of time. Industrial property includes inventions (patents), industrial designs, trademarks, service marks, layout-designs of integrated circuits, commercial names and designations, geographic indications of source, trade secrets and undisclosed information, and protection against unfair competition. An invention that is protected by patents is an *idea* that proposes a solution to a technical problem. It is this idea that is registered, publicly available and protected by law, usually for about 20 years. Copyright includes literary and artistic works such as books, poems, plays, films, musical works, drawings, paintings, photographs, sculptures and architectural designs, as well as computer programs and electronic databases. Unlike inventions, copyright does not protect ideas, but *form of expression of ideas*, in other words the choice of words, notes, colours and shapes, rather than what they express. Legal protection here does not require registration, as in patents, but only specific conditions, and lasts longer than patents: according to the Berne Convention, lasting until 50 years after the death of the author, a period that some have even extended to 70 years after the author's death (WIPO, 2010).

In setting up new rules for global trade, the World Trade Organization (WTO) negotiated the Agreement on Trade-Related Aspects of Intellectual Property Rights (TRIPS) during its Uruguay Round between 1986 and 1994. What was signed by more than 100 ministers in Marrakesh 'marked the beginning of a quiet revolution in the way that property rights in information were defined and enforced in an emerging global knowledge economy' (Corner House, 2004: 1). It drew on the Paris and Berne Conventions and added new areas, where these conventions had been silent or perceived to have been inadequate (WTO, 2010). The agreements that emerged in the nineteenth century about claiming exclusive rights over ideas and expressions, therefore, are the foundations that are still used to regulate an increasingly important part of international trade. As the knowledge economy is based on the production and exchange of ideas and expressions, establishing global agreements on their trade appeared to be urgently needed.

The aim of TRIPS was to introduce harmony and predictability among the various ways that different states dealt with intellectual property issues, and find a way to settle international disputes. TRIPS was based on three basic principles: national treatment (treating nationals and foreigners alike), most-favoured nations treatment (treating all nationals within WTO equally) and balanced protection (contributing to technical innovation and the transfer of technology, benefiting both producers and users). It set out standards for minimum protection, procedures for domestic enforcement and procedures for settling international disputes (WTO, 2010).

Sharing knowledge or rewarding vested interests?

What appears to be a commonly agreed convention from which everyone benefits, however, is subject to severe controversy and criticism, even by the supporters of globalization. The critique revolves around how IP damages the cultural commons, privileges the vested interests and rich nations and undermines the poorer nations and regions, limits access to natural resources and weakens local cultures (Gallagher, 2007).

Research into the origins of the TRIPS has shown how a handful of powerful companies persuaded the US government and the European Community to develop an international regime of intellectual property rights. The developing countries that joined this agreement, it is argued, gave up part of their ability to provide public goods for their people (Drahos and Braithwaite, 2002). Even ardent supporters of globalization find TRIPS questionable, calling it the 'hypocrisy of the high-income countries' and 'a rent-extraction device' (Wolf, 2005: 216–7). While some of the more economically advanced developing countries may benefit from the international IP agreements, for the rest it is a drain on their limited resources, which could have disastrous impacts on their ability to develop their economies: copyright prevents them from educating their people or adapting designs for their own use, while facing serious public health challenges. According to the World Bank estimates, the licence fees that the poorer nations pay to rich corporations in high-income countries would grow four-fold from the current level of $15billion, offsetting all development assistance (ibid). The export of intangible products, the cornerstone of the knowledge economy, which is so eagerly embraced by the US and Europe, therefore, can lead to unjust results for lower-income countries (Wolf, 2005: 217).

A study of 11 developing countries found that the space for public access to knowledge is shrinking, which is not only due to the assertion of these rights by copyright owners through the international copyright treaties, but also that the developing countries do not safeguard the public rights to the copyrighted material. These countries do not take advantage of the flexibilities that are part of the international copyright regime, whereby public access to knowledge can be available for personal non-profit or for education and research purposes (Kanniah, 2006).

In particular the way local cultures from around the world may be exposed to exploitation has become hotly debated. If a tribe believes in the religious and healing features of a plant and uses it for medicinal purposes, this information is not subject to patent; but a pharmaceutical company from outside can patent this local knowledge and use it for commercial purposes.In response, many local communities, from Australian aborigines to Andean farmers, have started campaigning for their right to control the use of their local knowledge and culture (Brown, 2003).

One of the areas of tension and controversy is the intersection of IP and biotechnology (Gibson, 2008), where patenting is considered to be an engine for new discoveries, as well as an unjust monopoly. The highly controversial cases of patenting human genes and limited access to drugs for AIDS/HIV have brought the tensions over intellectual property to widespread attention. In a landmark case in 1980 (*Diamond v. Chakrabarty*), the US Supreme Court decided that genetically engineered bacteria that were able to break down crude oil spills were patentable. According to the majority of judges (five to four), 'anything under the sun that is made by man' could be patented, with the exception of 'laws of nature, physical phenomena, and abstract ideas'. As they considered the bacterium to be either a manufacture or composition of matter, they ruled that it was subject to patenting (Hollaar, 2002). Following this line of argument, human genes were also subject to the same treatment, as they could only be deciphered through human work.

The international regime of intellectual property rights puts forward new limitations on the creation and exchange of knowledge as a public good. The natural tangible resources such as pastures, fisheries or forests, which are held in common, may be overused by private interests, depleting what belonged to everyone. Private property rights are advocated as a solution to the 'tragedy of the commons', regulating access to the common property. Critics, however, refer to historic examples in which self-organized groups have managed to avoid the tragedy of the commons without resorting to private rights or government intervention. In the case of intangible public goods such as information, it is argued, the establishment of intellectual commons would avoid giving way to monopoly control over knowledge. If the rules of arithmetic and the works of Shakespeare are part of the intellectual commons, why should there be exclusive rights over human DNA? The open use of information helps it grow rather than deplete, which is why it is argued that monopolies over information are counterproductive to the development of science and culture and to human ability to solve problems and to increase citizen freedoms (Drahos, 2006a).

Intellectual commons is a political expression of collective arrangements; it is different from public domain, which is an application of the intellectual property laws and regulations. An example of the intellectual commons is the Free Software movement, in which users are given access to the source code of the program. This software is subject to copyright, and hence allowing the programmers to benefit from their work, but also allowing the users to copy, change and redistribute the program according to their needs, on the condition that they do the same with others down the chain. The shared knowledge grows, rather than be restricted and monopolized by a few (Drahos, 2006a).

Intangible assets, tangible places

A key theme in the discussion of knowledge-based economy is the distinction between explicit and tacit knowledge (which will be discussed at more length in Chapter 5), with direct implications for how knowledge is generated, transmitted and applied. Knowledge economy is thought to rely on the systematic exploitation of tacit knowledge, which is embedded in the individual as know-how and experience, rather than the codified or rule-based knowledge, which can be written down, stored and transmitted (Brinkley, 2006). According to Powell and Snellman (2004: 199), 'The key component of a knowledge economy is a greater reliance on intellectual capabilities, rather than on physical inputs or natural resources.' It is characterized by the growing role of 'intangible' capital (Abramovitz and David, 1996) and a transition from tangible goods to intangible or information goods (Shapiro and Varian, 1999). Intangible assets, which draw on a highly skilled workforce, are the bases with which the high-cost regions can move up the value chain and compete with the low-production-cost regions (OECD, 2006). However, the picture is more complex than it seems, as some low-production-cost regions have moved up the value chain, R&D activities are more internationalized and widespread than before, and some services are also being outsourced from the high-cost regions (OECD, 2006).

A central feature of knowledge-based economy is the primacy of investment in intangible assets. The World Bank considers R&D, software and education as intangible assets, where investment has taken over from investment in fixed capital, which is a key indicator of transition to the knowledge economy (World Bank, 2008a). There is a growing level of investment in knowledge, measured by the OECD as investing in R&D, higher education and IT software (OECD, 2008). Investment in physical capital in the form of equipment is considered to have a causal link to economic growth through knowledge transfer and diffusion (DeLong and Summers, 1991; Martin and Sunley, 1998; Simmie, 2003). But what is the relationship between these intangible assets and the physical capital in the form of the built environment?

Cities are places where knowledge is produced, managed and exchanged in the global economy (Sellers, 2002). On the surface, therefore, it appears that the renaissance of cities is a direct contribution to the development of cities as the nodes of knowledge-based economy. Meanwhile, knowledge-based economy is said to rely on intangible assets, rather than fixed capital. Is there a contradiction in these two statements? Is investment in tangible assets, such as the urban environment, taking away resources from the intangibles, hence undermining the possibility of moving towards a knowledge-based economy? For a long time, critics in housing and urban development had argued against investing in bricks and mortar, and had directed the attention of policy-makers to people's other needs, which included health, welfare and education, amongst others. There was a tension in public investment in urban regeneration: whether to invest in people, who might move away when empowered, or in places, which might be very costly without any necessary improvement in economic performance and social conditions (Keating and Krumholz, 1999). However, under both Conservative and Labour administrations in the UK, investment in physical capital was seen as a prerequisite to the regeneration of cities (Madanipour, 2005; Urban Task Force, 1999), and research shows that investment in physical infrastructure intensified to compensate for previous underinvestment (Brinkley, 2006).

By defining tacit knowledge as personal knowledge, some have argued against public investment or subsidization of R&D activities, arguing that the resulting innovation would travel freely to other countries and regions. Their opponents, meanwhile, have argued that such investment is essential as part of a strategic innovation policy (Cowan *et al.*, 2000). This showed tensions between investment in physical and human capital, and between individual and social capital. It poses new questions about the relationship between the knowledge economy and the urban environment. The first question is whether and to what extent the significance of physical inputs and natural resources has disappeared, so as to make intellectual capabilities the centre of the economy. Other questions include the location of the knowledge economy and the physical conditions that are conducive to the development of intellectual capabilities.

Take the example of Charles, who is a computer engineer living in the north of England and working from home. On the surface, he is a knowledge worker based in a post-industrial location, as he only writes software, but he is in fact part of a global network of manufacturing the essential parts of digital devices from mobile phones to computers and other gadgets. For a number of years he was employed by a Canadian company, which was recently bought by an American company based in Massachusetts, where he was reassigned to a section run from southern California. He is now employed by a segment of this multi-site company, which employs individuals and groups around the world. Charles visits the California base once in a while, but his work is from home, accessing computers remotely with other colleagues, primarily writing software on computers that are based in Canada, for machines that are made in China and bought by companies in Europe or Asia, where he also visits once in a while, to make sure the buyers of the machines have the necessary software and expertise to use them. His pattern of connections are international and instant, crossing all time zones and communicating with many sites in order to undertake his work of developing software and supporting the machines. His company is a flexible organization, which acquires new teams and companies in some parts of the world, or lays off other teams and sections, in a fluid pattern of growth and contraction, adjusting to the changes in the market and its internal organization of production and sale.

While Charles and his company may appear to have contradicted the limits of time and space, both he and his company have fairly clear spatial and temporal patterns. Their location of production and consumption, their movement between places and their collaboration across time and space all have a clear material and spatial dimension. The technologies of transport, information and communication have allowed them to make connections between these places and people, and so they are able to undertake activities that would be impossible without these technologies. But this does not annihilate time and space; it only renders its experience different. Much of their daily life may be as normal as any freelance worker, their trips as normal business trips, their machines as material as any other good and their spatial practices not much different from the sectors of the economy that are not included in the statistics of the knowledge economy.

At a global scale, the emergence of the new international intellectual property regime, with its central role in the knowledge-based economy, has reflected an existing and widening gap between the centres and peripheries of the global economy. An investigation into the way decisions were made about the establishment of this new regime led the researchers to four cities: Washington (the seat of US government), Brussels (the centre of the European Commission), Geneva (the centre of the United Nations' WIPO and WTO) and New York (Wall Street and business headquarters). These were the cities where a network of influential actors met and planned the introduction of the new international property rights, while much of the rest of the world remained on the margins of these plans, as rather passive recipients of an agreement. According to the researchers, out of these four epicentre cities, the laws of intellectual property travelled to developing countries like 'invisible tsunamis', turning their innovation systems into 'so much debris' (Drahos, 2006b). The regulation of the intangible products, therefore, reconfirms a centre-periphery relation in the global space, which is also visible through other indicators of wealth, health and political stability.

At the local and urban levels, the introduction of the intellectual property rights creates a new hierarchy of significance. Ideas and practices that could be converted into commercial use are given priority, while others may be undermined and neglected. While this generates innovation in activities that may find economic value, it tends to ignore those cultural and scientific activities that would not lead to obvious and short-term commercial results. The differential pattern of investment that follows can change the urban landscape in important ways.

The changing nature of products would change the nature of places in which economic products are made. As manufacturing has been replaced by information processing, factories have been replaced by offices. As knowledge is embedded in people, artefacts, practices and processes, the space of cities is transformed accordingly, facilitating symbolic exchange and accumulation of knowledge capital, favouring some actors and activities while ignoring and undermining others. Cities become increasingly entrepreneurial and competitive, investing in buildings and places that might distinguish them from their competitors. Old factories are removed to make way for new offices, working-class neighbourhoods are transformed for white-collar workers, places of learning find new economic priority, possibilities for new economies of scale are created through clustering knowledge-intensive activities and the recreational spaces that would support them.

The changing nature of economic products would have a direct impact on the nature of processes of production, exchange and consumption and their social and spatial configuration. The transition from manufacturing to office work, from producing and transporting physical objects to intangible products, and the variety of ways in which the consumption of new products would differ from the past would all have social and spatial impacts for the city. We will return to the practices and social relations that evolve around new ways of working and consuming, as well as the places of work and leisure, their locations and relationships in later chapters.

Conclusion

The nature of economic output has changed in some cities: from manufactured goods to symbolic products. This change has been considered a transition to a post-industrial economy, while in fact it marks the relocation of economic activities from one place to another in global economy. This change has also been considered a transition to an immaterial and aspatial economy, while in fact it is a material process of embedded and embodied actors involved in material exchange of goods and services. Symbolic products may not be bulky and tangible, but they find weight in their conversion to economic value and in the processes through which they are produced and consumed.

The rising significance of intangible assets in the economy has brought about the need for a way of measuring these assets. This process, however, is difficult and often falling short of a full account through the use of measurement systems devised for physical capital and tangible products. The development of talents, knowledge and skills is thought to be the pathway towards expanding these assets, hence the importance of the learning infrastructure, both at the individual and collective levels. Governments and international organizations are all at work to facilitate their entry into the knowledge-based economy, through providing the necessary regulatory and financial support, education and development of knowledge workers, spread of the ICT infrastructure and investment in research and creative industries. Meanwhile, capturing the economic value of these activities has so far relied on the expansion of intellectual property rights, in the form of patents and copyright, which is at odds with the need to share and collaborate, which fuels innovation and creativity.

The change in the nature of products, and the processes of their production, exchange and consumption, has inevitably had major impacts on the urban environment, which is the main site of these changes. The city has not become aspatial or weightless; indeed, it has gained much more weight than before, as the growing population of the world's cities testifies. Investment in physical capital has not disappeared in favour of intangible assets; it has continued to be an important part of the economy, indeed so important that the subprime mortgage scandal could trigger a global financial meltdown.

5 Knowledge as productive capacity

If we are entering, or hope to enter, a dramatically different period in which knowledge takes over as the basis of the economy and society, is there a corresponding change in the nature of knowledge? Do we still hold knowledge to be the same as we did before the current era, or has there been an epistemic rupture, in which the nature of knowledge has changed, and we now approach knowledge differently from our predecessors? A key theme in the discussion of knowledge-based economy is the distinction between explicit and tacit knowledge, with direct implications for how knowledge is generated, transmitted and applied. Has there been a fundamental change in the nature of knowledge? Is knowledge an asset, a new form of capital? Cities and national governments from around the world prepare policy documents and publish marketing material on their relationship with the knowledge economy, while international organizations compare and rank these countries in their readiness to join the club. What do they all mean when referring to knowledge, and how do they intend to promote a knowledge-based economy and society?

In investigating knowledge economy and society, the role that knowledge plays in economic production, and the social and behavioural aspects of dealing with knowledge, are expected to find a central place. The knowledge economy appears to give priority to codified scientific knowledge, used as an instrument, a product and a commodity. In this process, the way knowledge is understood undergoes major changes, which is at odds with the traditional notions of knowledge as a public good that should be made widely accessible. The key argument in this chapter, however, is that knowledge is not merely scientific or codified; it is a cognitive as well as productive capacity, which includes other forms of knowledge, far beyond theoretical and codified knowledge. So we can see how knowledge is both embedded and embodied, allowing us to understand knowledge in its various dimensions, rather than being a simple commodity put to instrumental use.

Kinds of knowledge

Knowledge has been classified into at least three different types: propositional knowledge (knowing *that* something is so), non-propositional knowledge (knowing *of* something, by direct awareness or acquaintance, such as knowing a person or a place) and ability knowledge (knowing *how* to do something). Propositional knowledge has been further divided into empirical (*a posteriori*, knowledge that depends on sense and experience) and non-empirical (*a priori*, knowledge that depends on intuition, memory and introspection). The relationship between these different kinds of knowledge has been the subject of philosophical controversy: e.g., can knowing-how be reduced to knowing-that, or can we have *a priori* knowledge at all? (Audi, 1995; Pritchard, 2006).

The distinction between different forms of knowledge goes back to ancient times. Aristotle (1998: 1139b11–1140b30) distinguished between scientific, technical and practical forms of knowledge. Scientific knowledge is 'a state of capacity to demonstrate' and its objects are necessary and unchangeable; technical knowledge is 'a state of capacity to make, involving a true course of reasoning'; and practical knowledge is the 'capacity to act with regard to human goods' (Aristotle, 1998: 141–3). Technical knowledge (*technê)*, which is also translated as art (Aristotle, 1998), skill (Hutchinson, 1995: 206), craft-knowledge (Reeve, 1992: 73), or productive reason (Audi, 1995: 796), deals with knowing what steps to take to bring things into being. Therefore, scientific knowledge dealt with knowing the nature of things, technical knowledge with how to make things and practical knowledge with how to decide on the best course of action. It was, however, the word for scientific knowledge (*episteme*) that was later used to denote the inquiry into knowledge. The Greek word *episteme* referred to both systematic and personal knowledge. The nature of this knowledge and how it could be accessible, therefore, was a significant subject of investigation, giving rise to a central branch of philosophy called epistemology, which is an inquiry into knowledge (Cooper, 1999; Steup and Sosa, 2005).

Ancient philosophy was an integrated approach to all branches of human knowledge. After the scientific revolution of the early modern period, however, the division of labour among different branches of science emerged, gradually leading to many different and disconnected fields of knowledge, with associated academic disciplines and professional and technological societies. The scientific revolution of the seventeenth century and the division of knowledge into branches was followed by the rise of industrial capitalism, where the division of work into smaller, more specialist tasks was thought to lead to higher productivity (Smith, 1993). The process of fragmentation and specialization, however, was challenged by holists, among whom the nineteenth century German Idealists and their long line of twentieth-century followers were prominent. According to these critics, subdivision of the world into smaller, researchable parts took away some of the significance and meaning of the world. Phenomenological analysis and sociological analysis (Schutz, 1962; Simmel, 1978) were among the methods used to argue against this fragmentation of the social and natural worlds.

This line of criticism has re-emerged after the traditional methods of division of labour and specialization were challenged in the production and application of science and technology. Integrated work routines, rather than mechanistic subdivision of tasks, and cross-disciplinary collaboration for knowledge production, have been associated with a holistic approach to analysing the social world.

Meanwhile, the process of specialization has continued, with further subdivision of fields and the emergence of new areas of knowledge and expertise, at once expanding and deepening as well as fragmenting and disconnecting the fields of knowledge. Compartmentalization of knowledge has had a direct impact on its nature and use, and on what an individual knowledge worker can do, while the argument against compartmentalization rejects the old division of labour, division of academic disciplines, division of professional practices, and argues for overlaps, bridges and collaborative endeavours.

The general trend since the advent of scientific revolution in the seventeenth century has been giving priority to scientific knowledge, which is a trend visible until today, as exemplified in the definitions of knowledge economy. With the advent of the industrial revolution, technical skills became dominated by manufacturing industries, undermining the traditional craft skills that involved personal engagement with the object under construction, and so alienating the worker from the product. The only place for overcoming this alienation was in the arts, but here the object that was created by the artist tended to lose its 'usefulness', becoming a medium of aesthetic experience. The sciences and the arts, which were integrated areas of activity even until the Renaissance, started to grow apart, to the extent that artists and scientists developed different ways of thinking and acting. Those who tend to emphasize the weightlessness of the information society tend to undermine the value of making in human development and emotional satisfaction.

Doubt as a measure of knowledge

The discussions in the analysis of knowledge often take place around propositional knowledge, concerned with the conditions that are individually necessary and jointly sufficient for knowing that such-and-such is the case. Knowledge has been traditionally defined as justified true belief, which poses questions on three conditions that are necessary and sufficient for knowledge: truth condition, belief condition and justification condition. These questions ask how we form our beliefs, how we can justify our beliefs, what truth is and how we can find truth in any such justification. In particular, the problem of justification has caused much debate: asking what turns true belief into knowledge. While some have argued for adequate evidence as a necessary basis for justification (evidentialism), others have argued that what is necessary is the reliability of cognitive processes (reliabilism), i.e., the relationship between the belief and the mental processes that produced it. Reliable cognitive processes, the latter group argue, can be found in non-humans, which can have knowledge about their circumstances without sophisticated intellectual operations that are involved in provision and acceptance of evidence (Steup, 2006; Pappas, 2008).This has put forward the idea of making a distinction between animal knowledge (whereby the knower is not required to evaluate the source of a belief) and reflective knowledge (whereby such an evaluation is required) (Sosa, 2001).

Much of the recent debate about epistemology revolves around two dichotomies: foundationalism versus coherentism, and internalism versus externalism.

Do we rely on some foundations for our beliefs (foundationalism), or can we hold our beliefs by linking one to another (coherentism)? Do we justify our knowledge through internal mental processes (internalism) or also draw on additional external factors (externalism)? These two dichotomies have created four possibilities: internalist and externalist foundationalism, and internalist and externalist coherentism. A long line of philosophers, from Descartes to Locke, Hume, Kant and others, can be identified by internalist foundationalism, a position that the majority of commentators now seem to argue against (BonJour and Sosa, 2003).

A recurring central theme in epistemology is the problem of doubt and scepticism (Cooper,1999). When confronted by limitations, as well as the diversity of ways of experiencing, understanding and interpreting the world, the question has been: how can we be sure about what we know? Doubt has been the driving force in the fight against superstition and the development of science, testing the limits of knowledge, weighing the evidence for any claim to knowledge and search for reliable accounts of the world. In its most extreme form, doubt has been used to question the possibility of producing any reliable account, acting as a weapon against all forms of knowledge.

If knowledge is the result of search for certainty, doubt is the measure with which this search is structured and its results are evaluated. Doubt, therefore, is the ordering principle for approaches to knowledge. On one end of the spectrum, there are those who believe in received wisdom, as authenticated by some traditional authority, and avoid exposing these beliefs to any doubt. Doubt would be unsettling, undermining their knowledge by removing the certainty with which they interpret the world. At the other end of the spectrum, there are those who use doubt as a means to question any belief, considering beliefs to be no more than personal stories. In between, there are many shades of opinion. There are those sceptics who look at any claim to knowledge with caution, asking for reliable evidence to support that claim, which has been the way of science. There are other sceptics who believe any such evidence is potentially unreliable. A further group are those sceptics who deny any possibility of objective knowledge, as distinctive from those who believe such knowledge may exist but we are unable to reach it. This is a distinction between those who deny the existence of any order in the world and those who doubt whether humans are capable of uncovering any such order with their limited methods.

The historic response to doubt has been resorting to a foundation for beliefs, which has been intuition or experience, as reflected in the views of, and debates between, rationalists and empiricists. For Plato (1993: 199, 478a), knowledge was access to some underlying essence, which would be different from mere beliefs: 'The field of knowledge is reality . . . Its function is to know the reality of anything real.' As he described in his famous cave story, what we see are the shadows of reality, images that stand for original, providing mere beliefs rather than knowledge. Knowledge was, therefore, the ability to go beyond the surface and appearance, and reach a permanent core, which constitutes the nature of things; the philosopher, as the knowledge expert, then could 'see each of these things in itself, in its permanent and unvarying nature' (p. 202, 479d). In the medieval period, the problem of doubt was suppressed, and the transition from the medieval period to Renaissance was marked by the appearance of doubt, which questioned dogmatic beliefs and paved the way for the development of modern sciences. In modern philosophy, Descartes famously set out to confront the problem of doubt by finding a reliable foundation for beliefs, which he found in his intuitive reason (Descartes, 1968). He started by rejecting all the reasoning he had previously accepted as proofs, and concluded 'that I who thought thus must be something' (Descartes, 1968: 53). The empiricists like Locke and Hume also looked for a reliable foundation for knowledge, but they argued that it lay in sense and experience, rather than in intuition or *a priori* principles.

In order to justify our beliefs, foundationalists argue, we build a two-tier structure, with basic beliefs as the foundation and inferential beliefs as dependent on these basic beliefs. According to Blackburn (1996: 123), foundationalism can be understood by the metaphor of building a pyramid, for which secure foundations and modes of construction need to be identified, so that the resulting edifice is shown to be sound. Some idea of the 'given' is used as the basis for knowledge, and a rationally defensible theory of confirmation and inference as the method of construction. However, the idea of given, and with it the theory of foundationalism, has come under attack for the past two centuries, resulting in modest foundationalism, which acknowledges that foundational beliefs need not be indubitable or infallible (Audi, 1995).

Foundationalism's main rival has been coherentism, which is represented by the metaphor of a boat or fuselage, where the strength comes not from foundations but from the stability of interlocking parts (Blackburn, 1996: 123). It is therefore the relationships between beliefs, and their part in a coherent system of beliefs, that would justify a belief, rather than their dependence on a foundation. A related anti-foundational approach is provided by contextualist epistemology, which argues that there are some contextual basic beliefs that provide the basis for other beliefs (Audi, 1995). According to contextualism, which was advocated by Dewey, Wittgenstein, and Kuhn, among others, some social or temporal framework can set the paradigms within which some basic beliefs are accepted without justification. By analysing these frameworks and their changes, therefore, it becomes possible to understand the epistemic character of any given period or culture.

Embedded knowledge: social framework of knowledge

In emphasizing the significance of the social context, contextualist epistemology overlaps with the sociology of knowledge. The sociology of knowledge has been developed in different forms, but its various practitioners seem to agree on its core concern, which is 'the relationship between human thought and the social context in which it arises' (Berger and Luckmann, 1991: 16). It downplays the cognitive explanation of scientific knowledge, placing more emphasis on the social construction of facts (Latour and Woolgar, 1986). The attempts to place human knowledge within its social and historical contexts go back to Hegel's challenge against Kant, holding a priority for context over agency; to Nietzsche's perspectivism and the analysis of deception, illusion and mistrust; and to Dilthey's historicism, which argued for understanding human events within their own historical contexts. In particular, sociology of knowledge is influenced by Marx's separation of the superstructure from substructure, which has been mechanistically interpreted by some as a form of economic determinism, but more broadly as how 'human thought is founded in human activity ('labour', in the widest sense of the word) and in the social relations brought about by this activity' (Berger and Luckmann, 1991: 18).

Sociology of knowledge was developed in the 1920s by the German philosopher Max Scheler, who believed that society can determine the presence of ideas and regulate the conditions under which ideas emerge, but it cannot determine the content and nature of these ideas. He argued for the existence of a 'relative-natural world view': what appears to an individual as a natural way of looking at the world is set by the order of meaning developed within a society. Individual experiences thus find meaning by reference to this *a priori* frame of reference given to them by the society in which they live. Karl Mannheim, who developed and transmitted the sociology of knowledge into English-speaking countries, was primarily interested in ideology. Society, he argued, determined both the frameworks and the contents of ideas, and no human thought was immune from the influence of ideology. Knowledge was always knowledge from a certain position, and to mitigate against the influence of ideology, it was necessary to develop a systematic analysis of as many socially grounded positions as possible. Participation in social processes placed limits and biases on a people's perspectives, but also enabled them to acquire genuine knowledge of social and historical phenomena (Mannheim, 1968; Berger and Luckmann, 1991).

The interplay of the social context and the individual subject in defining human knowledge was a theme of Alfred Schutz's work, which combined Husserl's phenomenological philosophy with Weber's interpretive sociology (Schutz and Luckmann, 1974). He envisaged the stock of knowledge to be related to the situation of the experiencing subject. Peter Berger and Thomas Luckmann drew on Schutz, but excluded methodological and epistemological problems from sociology of knowledge, arguing that it should be concerned with 'everything that passes for "knowledge" in society' (1991: 26). Berger and Luckmann were interested in knowledge that can be found in common-sense, everyday life, rather than the specialist theorization of ideas. Sociology of knowledge, they argued, must be concerned with 'what people "know" as "reality" in their everyday, non- or pre-theoretical lives', the common-sense knowledge which 'constitutes the fabric of meanings without which no society could exist' (1991: 27). Following Durkheim, they considered social facts as things, and following Weber, that society is built up by activity that expresses subjective meaning. Sociology of knowledge then becomes concerned with social construction of reality, with how subjective meanings become objective facts, and how human activity produces a world of things. Drawing on the philosophy of language and mind, John Searle (1995) took up the challenge of explaining the construction of social reality, which echoed and extended these phenomenological approaches. Searle distinguished between brute facts, such as the existence of physical objects, and institutional facts, such as government and marriage, which only exist by human agreement, which means institutional facts are ontologically subjective but epistemologically objective. Social facts, he argued, are socially constructed, through collective intentionality and symbolization, which assigns function and meaning to phenomena, particularly through language.

The logic of science to explain its own workings was challenged by social sciences, which argued for a sociological understanding of how scientific knowledge was produced. Challenging the structural analysis, which was interested in macro-social studies, later studies used ethnographic methods to conduct micro-social investigation into 'the local settings of fact production', i.e., the laboratory in which scientific knowledge was constructed (Latour and Woolgar, 1986: 278). A key argument is that work in the laboratory should not be seen as separate from everyday life; the scientific and the social are both subject to the same human dynamics within which individuals operate: 'The construction of scientific facts, in particular, is a process of generating *texts* whose fate (status, value, utility, facticity) depends on their subsequent interpretation' (Latour and Woolgar, 1986: 273). But as it becomes clear that all interactions are social, the term social loses its meaning and value. It was useful as a weapon against the separation of the scientific from the social, but if this separation was no longer held, the result would be that 'the social study of science has rendered "social" devoid of any meaning' (Latour and Woolgar, 1986: 281). The result is 'science studies', which locates scientific knowledge in the practices of science, where in laboratories, experiments and groups of colleagues, facts are 'fabricated' (Latour, 1999: 15). The anthropological approach would show how people and objects were parts of the process of developing a culture within which scientific facts were made and interpreted, envisaged as a network of actors and their relationships. Just in the same way that anthropologists and archaeologists had understood distant cultures through their material belongings, it was now possible to have a better understanding of scientific practices by including the machines, laboratories and other 'non-human' elements, which were as much significant in the process as the human agents.

While for the Marxian analysis, social class was the context in which the generation and application of knowledge was embedded, the recent emphasis on social diversity suggests gender, ethnicity, age and lifestyle as the new contextualizing frameworks, sometimes operating through a conscious social platform and sometimes through the unconscious core of human mind.Structuralist analysis placed language at the heart of these contextualizing forces and some analysts such as Lacan focused on the interplay between language as the structure with which the unconscious of humans engaged (Bowie, 1979). In response to the Cartesian and Kantian belief in a stable and coherent self as the basis of knowledge, which had been adopted and radicalized by phenomenology, a new emphasis was being placed on contexts and frameworks: primacy of concepts, systems and structures replaced the primacy of experience or reflexive consciousness (Canguilhem, 1994: 88–9).These concepts, systems and structures were incorporated into the structure of a scientific community, as exemplified in academic disciplines and institutions, which in turn influenced how new members thought and behaved(Bourdieu, 2000). These structures could also be a feature of a wider temporal context: 'Scientific reason turns out to be subordinate to, and intelligible only in terms of, historical reason' (MacIntyre, 1980: 66).

Paradigms and epistemic ruptures

If knowledge was socially contextualized, then revolutions and upheavals were required to change that context and the nature and character of knowledge itself. Two of the influential formulations of this idea have been advanced by Thomas Kuhn and Michel Foucault, among others.

Kuhn's analysis challenged the basis of the authority of science, which has come to be 'the only generally recognizable cognitive authority in the world today' (Gutting, 1980: 1). Rather than a rule-governed method of inquiry, he argued for the scientific community as the source of that authority. Kuhn argued for a temporal and social context for science, which he called a paradigm: 'the entire constellation of beliefs, values, techniques, and so on shared by the members of a given community' (Kuhn, 1970: 175). The way scientists are socialized – undergoing similar education, involved in similar professional institutions, absorbing similar literature – turns them into a community, with its sense of identity and purpose. The existence of this paradigm made it possible for scientists to work, as they drew on shared paradigms and were committed to the same rules and standards. Kuhn likened scientific knowledge to language, as 'intrinsically the common property of a group', and to understand it, what was needed was 'to know the special characteristics of the groups that create and use it' (Kuhn, 1970: 210). There was therefore a sociological component to the way science was conducted and knowledge produced. Scientific revolution took place when one paradigm changed to another, which was 'the usual developmental pattern of mature science' (Kuhn, 1970: 12).

Foucault's analysis of epistemic ruptures in Western knowledge attempts to show how they have been transformed through distinctive paradigmatic phases in the past five centuries. He identified two major epistemic ruptures in this period: one in the middle of the seventeenth century, marking the start of what the French call the classical age, and the other at the beginning of the nineteenth century, at the start of the modern age (Foucault, 2002: xxiv). The sixteenth century was marked by a search for similarity and resemblance, as exemplified by painting and writing, which repeated and imitated nature. With the rise of rationalism, the seventeenth century abandons the search for similitude and looks for identities and differences, which are compared to one another and ordered in taxonomies, using mathematics as a universal science of measurement and order. The result is a systematic display of order in phenomena: 'The centre of knowledge, in the seventeenth and eighteenth centuries, is the *table*'(Foucault, 2002: 82). The transition from mercantilism to industrial capitalism marks the start of the modern age at the beginning of the nineteenth century, with its associated epistemic rupture, which abandons this analytical systematization of phenomena and looks for temporal and causal connections. The general area of knowledge is now 'an area made up of organic structures, that is, of internal relations between elements whose totality performs a function', which are connected together through analogy and succession (Foucault, 2002: 236). In the transition from the classical to modern age, Order gives its place to History, which Foucault finds still to dominate his own age: 'History has become the unavoidable element in our thought' (Foucault, 2002: 238).

Foucault (2002: 376) famously argued that 'man did not exist' before the nineteenth century: that systematic attention to human beings in the nineteenth century invented a conception of humans that was essentialist and universal, focusing on sameness rather than difference. By arguing for a decentred and differentiated subject, who could be analysed through psychoanalysis and ethnology, it was possible to smash this invented concept into pieces and realize that a coherent and stable self did not exist. The end of this narrow conception of humans was marking the end of modernity, and entry into a new epistemic era. He(2002: 406) argued for human finitude and against historicism: The nineteenth century had tended to 'historicize everything', but humans were finite, i.e., 'trapped in the laws of a perspective which . . . prevents it from ever being universal'. The result is context-dependence and difference, rather than universality and timelessness. 'All knowledge is rooted in a life, a society, and a language that have a history; and it is in that very history that knowledge finds the element enabling it to communicate with other forms of life, other types of society, other significations' (Foucault, 2002: 406).Foucault argued against the phenomenological approach, which gave priority to the observing subject, and rather than 'a theory of the knowing subject', he looked for 'a theory of discursive practice' as the basis for the historical analysis of scientific discourse (Foucault, 2002: xv).

Human sciences were not, therefore, inquiries into human nature, but into how humans live, work and speak. Foucault's primary interest is in analysing how representation, i.e., the relationship between words and things, has changed through these epistemic ruptures. Since the nineteenth century, three models have unfolded to address three epistemological regions: a psychological region, which studies functions and norms; a sociological region, which studies rules and conflicts; and a study of literature and myths, which focuses on the analysis of significations and signifying systems. These models unfolded one after the other: first the biological model reigned, then the economic one, and then a philological one, 'just as Freud comes after Comte and Marx' (Foucault, 2002: 392). The last model, which focuses on language and is 'a matter of interpretation and the discovery of hidden meanings' (Foucault, 2002: 392), which is closer to Foucault, shows a shift from formalization to interpretation: 'Interpretation and formalization have become the two great forms of analysis of our time – in fact, we know no others' (Foucault, 2002: 325).

If epistemic ruptures have occurred twice in the modern history, are we witnessing another such rupture as we enter the knowledge economy? In the apparent transition of the economic base from manufacturing industries to services, can we detect a new epistemic rupture? Could Foucault's anti-essentialist and spatial thinking (Flynn, 1994) characterize the new *episteme*? We will see in later chapters whether we can detect a socio-economic rupture of the magnitude that would warrant a parallel epistemic transformation. Industrial capitalism introduced a particular way of looking at the world; with its passing in some regions, are there new forms of knowledge that are radically different from the past? The critics of modernity have paved the way for this new outlook, by attacking the ways of modern industrial culture. These critics may be characterized by their wholesale scepticism and their deconstructive attitude to modernity. So a complete demolition appears to have been needed to remove the traces of the past, to inject doubt into the solid foundations that were accepted as given, so as to open new ways for future development.

However, a complete break between one epistemic context and another is impossible. Some proponents of contextualism in knowledge appear to take that context as fixed and unitary. They appear to assign a set of clear and unproblematic features to a period, and see rupture and revolution as the only way that change is possible. There is, however, conflict and diversity within each context, which are often the source of challenge to the dominant paradigms and major contributors to the new paradigms. As it has been argued against Kuhn (MacIntyre, 1980), and can be extended to Foucault, in epistemological crises, it would be impossible to forget one tradition completely and move on to a new one. Indeed, the only way to make this move is to use the tools provided by the existing tradition and to tell a narrative of change from one perspective to another. Epistemic ruptures and paradigm revolutions, therefore, show as much continuity as disjunction.

Furthermore, the notion of embeddedness of knowledge has its own limitations. While the development, interpretation and use of knowledge are context-dependent, the existence of some relatively stable and cross-contextual patterns of knowledge cannot be denied. It is on these bases that computers work, airplanes fly and medical sciences provide cure for human diseases common across the globe. Their development takes place in a variety of contexts and they are interpreted and used completely differently, but there are areas of knowledge that are without a doubt replicable and transferable. Embeddedness may explain the processes of how knowledge comes about, but the result of these processes, i.e., the content of knowledge, can and does go beyond these processes.

Embodied knowledge: personal knowledge

Alongside the attempts to contextualize knowledge in an epistemic context formed by history and culture, there has been a move towards contextualizing knowledge in human bodies, or in other words supplementing the notion of embedded knowledge with the idea of embodied knowledge. Knowledge production and acquisition is a social process, which is embedded in a social context, and is conducted by people who had internalized particular ways of thinking and behaving. A key term, which has been widely used in the context of the knowledge economy, is tacit knowledge.

The 'tacit dimension' of knowledge was introduced by Michael Polanyi (1958; 1983), as a form of knowledge that differed from, but complemented, the conscious cognitive processes. His notion of tacit knowledge originated in Gestalt psychology, which argued for holistic, rather than reductive and analytical, accounts of the world. Polanyi's work was an inquiry into the nature and justification of scientific knowledge, but he rejected 'the ideal of scientific detachment' and regarded 'knowing as an active comprehension of the things known, an action that requires skill', and 'the personal participation of the knower in all acts of understanding' (Polanyi, 1958: vii).

Faculty psychology, which was an influential approach to psychology during the eighteenth and nineteenth centuries, classified mental activities into three faculties: cognition, emotion and volition, or in other words, knowing, feeling and choosing. Inspired by Kant, faculty psychology's main theme was that the structure of the mind shapes the structure of experience; cause and effect relations could not be proven between phenomena, and so it was up to the mental faculties to make sense of the phenomena (Benjafield, 2007). By the end of the nineteenth century, methods of systematic observation in physics, chemistry and biology were beginning to be employed in human cognition, first through the method of introspection and later by observing behaviour. Behaviourists, such as B.F.Skinner, believed that research should focus on the observable phenomena, rather than the hidden contents of the mind (Smith and Kosslyn, 2007; Matlin, 2005). A parallel approach to scientific psychology was functionalism, developed by William James in the United States, which theorized everyday psychological experiences, focusing on function rather than the nature of mental activities, particularly in relation to the tasks people performed. Functionalism relied on the Darwinian notion of adjusting mental and behavioural activities in response to the world, a trend that has been followed by evolutionary psychologists and pragmatist theorists today. Meanwhile, Gestalt psychology was an approach in Continental Europe that opposed the experimental methods of breaking down psychological phenomena into their component parts, or behaviour into stimulus-response units. Instead, it argued for the unity of psychological phenomena, in which the whole is larger than the sum of its parts (Smith and Kosslyn, 2007; Matlin, 2005). It was a reflection of a holist challenge against methodological individualism.

With the advent of computers, cognitive psychologists have emerged who compare the brain to a computer and investigate the internal mental events that produce behaviour. The idea that the mind is 'an information-processing network with capacity limitation' has been a basis for theorization and empirical investigations with the help of brain imaging techniques (Benjafield, 2007: 11). Drawing on theoretical linguistics and experimental psychology, the computer analogy has enabled cognitive psychologists to focus on how representations convey information within a processing system with well-defined principles. Information-processing analysis uses flowchart models to show the step-by-step stages of sensory input and interpretation. An alternative approach has been called connectionism, which tries to capture the way the brain might be seen as 'an enormous number of interconnected neurons' (Benjafield, 2007: 19). Some philosophers of mind, however, are sceptical about the usefulness of comparing the human mind to computers. John Searle, for example, has said that the 'computationalists"invest an almost religious intensity into their faith that our deepest problems about the mind will have a computational solution' (Searle, 1998: 189). Drawing on machines to understand mental activity, he argues, is a reductive process, unable to capture the holistic nature of consciousness. This partly draws on how we are smitten by technology and aim to interpret our lives through technological metaphors and concepts (Madanipour, 2007a).

As Thomas Kuhn interpreted it and used it to refer to his own ideas, tacit knowledge is 'learnt by doing science rather than by acquiring rules for doing it' (Kuhn, 1970: 191). The notion of tacit knowledge, however, attracted criticism towards Kuhn, as it was seen to mystify knowledge by locating it in intuition and not open for analysis. In response, Kuhn argues that he is referring to intuition at the collective level, as the tested and shared possessions of a group, which are important in the socialization of new members. Knowledge, therefore, is embedded in shared exemplars, rather than in rules and laws.

In the discussions on knowledge economy, the distinction between tacit and explicit knowledge plays a central role. The subsequent use of the notion, however, has moved away from this earlier meaning, though retaining the personal dimension of knowledge. The widespread and loosely defined use of this notion in the literature has caused much confusion between knowledge and skills, between theoretical and practical knowledge, between procedural knowledge (know-how) and declarative propositions (know-what and know-why), between an abstract form of knowledge and what is particular to a context, and between what can be codified and what is unlikely to be codifiable (Cowan *et al.*, 2000).

The tacit–explicit distinction partly reflects the distinction between knowledge and information. The propositional knowledge deals with information, as it is the sense of the word whereby 'to know' means 'to apprehend that something is information' (Lehrer, 1974: 2). As we saw from Aristotle's (1998) definition of different types of knowledge, he sees knowledge as a 'capacity' to demonstrate, to act and to make. The difference between knowledge and information is widely held: information is only 'raw data, the basic material for generating knowledge' (UNESCO, 2005: 47), a fixed form of knowledge, which can only make sense in a wider context, through reflection and critical judgement. Knowledge is, therefore, a wider concept, defined as 'a dynamic framework or structure from which information can be stored, processed and understood' (Howells, 2002: 872). It is therefore possible to have access to a large amount of information, but not be able to understand, implement and use it.

While this difference between knowledge and information is generally held, their distinction is not very precise, and there are many areas of overlap and ambiguity. Furthermore, information is not limited to the propositional knowledge. Both non-propositional and practical forms of knowledge also involve information. In practical knowledge, in which I show competence to perform a task, say playing a musical instrument, I need to have at least some information about that instrument to acquire the necessary competence. In non-propositional knowledge, in which I am acquainted with a person or a place, I similarly need some information about that person or place to be able to say I know them (Lehrer, 1974).

Embodiment, embeddedness and spatiality

The notions of embodiment and embeddedness lead us to the materiality and spatiality of knowledge, both in its social and individual dimensions. The places that individuals occupy and the social context in which they are framed take material and spatial dimensions, which reflect, as well as frame, their social conditions. Many of the attempts to contextualize knowledge tend to focus on history, i.e., on time rather than on space. Sociologists of knowledge and epistemological contextualists have placed emphasis on a social and epistemic context in which knowledge is embedded. Very few, however, appear to pay attention to the spatial context in which knowledge is developed and used. While some have noticed the geographical dimension of knowledge (Burke, 2000), the notion that knowledge is embedded in a spatial context has not been advanced outside spatial arts and sciences. Even those who have emphasized simultaneity rather than sequence, such as Michel Foucault with his spatial thinking and critique of historical analysis, do not show much interest; Foucault depicted an epistemic landscape for his archaeology of knowledge (1989), but even he used a temporal structure for his analysis of epistemic ruptures (2002).

Any form of knowledge can be identified to have originated from and be drawing on a particular epistemic milieu, which will have its own social, temporal and spatial dimensions. The connections may not always be visible, but a concentration of particular ways of interpreting the world can be detected in particular places during particular periods. Scientific or artistic flourishing of some cities and countries during some periods of their history is remembered as a golden age, as exemplified by Vienna and Paris at the turn of the last century or New York after the mid-twentieth century. These flourishing periods provide strong historic evidence for the existence of a distinctive socio-spatial-temporal milieu and its significance for the development of scientific and cultural knowledge. Such innovative milieus may be observed at all geographical scales: we can identify characteristic features for cities, regions, countries, continents, or any combination of these scales. Their temporal scales may also be observed at all levels: some places flourish for only a few years, while others can go on for generations and even centuries. Beyond these historical and geographical peaks, however, the significance of the context for the character and content of knowledge does not diminish: epistemic frameworks may change, but they are always present as the ground on which knowledge develops and grows.

Emphasis on tacit knowledge, as embodied in knowledge workers, appears to be an attempt to break free from the context, at least in its spatial sense. If in the past knowledge resided in particular places, such as libraries and universities, and its application was primarily in the places of industrial production, now there is a larger range of possibilities for knowledge to be developed in different places. The possibilities that the information and communication technologies seem to offer, it is felt, would allow this decontextualization and spatial mobility. As the places for knowledge production and application associated with manufacturing industrieshave declined, and as ICT offers more flexibility in the choice of location, it is assumed that the significance of the context (spatial, temporal or social), has declined. Nothing could be further from reality. What is indeed taking place is the shaping of new contexts, rather than the irrelevance and disappearance of all contexts. Although ICT affords more spatial flexibility, it is the formation of new centres of knowledge economy that has signified its arrival and has attracted the attention of local authorities and national governments.

The emphasis on tacit knowledge in the knowledge economy displays a shift from explicit rules and institutions to personal skills, which can also result in a shift from fixed places and organizations to mobile persons. It therefore appears to allow for the development of new connections between individual, skilled, knowledge workers, who can move around and interpret and employ their knowledge creatively. By connecting different epistemic and social contexts together through technological and institutional globalization, emphasis on personal knowledge is a shift of emphasis on the individual's journey through partly connected contexts, establishing new links and reformulating the existing ones.

The notion of personal or embodied knowledge can be interpreted in two opposite ways. On the one hand, personal knowledge tends to envisage a new context for knowledge: it is not abstract and placeless, but created, embedded and carried by individual human beings. These humans are in turn embedded in a social and cultural context, which makes the conditions for knowledge creation and use possible. On the other hand, placing emphasis on personal knowledge may be seen as a challenge against the context, seeing knowledge as the property of individuals, rather than mystified contexts with imagined influences. Rather than rules and methods, which are thought to determine the shape of knowledge, it is the individual agent who is responsible for generating knowledge. Both these preferences, for the context and the agency, however, are present in the debates about how knowledge society and economy emerge: while some, such as evolutionary and institutionalist economists, look for contextual reasons for the emergence of a new economic formation, others, such as the neoclassical economists, argue for the significance of the agency in transaction.

The embedded and embodied notions of knowledge can, therefore, point towards diverging political positions. In the debate between Popper and Kuhn, it has been argued, libertarian and authoritarian notions of science have come to a clash (Fuller, 2003). While emphasis on the social context has underplayed the significance of the individual in knowledge, the acknowledgement of the embodied knowledge shifts the attention towards the individual. There have been a number of attempts at bridging the gap between the structure and agency, without necessarily addressing the production and use of knowledge. Anthony Giddens argued for a two-way interaction between structure and agency, rather than assigning primary significance for one or the other (Giddens, 1984). With his notions of 'field' and 'habitus' Bourdieu (2000) referred to this social and individual contextualization and tried to reconcile them, even if more in favour of the context. The notion of 'actors' and 'networks' appeared as an attempt to reconcile the role of agency and structure while taking into account the material dimension of social interactions (Latour, 2005). It is clear, nevertheless, that the notion of dichotomous parts and wholes has occupied the minds of analysts, to the extent that they have felt the need either to take sides or to try to build bridges between them. By considering the embodied and embedded notions of knowledge, however, we can move away from dichotomy and develop a multi-layered perspective into knowledge processes.

Knowledge as a social and psychological process

Now that we have seen how the embedded and embodied knowledge has been contextualized in temporal, spatial and cultural terms, can we say that knowledge is now dramatically different from the past? Can we say that the nature of what we know has changed in an age in which new technologies, new scientific discoveries, and maybe new knowledge paradigms, have arisen?

As scientific knowledge has substantially expanded, our approach to knowledge may have changed: the earlier naïve beliefs in undeniable truths have given way to the contextualization of knowledge, dramatically expressed as the end of grand narratives (Lyotard, 1984). This is evident in the changing approaches towards expert knowledge, from full trust in the skills of the expert to a qualified trust, which places a higher burden of judgement on the individuals and the society. A major shift from 'science' to 'research' is identified in the production of scientific knowledge. According to this shift, knowledge becomes less final and more open to change. Science was associated with 'certainty, coldness, aloofness, objectivity, distance, and necessity', but research was, in contrast, 'uncertain; open-ended; immersed in many lowly problems of money, instruments, and know-how' (Latour, 1999: 20).

How far is this shift a change in the nature of knowledge, or a change in the focus of attention by the observers of science? It appears at once to indicate two interconnected phenomena: on the one hand, it refers to a more uncertain and humble attitude by the scientific community, as the results of many confident uses of scientific knowledge have been revised or led to unintended consequences and human and environmental disasters. It also refers to a distinction between a verb and a noun: while research is the verb that refers to the scientific process, science refers to knowledge as a noun. The nature of the verb may constantly be changing according to circumstances, but has the nature of the noun also changed? A further distinction is between knowledge that may change with improvement in scientific endeavours, and what knowledge is *per se*. What counts as knowledge may change with improvements in science, but does the nature of knowledge also change?

If we see knowledge as a capacity, a belief and a personal involvement in the process of learning and investigating, in other words if we see knowledge as a social and psychological process, we would have a dynamic understanding of knowledge. This is markedly different from seeing knowledge as something final, complete, consolidated and external to human activity. Even information, which may refer to a stock of data, is not imaginable without human involvement and interpretation. Knowledge, therefore, is an active and dynamic process of becoming aware of phenomena and their relationships, implying a high degree of certainty in this awareness. Although we acquire knowledge through our senses, it is through connecting our pieces of information together that we make sense of them. So the method of information collection may be foundational, but the method of analysis is coherential. Without connecting together different pieces of sensory input, it is not possible to understand them. Connectivity of mental processes, as well as the connectivity of codified and explicit pieces of information, is the necessary premise for acquiring knowledge.

At least three features might be identified that could have an impact on the changing nature of knowledge: supply, process and communication of information.The digital technologies make it possible for information to be compressed, processed and communicated, and communication technologies provide a readily available, constantly changing, multi-layered and substantive supply of information. There are huge processing capacities, which are made available by powerful computers, and the Internet has made instant connections and communication across the world possible. So the supply, process and inter-human connections are considerably magnified. If knowledge is the capacity to analyse and understand this information, there is clear evidence that this capacity has been expanded through new technologies. Meanwhile, we can also see the limits of human capacity to deal with the accelerated supply of information, as evident in the difficulty of handling information overload. Furthermore, we can see the problem of reliability of information, which makes it hard to distinguish between different pieces of information.

We can see continuities, as well as ruptures, in the formation of beliefs and the process of their justification. What has changed is intensification in the use of doubt as a measure of these beliefs and the way they are formed. The reason for this doubt is the expansion of scientific discoveries (Lyotard, 1984) and revision of trust in the way they are used, rather than abandoning the process of searching for and justifying beliefs. The main change is in how knowledge is produced, shared and applied; in other words, in the social conditions of knowledge.

Three applications of knowledge

The uses of knowledge and information have increasingly been defined within an instrumental framework: how they can contribute to wealth creation and economic development. The EU2020, the European Union's strategy for the future, counts on knowledge as its primary asset, as a pathway to overcoming the economic crisis that spread in 2008 and 2009: 'The exit from the crisis should be the point of entry into a new sustainable social market economy, a smarter, greener economy, where our prosperity will come from innovation and from using resources better, and where the key input will be knowledge' (EC, 2009a: 2).

For some who believe in the intrinsic value of knowledge, it is an end in itself, as it satisfies an internal need to know and contributes to personal development and satisfaction. Others argue that knowledge is useful in providing an account of the world, help us with finding our place in the world and guide us on how to act (Cooper, 1999). In a discussion of the knowledge-based economy, the uses of knowledge become even more instrumentally defined, as knowledge plays a central role in social and economic relationships. Knowledge becomes an asset to draw on in pursuit of economic value. As such, the value of education also is redefined as a preparation for economic activities, rather than personal development or expanding a person's horizons.

In the discussions of knowledge society and knowledge economy, the focus of interest is not on knowledge *per se*, as conducted by philosophical and sociological investigations. The inquiries of epistemology and sociology of knowledge are into the nature of knowledge, its validity and its relationship with its social context. As such, these problems of knowledge can be identified in all human societies and individuals. In knowledge economy, however, the focus is on an instrumental aspect of knowledge: knowledge that can be accumulated and used as a basis for economic development. This is the reason why the issue of intellectual property rights has become increasingly important and controversial, as it collides with the traditional idea that knowledge was thought to be a common good, rather than a commodity.

When accumulated and purposefully employed for economic ends, knowledge becomes a new form of capital. Knowledge has always given its owner some advantage over the others, hence the term 'knowledge is power'. We can distinguish between knowledge as potential and actual power: a person with knowledge has the potential to use it, but may or may not do so given the circumstances. Many people who are considered to have knowledge may have merely accumulated information, without being transformed into knowledge, in the absence of a way of making sense of this information. Knowledge remains dormant, with potential that may or may not be realized. When knowledge is effectively used, however, it has been turned into an actual resource.

We should distinguish between a narrow definition, in which particular forms of knowledge are valued for their economic worth, and a wider conception of knowledge, which permeates society in different areas. In the narrow economic sense, only some forms of knowledge and expertise count as relevant. This then determines who is counted as a knowledge worker, what is considered to be a knowledge firm and which sectors of the economy are knowledge-based and therefore included in the relevant statistics. On the broader definition, however, different forms of knowledge in different aspects of society would all be considered worthwhile, each making a contribution to the development of a knowledge society. This would include local, informal and everyday forms of knowledge, which are taken for granted, but their absence is felt when people try to recreate them in other contexts.

We tend to distinguish between scientific knowledge, which has gone through a systematic and methodical process of observation, reflection and interrogation, and the everyday common-sense knowledge, which is more based on trial and error and on examples and precedent. A concern about the knowledge economy has been placing a high priority on scientific knowledge at the expense of other forms of knowledge. However, in a knowledge society, all these types of knowledge would presumably flourish, rather than giving the ultimate priority to the scientific knowledge, which could be exploited through technology. A key argument has been that in the drive for the knowledge economy, everyday local forms of knowledge may be undermined in favour of a systematic and instrumental approach to knowledge (UNESCO, 2005).

In practice, however, the application of knowledge in economy and society, which is the key concern of knowledge economy, does not appear to make marked distinctions between propositional and non-propositional knowledge. Instead, it appears to include all scientific, technical and practical forms of knowledge, plus any other intuitive forms of knowledge that may be held by a knowledge worker. Overall, knowledge economy, broadly conceived as a collection of different knowledge-based activities, appears to be interested in whatever passes as knowledge in society, as long as it can be turned into an economic asset through finding exchange value. Perspectives on what is useful in the knowledge economy vary, depending on the person's position and outlook. The type of knowledge that is needed in high-tech industries is different from that in creative industries, and both are different from the knowledge needed for managing and supporting economic development.

The reliability and validity of knowledge, therefore, becomes less significant than its application in economic exchange. In the Internet-based economy, the volume and reach of information has dramatically increased, but not necessarily its reliability. In the Internet age, through cultural differentiation and in a primarily commercial context, the problem of reliability of information has become paramount. Information is widely available, but no longer subject to editorial control, which would give it a sense of reliability. Commercial, cultural and personal interests are associated with many arguments, as well as with what is presented as fact. Tobacco companies that commission research into the health effects of smoking, for example, may or may not be mentioned when the results are published. Wikipedia becomes the primary source of information, where information is shared but its reliability is difficult to establish. To cope with the overload of information, many resort to familiar anchors, such as advertising, media and traditional authorities, to help us make judgements about what to believe and how to act. While ICT has provided society with a continual stream of information, and the freedom to produce and disseminate information, the trust in information and the ability to judge any given information becomes ever more complicated for individuals to develop. Both processes of forming beliefs and justifying them become open to influences that are not easy to judge or manage.

If the economy is the collection of goods and services and the processes of their production, exchange and use, then knowledge-based economy is one in which knowledge is an essential part of these processes and their products. In other words, knowledge economy is an economy that uses knowledge in the production, exchange and use of goods and services; which produces knowledge goods and knowledge services; and which creates and accumulates knowledge as an asset.

Knowledge, therefore, can be used in the economy in at least three main forms: knowledge as an instrument of producing goods and services; knowledge as goods and services; and knowledge as capital.

The first form, knowledge as instrument, is the age-old way that knowledge has been an essential part of creating the material and social world. From basic equipment and simple social arrangements to newest technologies and highly complicated organizations, knowledge has always been an essential part of making goods and providing services. Both as information that is needed in developing new tools and new ways of doing things, and as the capacity to interpret and transform the world, intelligent human beings have always employed knowledge to improve their living conditions. At this level, therefore, knowledge is, and has always been, integrated in the development of human societies; in other words, all cities have always been knowledge cities and human societies have always been based on knowledge, both individual and collective. The rise of new tools and technologies, which have brought about new and more effective ways of production and delivery of traditional goods and services, therefore, is one of the manifestations of the knowledge economy. It is here, in the application of new technologies and the transformation of business organizations, among others, that some have looked for the defining features of the knowledge economy: how science and technology have transformed the production, exchange and consumption of goods and services. Much of the literature on knowledge economy and information society tends to be focused on the role of new information and communication technologies. There are, however, other key features of the knowledge economy that are not covered in these investigations.

The second form is knowledge as product, where knowledge has itself become produced as goods and services; in other words, the economy produces new goods and services that have knowledge as their main component part. Again, knowledge goods and knowledge services have always existed, as an essential element of the division of labour that made urban living possible. While some people were involved in manufacturing or agriculture, others were involved in sciences or the arts, which were not necessarily material-producing activities. But as the number and extent of these knowledge products have increased, they have become the primary output of some economies. This is the condition that has emerged in the advanced industrial economies in recent decades, as the creation of material goods has been taken over by the creation of knowledge products (Stiglitz, 1999). This feature is another defining character of the knowledge economy. While using knowledge as an instrument may be widespread around the world, as exemplified in the phenomenal growth in the use of personal computers and mobile phones, without the development of knowledge products, an economy may not become a knowledge-based one. A focus on this feature of the economy may lead to a search for identifying and encouraging further growth of knowledge-intensive activities and the associated knowledge workers and knowledge firms.

The third form is knowledge as capital, where knowledge is used as productive capacity, created and accumulated as a driving force for the economy. This is the condition to which most economies appear to aspire, so that their output is not only knowledge products, but also knowledge producers. As knowledge goods and services shape the backbone of the economy, their creation requires the development of knowledge as a productive capacity. Emphasis on the development of knowledge and skills, and attempts at expanding the number of highly educated workforce, is a step towards creating knowledge powerhouses, which have the possibility of innovation and development of new knowledge products. Investigating knowledge as productive capacity would reveal a variety of factors at work to change the structural conditions in society.

Knowledge as epistemic capital

Knowledge has come to be known as the new basic form of capital, its accumulation driving economic growth, and its generation and application providing competitive economic advantage (Romer, 1986; Simmie, 2003). Knowledge, however, is not created and transmitted in a vacuum: it relies heavily on the material and institutional contexts in which it is produced and utilized. The contexts that generate knowledge but are not well equipped to commercialize it, for example, tend to lose out to the contexts that are. This means not only the necessity of the spatial context for knowledge generation and transmission, but also the necessity of its reliance on, and conversion into, applicable and exchangeable forms, if knowledge is to fuel economic development.

Different forms of capital, Bourdieu (2000) thought, would need to be converted into symbolic capital, which is necessary to acquire status. Knowledge, therefore, like other forms of capital, follows the pattern of conversion into monetary, and eventually symbolic, forms. This would mean that its accumulation would correspond to the general patterns of capital accumulation, which has already created an urban space in its own image (Lefebvre, 1991). If knowledge economy is a phase in capitalist economy (UNESCO, 2005), are there substantive similarities with its predecessor? If knowledge has become a key factor of production, then we may expect that many features of capitalism may continue to be the same, such as commodification, competition, creative destruction, accumulation, uneven distribution of resources, etc. However, the spatial implications of change from physical capital to epistemic capital could be substantial: factories are replaced by offices; blue-collar workers with white-collar ones; spatial relations between living, working and recreation areas become revisited and reframed. Gentrification becomes the process through which one group replaces another, especially at the centres of knowledge economy.

The changes in the these forms of knowledge application distinguish the knowledge-based economy from the industrial economy and other economies of the past, as knowledge as instrument is enhanced through new technologies, knowledge products replace manufacturing or agricultural products, and knowledge is accumulated through education and training, concentration of experts and control of intellectual property rights. The rise of knowledge economy, however, cannot be divorced from the presence of other economies, or other sectors in the same economy, in which manufacturing and agriculture continue to play an important role. Knowledge products are part of an international process of specialization, occupying a higher place in the hierarchy of goods and services, which include manufacturing and agriculture, now distributed across the world in interdependent regions.

All of these three applications of knowledge (instrument, product, capital) are present in the knowledge economy: new knowledge is used to produce, exchange and consume goods and services; new knowledge products are created; and knowledge is accumulated as a productive capacity and an asset. The extent of their presence and their relationship with one another may vary, and any one form may be converted to others. They also stimulate the development of a new division of labour. At local scales, there may be a specialization of some forms of knowledge, so that some economies focus on knowledge as instrument and others on knowledge as goods and services and knowledge as capital. At the larger scale of the global division of labour, these forms are interlinked and occupy their own place in relation to others. At this global scale, indeed, all forms of knowledge are ultimately stepping stones towards the instrumental form of knowledge application.

Knowledge capital is not the same as human capital. Although emphasis on tacit knowledge has shifted the emphasis from computers to humans, much of knowledge is still highly coded and expands at a rapid rate. Knowledge capital, therefore, is a combination of coded and tacit dimensions, with the tacit dimension enabling humans to decipher and make sense of the code, and understand and use coded knowledge. Tacitness also includes other forms of local knowledge, which may not be coded or commodified, which is more of a practical and cultural nature, rather than scientific and theoretical.

Knowledge may be a form of capital, but not in the same sense as money is, for the reason that some forms of knowledge are not valued and would not add anything to a person's privileges, while money is the abstract form of value that is translatable to different goods and services. In other words, money can help acquire knowledge, but the opposite is not necessarily the case. Some forms of knowledge are used in conducting everyday life, but they are not economically valued *per se*. Knowledge and skills of this kind may be absolutely essential in living in complex urban societies, but they are not the sort of knowledge that a person can be hired for. Even scientific knowledge cannot guarantee a person's economic well-being. An unemployed or retired scientist has accumulated information with a highly developed cognitive capacity over the years, but may not be able to use this knowledge to pay the bills. The only way this is possible is through translating epistemic capital to financial capital, through converting knowledge to money, which can then be used as a flexible tool for various purposes.

Money is a social fact, in the sense that human society has decided to assign exchange value to a physical medium, some metal or piece of paper or even a figure in a computer, which can be attained through some forms of activities (Searle, 1995). This externalized form of value can be used in a wide variety of circumstances, but its use is ultimately dependent on human agreement. Without such agreement, which is institutionalized through conventions and social practices, it remains merely a piece of metal, paper or electronic signal. Such agreement, however, is not given to other forms of capital, other forms of accumulating privilege, such as knowledge and status, which are acknowledged as assets, but not liquid enough to be transferred to others so easily or exchanged for goods and services. Social capital and epistemic capital, therefore, are forms of accumulated privilege, which are themselves dependent on conventions and social institutions. They may ensure a person's social position and influence, or enable a person to perform very specific tasks that no one else is capable of, but they would ultimately need to be converted to economic capital if their owner wishes to exchange them for goods and service.

If knowledge is a new form of capital, then knowledge-based economy is the series of relationships that emerge around the production, accumulation, exchange and use of this capital. These relations can be studied at a structural level, mapping them from a bird's eye view, as well as individual, household and community level, through life experiences and everyday routines, to see how these emerging relations affect society and economy at all levels.

The idea of knowledge as capital, combined with the idea that all meaning and value are based in human thought and action, support the notion of embedded and embodied knowledge. Forms of knowledge and information can survive in libraries, but to use knowledge as productive and cognitive capacity an active human home is required. That is why accumulation of this capital tends to take place through the clustering of knowledge workers. But the final key is still held by the financial capital. If we compare knowledge with finance, we see clearly their different values in the marketplace. If finance dries up, the architecture of the global economy is jeopardized. But knowledge is not accumulated and concentrated in the same way, cannot float and be transferred in the same way, and cannot dry up and cause crisis in the same way, as it is differently distributed. It is ultimately the availability of finance that can invest in research and development and that can secure the clustering of knowledge workers. At the same time, the value of knowledge in the knowledge economy is not knowledge *per se*, but an instrumental and commodified use of knowledge, hence the significance of converting knowledge into money.

If we see knowledge as a form of capital, then the implications are that it can be private (hence intellectual property rights becoming a key issue in knowledge economy) or public (which is the traditional notion of knowledge as public good). There is a tension between these visions: on the one hand between the control of the knowledge economy, whether by or in the interests of the public or private sectors. The other tension is between the pressure for private control of knowledge and the need for its distribution as a foundation for the knowledge-based economy. The drive for private control of this capital may stimulate its growth, while there is simultaneously the need to make it widely accessible as an essential part of the development of a knowledge-based economy. Within this context, education becomes a key path towards this growth, both as a means of transition into a new situation that requires new skills, and the primary preparation for the development of knowledge.

Conclusion

Knowledge has historically been defined as justified true belief, which has been subject to controversy about what these conditions entail. In the age of scepticism and information abundance, the problem of justification has become more challenging than ever. The challenge to industrial modernism's hierarchies and routines, and the technological possibility of making connections between dispersed individuals and institutions, has inspired an interpretation of information growth and distribution as networks and rhizomes, in contrast to vertical organizations and hierarchical classification. Knowledge involves sorting and classifying information, and understanding it by placing information in ever-changing contexts. Knowledge is a dynamic process, rather than a stagnant object.

Knowledge is embedded in temporal, social and spatial milieu and therefore information inputs, from simple sensory inputs to complex pre-processed data, can only make sense within a context. This context-dependency applies both to everyday knowledge and the more systematic scientific knowledge; it applies to different forms of knowledge: know-what, know-of and know-how. Knowledge is also contextualized in the human body, as part of the cognitive processes that connect sensory inputs to memory and existing mental patterns. At the personal level, knowledge is the capacity to make connections between different pieces of information and interpret them. Knowledge, therefore, is embedded in socio-temporal-spatial contexts and is embodied in intelligent human bodies. This contextualized knowledge is subject to change when these contexts change.

The change at the large scale takes place through epistemic ruptures and paradigmatic revolutions, often in line with macro-scale structural changes in society, which changes the frameworks within which knowledge is produced and understood. At the personal level, change is through transmission of capacity, via education, training and research; through physical movement of knowledge workers from one place to another; or through the meeting of minds in which new ideas emerge. Information and communication technologies, a new global division of labour and the drive to find a new rationale for de-industrializing economies, have led to the accumulation and instrumental use of whatever passes as knowledge, as a new source of power, a new form of capital. To make economic use of the epistemic capital, however, it needs to be converted to money, as the most liquid and mobile form of value. The instrumental and commodified use of knowledge creates tensions and controversies at the intersection with the traditional notion of knowledge as a common good and in the context of the need to spread knowledge as the foundations for a knowledge-based economy.

6 Digital technology and the mediated city

For many, the idea of knowledge economy is intertwined with information and communication technologies. In this chapter, we explore the relationship between technology and economic change, the conditions of the mediated city and the implications of digital technology for urban form through dispersion and agglomeration, as played out through spatial compression, temporal acceleration, social decontextualization and functional augmentation.

Changes in technology

Information and communication technology (ICT) is considered to be the lifeblood of the information economy, the path to innovation and higher productivity. New information and communication technologies have transformed the way information is produced, stored, transmitted and exchanged, with far-reaching implications for how people live and work. As a driver of productivity and economic growth, knowledge leads to 'a new focus on the role of information, technology and learning in economic performance' (OECD, 1996: 5). According to the European Union:

> We belong to the information society. Mobile phones, the internet, high-speed digital delivery systems, which bring together the previously separate worlds of telecommunications and broadcasting, have created the information revolution – at home, at school and at work. We can communicate to and from any place at any time.
>
> (EU, 2009)

National governments and international organizations look for ways of facilitating ICT development and access across their territories, as these technologies are thought to be essential for economic development. The United Nations believes that ICTs 'offer unique opportunities for developing countries to narrow the development gap with industrialized countries. They have the potential to assist developing countries "leap frog" entire stages of development' (UN, 2009). The reason for the Soviet Union's collapse was seen as its inability to master the ICT revolution and hence stalling its productive capacity (Castells, 1996).

By developing indicators on the basis of ICT access, use and skills, the degree to which a society has become an 'information society' is measured (ITU, 2009). Nations are constantly compared with one another for their ownership and use of computers, the quality of their communication infrastructure, the number of connections to the networks, the price of communication and the speed of their networks (ITU, 2009). Access to, and use of, ICT for those segments of society, such as women, small firms or low-income groups, or those parts of the world, such as rural areas or developing countries, which are not yet connected, are targeted by researchers, policy-makers and service providers. By the end of 2008, there were more than 4 billion mobile cellular subscriptions, 1.3 billion fixed telephone lines and close to a quarter of the population in the world were using the Internet (ITU, 2009: 71). ICT's phenomenal expansion and social significance have made it a defining feature of the economy and society, expressed in terms such as the electronic age or computer age (McLuhan, 1964), the Internet age (Raymer, 2009; Cavanagh, 2007; Nicholas, 2000), or, more widely, digital age and information age.

The label of information age is used to characterize contemporary society, as can be seen from a handful of examples from a sea of studies: from the use of computers as its tools (Capron, 1996) to a wide variety of ICT applications in libraries and museums (Brophy, 2001; Keene, 1998), in arts, architecture and archaeology (Riewoldt, 1997; Reilly and Rahtz, 1992; Collins, 1995), in health, transport and crime (Millenson, 1997; Hepworth and Ducatel, 1992; Wall, 2007), their implications for children (Sendov and Stanchev, 1986; Holloway and

There are three mobile phone subscriptions for every five persons in the world (Seoul, Korea).

Valentine, 2003), for rural communities (Allen and Dillman, 1994), and for society as a whole (Castells, 1996; Melucci, 1996; Stehr, 2001; Terranova, 2004; Quinn, 2005). Technology provides the lens through which society is seen, and even characterized, as expressed in the widely used label 'network society', which describes 'the emergence of a new social structure' (Castells, 1996: 27).

With the growth of new digital technologies (in audio and visual technologies of radio, television, cameras, etc.), the term 'digital age' has spread more widely recently (Avery *et al.*, 2007), apparently taking over from 'information age', while covering similar and new issues: language (Hale, 1996), publishing (Cope and Phillips, 2006; Inman and Picton, 2008; Berry, 2004; Thompson, 2005), education (Nelson, 2008; Beetham and Sharpe, 2007; Eisner and Vicinus, 2008; Goodwyn, 2000), engineering (Hopkinson *et al.*, 2005), sports (Hamil, 2000), arts (Sutton *et al.*, 2007), cinema (Le Grice, 2001), music (Folkestad, 1996), architecture (Kolarevic, 2005), culture (Jonscher, 1999; Tredinnick, 2008), crime and security (Grabosky and Smith, 1998; Eriksson and Giacomello, 2007), and politics (Dutton, 1999; Godwin, 1998), among others. With its vast spread and deep penetration, ICT is identified as a driving force in social change, assuming a more marginal, less significant role for other factors.

The significance of technology for society cannot be ignored. However, technology alone cannot shape society; it is only a tool, one factor among many. The development and spread of any technology are intertwined with complex social processes from which they cannot be separated. Furthermore, there are important

New technologies have facilitated the spread of information and communication to unprecedented levels (Fez, Morocco).

parts of life, and significant parts of the world, that are not reached by new technologies. Technological determinism, which may be detected in much of the work on the impact of ICT on society, assumes a central causal force for technology, therefore, tending to be reductionist, ignoring complex and multidimensional social processes that are involved in its development and use. There is a long tradition of technological determinism, which sees social relations as a by-product of technological change. According to a famous quote from Marx, writing in 1847:

> The social relations are intimately attached to productive forces. In acquiring new productive forces men change their mode of production, and in changing their mode of production, their manner of gaining a living, they change all their social relations. The windmill gives you society with the feudal lord; the steam-mill, society with the industrial capitalist.
>
> (Marx, 2008: 119)

It would then be tempting to update Marx's formula and say that the computer gives you society with the global corporation. Technological change has been used to periodize human history, as reflected in the stone, bronze and iron ages. Even human evolution is closely related to the development of tools, and the shape of the human hand has been associated with the ability to use and make tools and the need to have a powerful and precise grip (Bradshaw, 1997). However, the long cycles of human evolution cannot be replicated in the shorter cycles of technological change, and even shorter cycles of enthusiasm for a new technology, as expressed in terms such as atomic age and space age.

Major scientific discoveries and technological developments have always created new waves of enthusiasm and interpretation, each used to characterize contemporary society and imagining a future shaped by that new technology. The second half of the twentieth century was identified by at least two such labels: the Atomic Age and the Space Age, before the rise of the Information Age. The discovery of radioactivity at the end of the nineteenth century triggered the start of the new Atomic Age, which came to worldwide attention after the explosion of atomic bombs in the Second World War and the use of atomic energy in civilian power generators. If we accept Marx's assertion on the significance of change from windmill to steam-mill, then surely a nuclear power station must be the next inline, producing completely new productive forces and social relations. While the use and unintended consequences of nuclear power have created enthusiasm, as well as anxiety, that still continue in national (Greenpeace, 2009) and international debates (BBC, 2009b), the notion of characterizing society with this technology, however, has disappeared.

Similarly, the development of space travel – which started by sending Sputnik, the first satellite, into the earth's orbit in 1957 – launched a new Space Age (NASA, 2009). This age was characterized by the space race between the Soviet Union and the United States and their ambition to explore other planets, culminating in the Apollo 11 moon landing in 1969, which was interpreted as 'a giant leap for mankind', capturing the imagination of the world and fuelling an explosive growth of science fiction. While the space scientific exploration programme continues with the International Space Station, the space shuttle, the Mars explorations (NASA, 2009; RSA, 2009), more countries develop their space programmes (ESA, 2009) and even private space tourism grows, the label Space Age has by now almost disappeared from popular discourse and priorities. The fiftieth anniversary of the dawn of the Space Age was celebrated in 2007 (NASA, 2009), but not generating the same level of enthusiasm as it once had done. From around the turn of the twenty-first century, what has replaced nuclear and space technology as a defining feature of the age is information and communication technology. While the age defined by atomic energy and space travel would be less directly experienced by individuals, the rise of information and communication technology has penetrated society at an individual level, hence making a more direct impact on the way people live, work and socialize. The strong relationship between technology and social relations is obvious; the causality of technology in determining social relations, however, is not so.

The terms information or digital age are used in a wide variety of subjects, primarily referring to the application of ICT to various parts of life. The information age started with the invention of computers around the middle of the twentieth century, supported by the existing and expanding innovations in communication networks.

Fascination with the Space Age has now been replaced by admiration for digital technologies (Kennedy Space Center, Florida, USA).

Alongside their impact on economic productivity, we also hear about the rise of individualism and the decline of social habits such as the face-to-face encounter, the death of books and the print media, and of institutions such as libraries, museums and universities, expecting that the new technologies may, or even should, make them redundant, changing the world beyond recognition. However, this characterization limits the interpretation of society and its range of options. As Gershunyand Miles (1983: 232) put it, 'It can be extremely misleading to talk of "*the* information society".' Indeed a wide range of information societies are possible if the range and scope of policy choice, technological application and the context are considered. According to UNESCO, 'It would be inadmissible to envisage the information and communication revolution leading – through a narrow, fatalistic technological determinism – to a single possible form of society' (UNESCO, 2005: 17). Such a narrow vision and particular forms of behaviour tend to privilege particular types of knowledge at the expense of others. Rather than a narrow, technologically determined identification for society and economy, which has been labelled information society, the term knowledge society has been increasingly used to refer to a wider range of issues and concerns. 'The idea of the information society is based on technological breakthroughs. The concept of knowledge societies encompasses much broader social, ethical and political dimensions' (UNESCO, 2005: 17).

In summary, the far-reaching implications of ICT for society cannot be ignored. However, technology is only one factor among many in shaping society, the waves of enthusiasm for technological innovations are often short lived, and there are other sources and forms of knowledge, with social relations that have been formed around them, making the social world far more complex than a single causal change can explain. Knowledge society and knowledge economy are designations that are associated with the phenomenal growth and expansion of information and communication technologies, but there are other dimensions to the dramatic changes in society.

Long waves and techno-economic innovation

Some analysts have tried to explain major social change by the temporal logic of biological processes, through recurring cycles of innovation, growth, destruction and decline. Borrowing from biology, Schumpeter describes capitalism as an evolutionary organic process, with internal dynamics of its own, which changes not due to outside events such as wars and revolutions, but from inside. The prime mover in this process is innovation, competition and creative destruction of the old. Innovation is the 'fundamental impulse that sets and keeps the capitalist engine in motion', which comes from 'the new consumers' goods, the new methods of production or transportation, the new markets, the new forms of industrial organization' (Schumpeter, 2003: 83). The process of innovation 'incessantly revolutionizes the economic structure *from within*, incessantly destroying the old one, incessantly creating a new one. This process of Creative Destruction is the essential fact about capitalism. It is what capitalism consists in and what every capitalist concern has got to live in' (ibid). Against a static conception of economics, in which the price mechanism reigns supreme, where the analysis focuses on a situation 'as if there were no past or future to it' (p. 84), Schumpeter argues for a dynamic understanding. He locates the economic activity within a temporal context, which is ruled by the regularity of long waves and business cycles, with an in-built capacity for renewal.

The Russian economist Nikolai Kondratieff (1935) had argued that the dynamics of economic life in capitalist economies were not simple and linear, but complex and cyclical. He proposed the idea of long waves in capitalist economies lasting on average 50 years, fluctuating between periods of high and slow growth, marked by a succession of expansion, stagnation and recession. Schumpeter combined this temporal cycle with his notions of innovation and creative destruction, to come up with a regular pattern of historic change, each cycle being a separate 'industrial revolution'. The first Industrial Revolution started in the 1780s, followed by other waves starting in the 1840s, the 1890s and the 1940s. Through innovation in methods of production, commodities, forms of organization, sources of supply, trade routes and market, these revolutions reshaped the existing structure of industry, initiating a period of prosperity, even though interrupted by shorter business cycles. The cycle moved on to the elimination of obsolete elements and ended with periods of decline and depression. This was a 'process of recurrent rejuvenation of the productive apparatus' (Schumpeter, 2003: 68).

Shorter economic waves have also been identified as harmonics of the long Kondratieff waves: Kitchin cycles of three to five years, Juglar cycles of seven to

The process of creative destruction renovates the productive apparatus, destroying the old economic structures and incessantly creating new ones (Newcastle, UK).

11 years, and Kuznets cycles of 15 to 25 years (Korotayev and Tsirel, 2010). Kitchin cycles are shorter crises of oversupply, in which information about the declining demand takes some time to reach the suppliers. As demand increases, suppliers flood the market, but the information about the point of saturation takes a while to be fed back to them. The Juglar cycles, better known as business cycles, are also the result of the crisis of overproduction, but regarding investment and innovation. Here investment in productive capacities grows on the basis of responding to growing demands, but it cannot be switched off quickly when the demand declines, hence taking a longer period to run. Kuznets swings or cycles are longer and were first proposed by Simon Kuznets to account for the periods of intensified migration and the impact of demographic change on construction activities in response (Kuznets, 1930). Kuznets swings are also known as building or infrastructural investment cycles (Korotayev and Tsirel, 2010). Kuznets proposed a curve that would show a sequence of stages for an economy: as it develops, the share of agriculture in GNP decreases, the industries develop and then decline, and finally the services grow. In his later work, Kuznets offered a hypothesis in which an inverted U-curve related this cycle to income inequality: as nations become more prosperous, inequality first rises but then starts falling at a certain point, a hypothesis that is hotly debated and tested (Pessoa, 2009; Angeles, 2009). This curve resembles a biological analogy, from conception and infancy to adolescence, maturity and old age, which has been used to analyse the life cycle of a technology (Ayres, 1997).

While Schumpeter's analysis of innovation is multi-dimensional, the long waves have been increasingly associated with the dominant technology of the time, attempting to establish a causal link between technological change and economic long waves. The driving force for change, according to neo-Schumpeterians, is innovation and diffusion of new technologies (Dosi, 1988; Magnusson, 1993). Techno-economic structural transformation causes the social and institutional sphere to go through a structural crisis to adjust accordingly. So the key factor in the second long wave was low-cost steam-powered transportation, in the third low-cost steel, in the fourth low-cost energy from fossil fuels, and in the fifth low-cost microelectronics (Perez, 1983). Long waves are taken as an indicator of total socio-economic and institutional systems, representing successive modes of development responding to successive technological styles or techno-economic paradigms (Perez, 1983). In the downswing of a long wave, a new key technology emerges, which promises to reduce costs and open new possibilities, hence helping develop a new paradigm for the most efficient organization of production. The widespread adoption of this new technology signals a new wave, and when the full range of these new possibilities have been utilized, a paradigm peaks and the downswing starts. This peak is frenetic and short, but appears to give 'the promise of everlasting upward progress', where the new technological style is extended to new products and processes and establishes 'undue confidence in the institutional mechanisms', sowing the seeds of rigidity and inertia and ultimately contraction (Perez, 1983: 356). A long wave, therefore, is interpreted as a learning process, running out of steam when its information content is exhausted, going through a sequence of a new knowledge phase followed by a consolidation phase (Modelski, 2001).

The idea of long waves is not widely held among the economists; even those evolutionary economists who accept the concept do not agree on the events and dates that signal the start and end of a wave and the data that would be significant to identify the cycles. The long wave theorists weave together a number of themes into epochal paradigms, which are explained through technological change and associated economic, social and institutional change. In doing so, the focus of innovation has been narrowed down to technological change as the main driver for social and economic transformation (Wymbs, 2004; Hilmola, 2007). Such large schematic frameworks generate a sense of clarity and regularity to historical events and processes, which are then used to explain major changes and historic events, and predict future trends. They are the underlying trends within which events would make sense, offering a framework with which to segment historical time into distinct periods identified by economic change (van Roon, 1981). This is why long waves become popular after major historic events and their place in the upswing or downswing of a long wave, such as the global economic slowdown in the 1970s (Mensch, 1979; Modelski, 2001), the fall of the Berlin Wall in 1989 and the following collapse of the Soviet Union (Kuznetsov, 1992), and the global financial crisis of 2008 (Thompson, 2009; Korotayev and Tsirel, 2010).

The notions of long waves and a beating heart give an overall shape to a mass of diverse activities across time and space, which is why they are found attractive. They offer a structural pattern, a framework within which to make sense of the data, tidying up the mess of historical change. However, they also seem to justify a particular perspective into the world. If Schumpeter's 'perennial gale of creative destruction' (2003: 84) is taken to be the heart of economic life, then a complete disregard for the past and present in the name of the future would become justifiable. It is an economic expression of modernism, with its break with the past, which was seen as obsolete, and its hope for the future, which was always inevitably better. Any deviance from the tyranny of an accepted innovation would be considered anachronism, while alternative innovations would be condemned to silence and rejected as irrelevant. Comparing social processes with biology, such as a long-term evolutionary dynamic and a vibrant life force inside the economic process, therefore, is misleading, as it implies a degree of inevitability in the structural process. It is a reminder of Voltaire's Dr Pangloss: 'It is proved that things cannot be other than they are, for since everything is made for a purpose, it follows that everything is made for the best purpose' (quoted in Gowdy, 1997: 380).

Progress is an inherent assumption in evolutionary notions, both in biology and economics, as under competitive pressure, some features are kept and others discarded, and the resulting organism is better able to adapt and survive. The negative impacts of economic development on the biophysical environment are a witness that the evolutionary economic process is not necessarily always progressive and resulting in the best outcomes (Gowdy, 1997). In biology, destruction of old generations happens through their death; in economics, this destruction needs to be induced through creative destruction, as the cycle is much shorter and physical objects that constitute the productive apparatus can last for generations. The Darwinian notion of evolution as adaptation through natural selection is a rather passive notion: organisms that are better suited to an environment are better represented in the next generation, and there is no will involved (Eldridge, 1997). In economics, however, we are confronted by agents who are actively struggling to survive; they do their best to compete and can overcome their disadvantages if they change course. Information in biological evolution is transmitted through genes, but in society through interaction and learning. The impact of external factors cannot be denied, as adaptation through selection will not be able to absorb some of the effects of the external environment (Eldridge, 1997: 397). Biological processes are very long term, taking many millennia for a complex organism to change in adaptation to its environment. Social processes such as economic activity, in contrast, are conducted by intelligent human beings in particular contexts, with a range of options available to them. Meanwhile, the long wave theory assumes a structural logic for economic change, and individual actions appear to have only a limited impact on the course of events.

When applied to developing economies, the ideas of creative destruction and development from within become more controversial. The main form of creative destruction in the direct and indirect colonization of much of the world in the nineteenth and twentieth centuries was an intervention from outside, transforming places and institutions not through an internal logic but an external, imposed one. Innovation in these cases could then be used to justify the domination of Western economies over the rest of the world. This may be an internal logic of the economic system at the core of the global economy, but it did not necessarily reflect the internal dynamics and needs of the periphery. These economies did not change from within, but did so as a result of outside intervention. A similar dynamic may be observed in the relationship between the core and periphery within the advanced industrial economies.

In short, historic change is not necessarily subject to a neat cyclical logic associated with technological change. There are many technologies that emerge one after the other, each changing society's capacity and tools, and so the way we assign value and significance to these technological innovations also changes with them as they are adopted and widespread. The technologies of information and communication have been in the making for two centuries, while technologies such as nuclear, space and genetic technologies are also taken to be epoch-making. It follows the way we write history: we connect the events to one another through a narrative after they have enfolded, which reflects our current priorities and sensibilities. These retrospective narratives, however, cannot be used to predict the future, as the order we created from the past was selective, identifying patterns that may or may not resurface. The ideas of cyclical repetition and creative destruction appear to be offering normative licences for calling some ideas, objects and practices obsolete and so demolishing them accordingly in the name of innovation and progress, without much concern about the social impacts of these dramatic actions.

Around the turn of the twenty-first century, the collapse of the Soviet bloc, a long period of economic growth and major advances in information and communication technologies convinced many commentators that we had entered a completely different era. Excited analysts were claiming that economic cycles had been abolished and a new dawn had arrived. Some commentators have portrayed the rise of the knowledge-based economy as a sharp break from the past, signalling a new economy in which ICT has allowed firms to benefit from continual innovation in scientific and technological knowledge, resulting in productivity gains and falling transaction and processing costs. This was a new economy in which business cycles were ruled out, and growth was fast, continuous and non-inflationary, as reflected in ever rising stock markets. This optimistic belief in a new economy, however, came to an end with the dot-com crash and resurfacing of business cycles as the underlying structural properties of market economies.

Some even question the existence of a knowledge economy, arguing that knowledge has always been embedded in much of what people do. Rather than a full and sudden transition from one economic formation to another, which labels such as post-Fordist or post-industrial suggest, some have argued that we have witnessed a 'soft discontinuity' (David and Foray, quoted in Brinkley, 2006: 5). Sceptics have insisted on continuity with, rather than break from, the past. Rather than the arrival of a new information age, they argue, the abundance of information in society had caused new adjustments to be made in society (Webster, 2006). This is a blurring of the lines of division between manufacturing and services, facilitated through the development of new technologies, in which new knowledge is embedded in both goods and services (Powell and Snellman, 2004).

Technological metaphors and urban form: clocks, engines and computers

At the level of urban space and form, we can observe associations between particular technologies and particular forms, for example how the invention of lifts made the construction of tall buildings possible. These associations, however, only make sense in a wider context. The question in our investigation is now about the role of digital technologies in urban transformation, for which we need first to go back in time, to see how different phases of technology-inspired worldviews have set out to transform cities, with varying degrees of success. Looking at the history of urban form after the Renaissance, many new technological innovations have made contributions to the way cities have been built and run, from print and gun powder to aviation and satellite technologies. With an eye on the theoretical significance of time, space and knowledge for our study so far, at least three technologies stand out: clocks, engines and computers, providing new tools to measure time, to control space and to manage information. These technologies have been widely used in a metaphoric sense to characterize historic periods and to shape cities accordingly.

In the first phase, mechanical clocks became a symbol for the interpretation of the universe. Mechanical clocks were invented in the fourteenth century, but it was not until the scientific revolution in the seventeenth century that they became the prevailing metaphor for how the world was ordered. Newtonian mechanics envisaged the natural world to work like a mechanical clock, following unchanging rules and absolute principles. The world as people experienced it was likened to the face of a clock, with an underlying order of wheels and springs that lay behind that face and needed to be discovered (Hollis, 2002). Kepler rejected the quasi-animated and magical ideas of the universe, which prevailed in the medieval world, and compared the universe to a clock, heralding a mechanistic conception of nature that was embraced by natural philosophy from Descartes onwards (Whitrow, 1972).

The city was then reshaped to be an appropriate reflection of this mechanical cosmic order, both in the way its face appeared and the way its underlying springs and wheels worked. This order took the shape of geometrical regularity, as mathematics was thought to be the way natural laws could be captured and understood. A system of nodes, axes and networks were superimposed on the medieval cities that were thought to be disorderly and haphazard in their shape and order. The period coincided with the rise of absolute monarchies and the process of creating nation-states, so the urban space was treated as an opera stage, on which this power could be displayed and celebrated. The city was a mechanical organization mimicking a mechanical universe ruled by timeless rules that could be understood and represented through a static and harmonious Euclidean geometry (Madanipour, 2007a). European city builders were trying to recreate the ancient Rome, as evident in the transformations of Paris by Colbert in the seventeenth century and Haussmann in the nineteenth century, both mentioning their inspirations from ancient Rome

Mechanical clocks, symbolizing an understanding of how the universe worked, were used to reorganize society and space (London, UK).

(Trout, 1996: 168; Horne, 2002: 265). This was even seen in L'Enfant's plan of Washington, DC, with its senate and its location, Capitol, both named after Rome's.

In the second phase, the static geometry gives way to a dynamic mobility, as the invention of engines, which gave rise to the Industrial Revolution, transformed cities in more profound ways, providing new patterns for spatial configuration. The nineteenth century was the century of movement, facilitated by the steam engines used in railways and ships. Railways facilitated mobility, uprooting people from their towns and villages and concentrating them in large industrial cities (Briggs, 1968). Railways opened up new continents and speeded up movement across space in a way that was not imaginable before. Cities became connected to one another, leading to the creation of standard time that would overcome differences between local times (Aveni, 2000). The Victorian cities themselves were opened up to allow new railway stations to be built at the heart of the city and the railway lines to cut through the city. This was a path to modernity that was considered absolutely necessary, even at the cost of removing large parts of the city altogether. In Newcastle upon Tyne, for example, the railway lines and station got dangerously close to the ancient castle from which the city bears its name.

The rule of engines continued in the twentieth century, though this time in the form of cars. The modern movement in architecture, which dominated the century's aesthetics and approach to urban form, developed a new visual and spatial alphabet, which mimicked the language of engineering and manufacturing

Engines facilitated mobility, reshaping the city accordingly, which grew horizontally and vertically (Tokyo, Japan).

industry's logic (Le Corbusier, 1978). Le Corbusier (1987: 3) recounts how he was impressed by the power of the car when standing in the middle of a street in Paris: 'Motors in all directions, going at all speeds. I was overwhelmed, an enthusiastic rapture filled me . . . The simple and ingenuous pleasure of being in the centre of so much power, so much speed.' His recipe, and that of the entire modern movement in the twentieth century, was to reshape the city to facilitate the car's reign. Modernism was a technologically determinist school of thought, which had used new technologies of construction and transport to transform the cities of the world. The new parts of cities were designed on the basis of car access, and so fast roads were cut through the old cities. The use of engines, as trains or cars, largely reshaped the urban space, especially at a time that much of the urban expansion was taking place.

Cities grew horizontally and vertically, made possible by the invention of cars and lifts. The power of steam that first ran the engines was also used to produce steel, used in construction of large spans, major bridges and high-rise buildings, which together with the invention of lifts helped change the scale and height of buildings and the density of cities. It was the motor car, however, which prevailed in the horizontal spread of urban areas and the suburbanization process that became the hallmark of the twentieth century. According to Frank Lloyd Wright, 'The outcome of the city will depend on the race between the automobile and the elevator, and anyone who bets on the elevator is crazy' (quoted in O'Sullivan, 2003: 167).

While nineteenth-century modernization had used the aesthetic language of earlier ages (Schorske, 1981), the twentieth century invented its own, which was the language of modern technology. It was inspired by movement (Giedion, 1967), but now it was individualized movement of cars, rather than the collective movement that the railways would allow. Rather than following the static geometry of the earlier centuries, the geometry of the modern city was now following the aesthetics of the Industrial Age, whereby the rules of perspective were abandoned and a dynamic depiction of the subject through an exploded geometry became the norm. The geometry of the city was a dynamic one, which integrated fast movement into the urban fabric, reshaping it to be experienced from inside a moving vehicle.

The third phase in these paradigmatic shifts is the rise of computers, as the technology that symbolically defines the character of the latter part of the twentieth century and the beginning of the twenty-first. The ability to collect, store, process, transmit and receive data in real time at high speeds and volumes has become the new technological paradigm. The initial phase of this new paradigm has brought about a sense of invisibility of change, a virtual world that appears to compete, and even take over from, the real physical world. With the arrival of this virtual world, it appears that there is little evidence that physical reality would need to be changed. The static geometry of the early modern age was partly replaced by the dynamic geometry of the modern city. In the late modern city of computers and communication networks, is there a major spatial component to a cyberspace, which is detached from these real and metaphorical geometries?

Fractal geometries may be used to explain how the world is ordered, but there is no attempt, or a need felt, to shape the world in fractal geometries. The mechanical conception of the universe dominated much of the age of engines, but it was started to be challenged by Einstein's theory of relativity, by quantum physics and by chaos theory. The concept of an overarching unchanging order gave way to a conception of order as determined by the behaviour of smaller component parts of ultimately unpredictable systems.

Mediated city: city of computers and communication networks

The use of ICT in the everyday life of the city, which started from small steps in more technologically advanced areas of activity, has now spread to many more spheres – from building and managing cities and delivery of public services to conducting economic and cultural exchange, as reflected in terms such as e-government, e-business, e-learning, e-museums, etc. Many urban affairs now seem to be mediated through these information and communication technologies, resulting in facilitating the delivery of services, cultural and economic exchange, and political struggle.

The sphere of government is one in which mediation of the digital infrastructure has been used to establish interactive relationships between governments and citizens. The idea of e-government has become systematically embraced by governments at all levels, and it is thought that the term digital city designates a

Digital technologies have found widespread application in urban life (Berlin, Germany).

city in which e-government is in place, allowing the citizens to have access to information and services online (Millham and Eid, 2009). In the UK, the e-government unit (eGU) is the largest unit in the Cabinet Office, responsible for formulating information technology (IT) strategy and policy, developing common IT components for use across government, promoting best practice across government and delivering citizen-centred online services (Cabinet Office, 2007). The central government also worked with the local governments to develop their capacity in delivering online services. At the local level, the Local e-Government Programme officially closed in April 2006, having met its target of ensuring that 'all local councils offer all local services online by December 2005' and assisting local governments to 'achieve 100 per cent capability in electronic delivery of priority services by 2005, in ways that customers will use' (DCLG, 2010). The levels of use, however, are still low, which is suggested to be due to the low levels of citizen engagement in the design, development and evolution of local e-government systems (Damodaran *et al.*, 2008). E-government has been spreading across the world in different countries, with varying degrees of reach and effectiveness, which partly depends on the level of economic development in these regions (e.g., Tsai *et al.*, 2009; Arpaci, 2010; Rorissa and Demissie, 2010).

The mediated relationship between the government and citizens, however, is not limited to public services; it is also reflected in the expressions of power from both sides, through surveillance and security concerns as well struggles for democracy and openness. Digital technologies have been used in surveillance of the urban scene for various reasons, including traffic monitoring and management and for crime prevention. In the UK, where the use of closed circuit television cameras and imaging technologies has been widespread for a variety of purposes, it is used by government departments in guarding perimeters and national borders, by small businesses in protecting their premises and goods, and by local authorities and police forces for public safety (Home Office, 2010). While the main rationale for the use of this technology is safety and security, critics argue that its effectiveness has not been proven, and while technology has become more sophisticated, safeguards and regulation for protection of privacy have lagged behind (Liberty, 2010). Various technologies such as face recognition, DNA identification and radio frequency identification have been used, and large amounts of data have been collected about citizens, leading to concerns about whether the data are kept safe and about how they are used.

While digital technologies facilitate the collection, analysis and storage of data, the implications for privacy and human rights are not yet fully known. The boundaries between public and private spheres in the digital world become more blurred than in the everyday physical world. A walk in the virtual space may appear to take place in the privacy of a person's home, but it is not anonymous; it is a recorded trip that can be viewed by others, shared for commercial purposes or monitored for security reasons without the knowledge or consent of the traveller. On the one hand, it has been argued that people should not be worried about this if they have done nothing wrong; on the other hand, it has brought about concern by those who are worried about the way this information is used and its impact on human rights and privacy. During the Cold War, socialist countries were blamed by Western liberal democracies for their cultures of surveillance and close monitoring of their citizens. Now critics argue that a somewhat similar attitude, even associated with racism, is embraced by the European states (Bunyan, 2010). Most citizens appear to accept, or even campaign for, the installation of surveillance cameras or other surveillance technologies, remaining somewhat indifferent to the concerns raised by academic researchers and human rights campaigners, which has posed a challenge to the commentators to explain the difference (Best, 2010).

Digital technologies are also used to challenge government authority, as the protest movements in the Middle East and political campaigners in China have shown. While these technologies are used for mass surveillance, they can also be used for mass mobilization, helping protesters to coordinate their activities, spread information about their struggles and mobilize new movements. In response, some governments have tried to control the Internet, placing limitations on sites that can be accessed, attempting to block the path of protestors and campaigners, as well as limiting the flow of information that they consider to be against their interests. The infrastructure of the Internet, however, cannot be blocked and information finds a way to go around and become accessible. Digital technology is being used as a weapon of social and political control, as well as a vehicle of free expression and democratic struggle.

In the economic field, digital technology has been considered to be the source of gains in productivity and economic growth, and the vehicle of globalization. The notions of e-commerce, e-marketplace and e-business are all used to refer to the way digital technology is used in economic transactions (e.g., Standing *et al.*, 2010; McCloskey and Leppel, 2010; Pastuszak, 2010). This application of technology appears to lie at the heart of the notion of knowledge economy, whereby it expands the possibilities of trade and exchange, facilitating new divisions of labour, finding access to new sources of innovation and new markets. E-business involves the application of digital technologies to all areas of business activity, which includes e-commerce, i.e., buying and selling goods and services through electronic networks, including everyday shopping. Here, too, there is a tension between open access to information on the Internet and the attempt by commercial organizations to charge for its use, as we saw in the intellectual property discussion, or use the recorded data for commercial gains. This area is subject to trial and error, leading to many controversial issues that need to be resolved. Examples include online access to music or newspapers' content, where the search is on to find an approach that would not create barriers to access and not disadvantage the producers of information and entertainment.

In the cultural field, there are similar possibilities of expanding access and the range of information and activities. Online universities and the online availability of digital libraries, museum exhibits, art galleries, music and movies, as well as the use of digital technologies to create new forms and expressions, are central to the notion of creative economies. The value of embracing these technologies, however, is not equally accepted and there are serious doubts about their impact on the social environment. For example, the claims made about the use of e-learning in higher education, whereby it can become the primary form of communication and replace human interaction or it can offer all knowledge in codified form, have been doubted (Njenga and Fourie, 2010). The value of universities as social spaces in which young people forge friendships and learn about their world through personal engagement, therefore, cannot be replaced by the functionalist delivery of lectures online. Libraries, archives and museums can converge the acquisition, documentation, representation and access to enduring knowledge (Given and McTavish, 2010). However, the mechanisms for doing so are open to question, especially when involving commercial benefits for large organizations. Some authors and publishers launched a lawsuit against Google for digitizing books in some libraries, which led to a settlement through which a Books Rights Registry will be set up to manage the issue. The establishment of e-museums, or the use of Augmented Representation of Cultural Objects, such as placing educational kiosks in museums, have been promoted (Johansson, 2001; Sylaiou *et al.*, 2010). Meanwhile, the debate is on whether the virtual presence of cultural objects can replace their actual presence.

Digital technologies, therefore, have spread widely and penetrated deeply into various spheres of urban life and spheres of activity, becoming new tools with which to exert or challenge political power and social control, conduct cultural and economic exchange, and enhance representation by adding a virtual layer onto the experiences of the physical world. Given this ubiquity, digital technologies have lent their names to the city, which has been called digital city, networked city, etc. This is a mediated city that is increasingly using and relying on a new

How far can the virtual presence of artefacts replace their real presence? (London, UK).

digital infrastructure, a city that is embracing additional, new forms of mediation between people, objects and representations. However, this is as yet a partly invisible addition, a hidden infrastructure the spatial impacts of which are yet to be fully developed.

Digital technology has had a major impact on how people live, touching all aspects of work, leisure and movement. There are many ways that the spatial implications of these technologies could be classified and discussed. Here we can identify four major forms of such impacts: functional augmentation, spatial compression, temporal acceleration and social decontextualization. Through these technologies, the dynamics of space and time for some activities are transformed, while augmenting the various functional activities and decoupling individuals and organizations from their social and spatial contexts.

Functional augmentation

It is not uncommon for people to live in old houses but with modern lifestyles. If we look at a house that was built a century ago and compare it to its original state, what are the changes, and can we attribute any of these changes to changes in knowledge? Most of the change is in technologies: refrigerator, land-line telephone, dishwasher, washing machine, tumble dryer, central heating, digital television, broadband Internet connection and mobile telephones, etc. There is also change in the way the householders live, dress and think. But there is little change in the spatial configuration of the house: it is more or less as it was before, with the addition of double glazing, added insulation and a few other minor changes. The streets are also the same as before, although they are now used for cars and buses, rather than horse-drawn carriages. Technologies have changed, infrastructures have transformed, but the essential spatial configurations of the house and the city, at least in the old parts, have remained almost the same. If we are looking for spaces that would reflect our current and forthcoming economic and social conditions, should we look for them only in technological, institutional and behavioural change, rather than in spatial change?

The philosopher and classical economist Adam Smith (1993) interprets technology as an abridged form of human work. This may have been an apt interpretation of the early stages of industrialization of manufacturing, where a single new machine could replace the work of dozens of workers. In our time, technology is still considered a vehicle of increasing productivity, allowing a higher rate of activity for a certain amount of human effort. While some forms of technology are abridged human work, others are tools that make new activities possible. For example, a microscope or a telescope enables an operator to magnify objects to such an extent that no amount of human effort would have made it possible. When it comes to computers and communication networks, the scope of possibilities that are opened up are unprecedented. In these cases, technology extends human capacities, allowing new activities to take place that were not possible or imaginable before. In both dimensions, abridging human work and extending human possibilities, technology augments human functions.

Since the arrival of digital technologies, the relationship between these technologies and the existing physical transactions has been a subject of trial and error, and businesses are encouraged to 'get the right mix of bricks and clicks' (Gulati and Garino, 2000). Augmented reality (or mixed reality) is a recent technology that aims to bridge real and virtual spaces, mixing computer-generated stimuli (visual, sound or haptic) with real ones, with the aim of helping user interaction in real time (Portalés *et al.*, 2010). The race is on to develop new technologies (Lee *et al.*, 2010) that would facilitate this interface between the virtual and the real, with applications in various fields of health, education, engineering and entertainment. Applications are found in surgery (Hansen *et al.*, 2010), education and learning (de Freitas *et al.*, 2010), product design and manufacturing (Ong *et al.*, 2007), photogrammetry (Portalés *et al.*, 2010), heritage and culture (Sylaiou *et al.*, 2010), and games (Tedjokusumo *et al.*, 2010), among others.

Augmented reality (AR) technology, it has been suggested, provides a seamless interaction between real and virtual environments, enhances the representations of reality and produces computer-generated objects that can be used as spatial cues for face-to-face and remote collaboration (Billinghurst and Kato, 2002;

New technologies have transformed many functions in urban life (Tokyo, Japan).

Portalés *et al.*, 2010). AR technology provides an interactive framework in which collaboration with other users and dynamic application of information and communication technology becomes possible. It helps spread the ubiquity of ICT in the city, embedding its use in a variety of activities in the home, office, library, museum, operating theatre and classroom. Mixed reality technology helps the deployment of interactive representation, in which an element of feedback is added to the everyday activities, enhancing the human capacity to execute tasks and collaborate with others.

Some have argued that the divide between real and virtual that is taken for granted by the design and planning professionals can be bridged through recognizing and drawing on the invisible digital infrastructure of the city (Aurigi, 2008; Graham and Marvin, 1996; 2001). In applying AR technology to the urban space, it is used to add layers of information to representations of the environment and to develop visions of the future environment through collaborative design and planning (Sareika and Schmalstieg, 2007; Wang *et al.*, 2007; Ismail and Sunar, 2009; Höller *et al.*, 2009). It has also been widely promoted in urban management, in which some municipal services and communication with citizens have been digitized, using e-services and e-government as the extension of ICT into urban management. With the ubiquity of information and communication technologies, however, the discussion is about the 'augmented city', in which the focus is changing 'from a technological, project-based view towards a more holistic view of urban space enhanced, and permeated, by technology' (Aurigi, 2006: 8).

Functional augmentation may enrich the way a city works, as previous forms of infrastructure have done, from water and electricity to trains, telegraph and telephone. A critique of augmentation, however, may be raised for undermining the physical and social contacts that were going on in various places of service delivery. This takes at least two forms. On the one hand, there is a reduction in physical contact by human hands with objects and practices. Engagement with a digital screen may be efficient in a wide range of activities, but in a physical sense it is a stationary activity, which removes the incentive to go out and to develop a multi-sensual relationship with the surrounding environment. All such connections are mediated through standardized objects designed and managed by others. On the other hand, the social contacts that people had with one another are sacrificed for the efficiency of the technologically mediated service. Some service providers such as banks and governments may offer easier and faster online services, but by doing so they also undermine some of the possibilities for sociability.

The private motor car, the personal computer and the mobile phone are the technological manifestations of the drive for individualization, and in turn fuel this drive further, allowing individual action that is independent of others. Other technologies have also had similar effects. For example, the technology of central heating had a major impact on the way the members of a household used their home. Whereas before, everyone had to congregate in the family room to benefit from the fire, central heating would heat up all of the house, removing the need for togetherness and allowing members of the household the freedom of their separate rooms. Although in some sense, the radio and later television set brought

Creating complicated architectural shapes has become possible through the application of digital technologies (Newcastle, UK).

household members together, ICT and the reduction in the price of televisions have made individual use of the media possible, once again removing the obstacles to individualization.

Further back in time, the technology of water network, which delivers water to individual units across the city, released households from travelling to the water source, which would be a spring, a river or a well. The social gatherings around the water well or fountain (and its modern equivalent the water fountain in the office) was part of everyday life of a city, bringing people together, acting as a place of information and socialization. In the individualized system that the water network provides, sociability is traded for convenience. It is of course far better to get water at home, rather than having to travel, sometimes long distances, for collecting water. Easy access to safe drinking water is an unquestionable human need, which is well answered by the establishment of water networks. The social result, however, is the loss of some of the spaces of sociability.

Dispersion and agglomeration

Spatial compression is one of the widely discussed features of new technologies. Through easier transmission of information as well as heightened mobility, the spatial barriers that kept people within strict limits have been loosened. For many the locality in which they live is only one dimension of their life experience, while they are able to communicate with people in other parts of the world for personal relations or work. The ability to keep in touch with others, to send and receive large amounts of information across invisible networks, has transformed the perceptions of space and time, as well as some spatial practices. The metaphor of spatial compression is then used to convey the sense in which space in between people in different places has been compressed, reducing what geographers have called the friction of distance (Dicken and Lloyd, 1990).

At first, it was thought that new technology would remove the need for physical co-presence and face-to-face communication. Even before the arrival of digital technologies, some had thought that cities had come to the end of their useful life (Webber, 2003). With the arrival of information and communication technologies, individuals who are connected to the network, it was thought, would live in a 'space of flows', in which location mattered less and distance even lesser. Spatial limitations would be removed and the relationships between individuals from across the world would be freely established, releasing the need for concentration in cities, questioning even the future survival of cities. However, investigations into the spatial impact of digital technology have so far failed to show any significant impact. While the possibility of communication has been intensified, its spatial effects have intensified urban living, rather than dismantling cities. One reason is that new technology is not able on its own to change the socio-spatial configuration of cities. Research has indeed shown that it intensifies the existing trends, rather than transforming the urban space in radically different ways. While digital technologies are at the heart of knowledge-based economies, the spaces of the knowledge economy will be shaped by a wider range of factors.

On the surface, a paradox seems to be at work with conflicting forces that shape the city, all made possible and assisted by new technologies. On the one hand, centrifugal forces facilitate the movement of people away from others and from the city; on the other hand, centripetal forces have continually fuelled urban expansion through creating new clusters and agglomerations. On the one hand, these forces encourage the atomization of individuals and households; on the other hand, they bring them together in new ways. Both of these processes have drawn on new technologies; in a sense, new technologies have been developed to help make these centrifugal and centripetal forces grow and influence the temporal and spatial conditions of increasingly urbanized societies. So how do we account for the apparent contradiction between their outcomes? How can dispersion and agglomeration be the results of the same technological and socio-economic processes?

Centrifugal forces operate through the twin processes of spatial decontextualization and temporal acceleration. From trains to cars, and from telegraph to the Internet, a continual process of technological innovation has facilitated the mobility of ideas, information, goods, services and people at unprecedented speeds and scales. At the level of individuals, this mobility has brought about a degree of freedom from the context, enabling people to move to other places, abandoning or keeping some contact with the place they left behind or setting up completely new connections. It has changed the way social and spatial contexts exert influence on the life patterns of their members. As people can choose to move about more easily, and form networks of communication with others who are based elsewhere, the membership in local socio-spatial contexts becomes looser than ever before.

These changes of decontextualization and acceleration have made it possible to reconfigure everyday spaces, opening up ever larger distances for daily activities of various sorts, while transforming and loosening the local ties. A significant consequence of this mobility has been overcoming some of the temporal and spatial limits that have been taken for granted for millennia. A parallel consequence has been atomization of the individuals, who have looked for ways to loosen the hold of the context. These twin processes of decontextualization and acceleration can be observed in the development of theories and practices of modern societies, as exemplified in their philosophical ideas and new technological innovations.

The notion of the modern autonomous individual was in the making for a number of centuries (Coleman, 1996). It was expressed in the philosophy of Rene Descartes (1968), who refused the influence of custom and tradition, which had dominated the medieval world, and argued for a rational foundation for belief and action. In this way, the centre of gravity moved from society and its metaphysical beliefs and conventions to the individual, who now stood at the centre of the world as the measure of all things. Other philosophers of the modern period have extended this individualization: from Kant to J.S.Mill and Nietzsche, each in his own way radicalizing the notion of individuals free from the constraints that society has placed on them, so as to remove obstacles that would prevent their flourishing.

This celebration of the human subject as the centre of the universe can be seen in the art and architecture of the Renaissance and what followed it (Pevsner, 1963); it can also be seen in the new technologies that have been created ever since. Transport technologies during the nineteenth and twentieth centuries had enabled the large-scale movement of people out of their towns and villages to go elsewhere in their country or abroad, where they thought they could have access to better living conditions. At the urban level, these technologies, particularly the motor car, were the symbols of individualization, which allowed for flexible movement in all directions, and hence fuelling suburbanization, the ultimate spatial form in decontextualization and atomization.

The Internet is the latest in a long list of inventions that have enabled human subjects to free themselves from the constraints of their contexts and accelerate the pace of their activities. In this sense, some intentions and interpretations of the Internet have been libertarian by nature, hoping to contribute to a radical individualization project. The period and the social milieu in which it emerged coincided with the rise of alternative lifestyles and the rejection of mainstream norms and moral certainties. Its pioneers seem to have seen in it the possibility of breaking with this mainstream society and enjoying a level of personal freedom that had never been experienced before. Technological innovation was seen as the pathway to this freedom. The result is atomized individuals with an accelerated pace of life and a wider spatial reach.

Information and communication technologies are the latest in a long list of inventions that have expressed the desire for loosening the connections between individuals and their contexts (Vienna, Austria).

Centripetal forces, nevertheless, bring these atomized individuals together in cities. At first, this seems to be a contradiction, a reverse process at work that goes against decontextualization and acceleration. For generations, people have thought about the end of the city, first through suburbanization and then through the spread of information and communication technologies. If people could live where they wanted, it was thought, they would surely abandon the overcrowding, noise and air pollution that characterize large cities. Why is it then that cities are growing more than ever before, to the extent that now the majority of the world's population is urban?

The processes of decontextualization and acceleration do uproot people from their spatial and temporal contexts, but these processes do not take place in a void, neither do they throw people into an atomized emptiness. They are uprooted so as to be absorbed in the new centres of economic production, which in the new globalized economies tend to be in cities. It is a process of creative destruction, which destroys one social milieu to create another one. The process of urbanization involves a large number of factors, which, as we saw earlier, bring about agglomeration and concentration of people, resources and activities. It is the magnet of agglomeration that takes people out of their contexts and attracts them. It is the logic of this magnet that accelerates the speed of life in large cities and invests in new technologies that would accelerate the pace even further to maximize the use of time and space.

The formation of these magnets transforms the map of the earth, creating agglomeration and accumulation in some places, while depopulating and bypassing other areas. In spatial terms, this is best manifest in the rise of cities in the last two centuries, a process that has continued and intensified to this day and is likely to do so in the foreseeable future. This is part of a general process of agglomeration and accumulation that is central to the emergence and growth of capitalism, as it facilitates the development of the economies of scale in production and consumption of goods and services.

These forces of course do not operate for everyone and in every context. While hyper-mobility may be the conditions of the elite at the heart of the metropolitan economies, these are not the circumstances of the majority of the world's population. In rich countries, people who are in weaker socio-economic positions have limited resources, and hence their spatial reach and temporal pressures are radically different from those who have better access to resources. The growing social divide inside these countries has created differential life trajectories and chances within the same territories. In marginal parts of metropolitan areas, or in smaller towns and cities outside the global cities, life may go on much as before, making gradual adjustments to come to terms with new technological innovations, which often arrive years after the hotspots of innovation. Outside rich countries, these technologies may take much longer to arrive, become accessible to a minority of the population and life stories may remain unaffected by the time–space compression that frames the lives of the metropolitans. When technologies that have been developed in one particular context are transferred to other contexts, their meaning and use could change, no longer necessarily used for the purposes they were designed.

As time and space are turned into assets, and as they are finite resources as such, the pressure is on to maximize their use. The processes of globalization and technological innovation, which feed on one another, are indeed expressions of the desire to maximize the use of time and space. By spreading activities in complementing time zones, a global operation can overcome the spatial and temporal limits of working in one location. In opposition to this spatial-temporal pressure for financial rewards, there are many different movements, resisting the use of new technologies and the spread of globalization. An example is the Cittaslow movement, which nostalgically looks to the slow paces of historic cities as a way of living that refuses to sign up to an ever faster pace of globalized life.

Conclusion

Digital technology is a central part of the notion of knowledge economy, allowing information to be codified and transmitted in new ways. However, it cannot be necessarily and fully equated with the complexity of a knowledge-based economy. This economy would involve finding economic value for activities in both science and culture, which may or may not involve computers and communication networks. It is true that artists and scientists both use the new technologies, and many of them would only be able to do their work through these technologies, but their work also involves processes of long-term research or artistic creativity that for some can take place without any computer applications. The creative and economic dimensions of the knowledge-based economy are enhanced and facilitated by new technologies, but they are not necessarily co-extensive.

The prevailing technology of the time has often influenced the framework of possibilities in the city. It has also been widely adopted in a metaphorical sense, used beyond its actual capacity and use. In the city of clocks, for example, the notion of a clockwork universe inspired a sense of order that could be understood and presented in Euclidean geometry. The urban form that was given to Western cities, between the Renaissance and the nineteenth century, was inspired by this notion of cosmic order that was expressed in Newtonian mechanics. In the age of engines, a new infrastructure of access and new spaces of production created at first a geometry of *laissez-faire*, to be reshaped and re-adjusted through the growth of social forces in the hope of creating a fairer and better ordered geometry through a visible network of railways and roads. Now, in the mediated city, the urban space is formed on the basis of an invisible infrastructure of information and communication, allowing the urban space to be shaped by different considerations, whereby the forces of individualization and agglomeration are at work. Digital technology may be an invisible infrastructure that would enhance and intensify existing patterns of social life and economic production. As such, its spatial implications would not be separate from the way society works, with its social stratification, political tensions, and economies of scale and market dynamics. In all these phases, the issues of social stratification and inequality, or the attitudes of indifference or even hostility towards the natural environment, have been present, each translating these issues into spatial configurations.

Alongside technological change, which has replaced human work with automated systems and has encouraged decontextualization and individualization, there is a process of agglomeration and clustering, which aims at creating economies of scale. The combination of spatial-temporal compression, atomization and agglomeration creates new urban landscapes in which knowledge economy is emerging.

7 Global organization of production

We have seen that the key features of the knowledge economy include innovation through the changing nature of knowledge to become a productive capacity and economic asset, facilitated by the use of information and communication technologies, transforming the nature of economic products. In this chapter we explore another dimension of this transformation, which is the social organization of production, finding spatial expression in a global division of labour.

Social organization of production

Alongside technological change, organizational change also plays a crucial role in economic change. The changing social organization of production has been used as a framework with which to explain change in the structural conditions of society, whereby the changing dynamics of production are taken to be the central feature of economic change, causing new social configurations. Different strands of these investigations have been grouped under the label 'post-Fordist', which include neo-Schumpeterian, flexible specialization and the regulation school (Amin, 1994). These are attempts at periodization, aiming to show a paradigm shift: how a transition from mass production to flexible production arrangements characterizes a new era.

The early-twentieth-century Taylorism was a model of management that rationalized production through intensified specialization. Industrial production could increase productivity and lower the price of commodities through mass production, conducted on assembly lines based on a detailed division of labour, where specialization and repetition could rely on lower-level skills. This method of mass production and specialization was used in Henry Ford's car-making factory, which is why Antonio Gramsci used the term Fordism to refer to this organization of work. Mass production, however, started to change from the 1950s onwards, as the phase of demand for, and the capacity for the production of, mass-produced goods gave way to the demand for variation and distinction, leading to the rise of more differentiated products and flexible forms of production (Jacobs, 1970). The twentieth century had been the century of organization (Aglietta, 2000), and new changes heralded the end of organized capitalism and the start of a so-called disorganized one (Lash and Urry, 1987).

The changing organization of work is a key driver of change in spatial economy (London, UK).

A new system of industrial production was emerging, which was characterized by flexible, customized specialization and the application of new technologies. The nineteenth-century triumph of mass production over craft production was the first industrial divide, now followed by a second industrial divide in which craft production re-emerged in new significant ways (Piore and Sabel, 1984). This new structure of production was thought to have the capacity for restructuring the society on a communitarian basis, and would be a challenge to Keynesian economics, large corporate organization, the separation of concept and execution, and production of standardized goods. Flexible specialization, Piore and Sabel (1984: 17) wrote, 'is a strategy of permanent innovation: accommodating to ceaseless change, rather than an effort to control it'. Flexible production had continued to exist in the areas in which the supply of skilled workers and the differentiated demand were high, as distinctive from the areas such as the US, where mass immigration of unskilled workers and demand for standardized goods facilitated the emergence of mass production (Sabel and Zeilin, 1997). The emergence of flexible production could therefore be seen as a sign of the affluence of the market, which embraced a diversity of lifestyles and patterns of consumption.

Piore and Sabel used the cases of southern Germany and Third Italy. Third Italy referred to some of the central and north-eastern parts of the country, where interdependent small firms and workshops emerged in the 1970s as the engines of economic development. In contrast to the organized labour in mass-production

First Italy, this area was marked by small units specializing in a range of related products and employing a flexible workforce (Brusco, 1982; Kumar, 2005). Another case was the way Japan had used teamwork and just-in-time methods of production, which were markedly different from the Fordist method of mass production. These changes were taken to signal the passing of the mass-production age. For the flexible specialization theorists, the general dichotomy between flexible specialization and mass production was taken up as an epochal transformation, which was extended to geographical distinctions by those trying to explain regional specificities (Storper, 1997). The flexible specialization school had an overall positive assessment of this transition into what they saw as a more humane pattern of work, with the possibility of social integration. It could reintegrate conception and execution, which had been separated from one another in the industrialization process and had alienated workers from their products (Bourdieu and Coleman, 1991). However, mass production did not come to an end, but only relocated to other regions in an integrating global economy in which large and small firms coexist. As we shall see, the separation between conception and

New, more flexible methods of organizing production distinguished Japanese companies from their Western counterparts (Tokyo, Japan).

execution has now been globalized, in a new division of labour in which some people and places are involved in design and management, while others in physical production.

The transition of some sections of Western economies out of mass production has been interpreted by others, such as the regulation school, in less favourable terms, owing to its negative impact on the lives of industrial workers. One of the main strands of post-Fordism is the regulation approach – one of the trends in institutional and evolutionary economics, which analyses capital accumulation in conjunction with the regulations that make such accumulation possible. It is rooted in Marxism, and especially seems to address Marx's concern about the relationship between base and superstructure. Marx's periodization had identified a linear progressive interpretation for history, in which capitalism had replaced feudal and mercantilist periods, and itself was going to be replaced by socialism. The regulation school's periodization focused on different episodes of capitalism and how its chronic crises were managed through changing organization of economic production. Regulationists focus on 'the changing combinations of economic *and extra-economic* institutions and practices that help to secure . . . a certain stability and predictability in accumulation' (Jessop, 2001: x–xi).

In his influential book, *A Theory of Capitalist Regulation,* Michel Aglietta outlined an approach, which was 'an offshoot' of Fernand Barudel's analysis of the history of capitalism (Aglietta, 2008: 62), attempting to give an account of the whole economic system. The book's essential idea was that 'the dynamism of capital represents an enormous productive potential but it is also a blind force' (Aglietta, 2000: 397). This force could not limit itself and was open to continuous crises, hence unable to deliver perpetual capital accumulation. To become stable and deliver the expected results, it needed mediation, which amounted to a mode of regulation. Aglietta (2000: 391) defines Fordism as a mode of regulation, which is 'a set of mediations which ensure that the distortions created by the accumulation of capital are kept within limits which are compatible with social cohesion within each nation'.

Fordism was the central regime of accumulation, giving rise to the post-war 'Fordist compromise', which involved 'subordination of workers to managerial staff and machines, in exchange for the promise of a steady job and steadily increasing consumer power' (Lipietz, 1992: 17). Fordism's corporate capitalism was successful in redistributing a share of wealth, correlating productivity gains with income distribution (Aglietta, 2008). A coherent mode of regulation is called a growth regime, whereby the mediation mechanisms bring the forces that are 'diametrically opposed but inextricably linked' to an acceptable compromise (Aglietta, 2000). This golden age, however, was no longer sustainable, and the crisis of Fordism was widespread by the 1970s (Lipietz, 1987). When international competition intensified and mass production ran out of steam, it entered a crisis, to be replaced by a new system of accumulation that relied on competition and markets (Aglietta, 2000).

Analysts of the regulation school, therefore, concentrate on the mediation mechanisms that are used to ensure stability for capital accumulation. A growth regime is a unique historical and cumulative effect of coherence in these mediation mechanisms, which comes to an end when it no longer plays its designated role. The underlying hypothesis of the regulation approach is that 'capitalism is a force for change which has no inherent regulatory principle' (Aglietta, 2008: 62). The implications of this argument are that these mediating mechanisms and regulatory principles lie outside capitalism. These mechanisms and principles are to be found in institutions: 'especially collective beliefs which express the common good', which in the long run lead economic trends (Aglietta, 2008: 62). Formal institutions embody these beliefs, and since these beliefs are different from one society to another, they result in the diversity of capitalism across the world, linked together through the globalization of finance (ibid).

But if capitalism is a domineering force that expands around the world and penetrates new areas all the time, how can these mediating mechanisms exist outside capitalism? How can we envisage mediating mechanisms that have kept their independence and can rule over the blind forces of accumulation, especially if they are coherently intertwined with the processes of capital accumulation within a growth regime? This is an apparent contradiction based on the idea that capitalism, or any other economic formation, can be separated from its institutional arrangements. Calling capitalism a blind force would ignore the particular contexts in which it has emerged, the cultural and political dimensions of the process of economic transformation. This separation of the different dimensions may be difficult to uphold: we may analyse an individual person's actions as led by blind desire, but the overall economic system has been built through centuries of institutional trial and error, and is highly institutionalized, rather than being merely a blind force. It may generate unintended and undesirable outcomes, as exemplified in its cyclical systemic crises and in ever-present social inequality, but these features are integral parts of the system, rather than added dimensions. What the regulation school calls the Fordist mode of regulation is indeed one of the central dynamics of capitalism to grow inwards through demand stimulation, as well as some efforts made to protect itself through managing the unintended or undesirable consequences of capital accumulation. At the same time, the regulation school can respond to such criticism by arguing that the sphere of social life is not entirely monetized, and the pressure to control capitalism can depend on these areas, drawing on other values such as support and collaboration rather than competition and greed. At its heart, the regulation approach seems to suggest a normative social-democratic agenda, in which it is desirable and necessary to frame and control the energies of capitalism, in the hope of steering it towards socially progressive gains. It is an ideal that seems to be reflected in the European social model, which attempts to reconcile economic competitiveness with social cohesion, an idea that is still embraced long after the apparent demise of Fordism.

The theories of post-Fordism and neo-Fordism have been criticized on a number of grounds, primarily on their opposition between mass production and flexible specialization, but also for many of their other assumptions and arguments (Kumar, 2005). The existence of a coherent Fordist regime of accumulation has been doubted. As the car industry was one of the significant features of the twentieth century, it has been tempting to see its methods as defining the era. When the Japanese car industry with its equally mass produced but differently organized system emerged as a successful competitor to Western car manufacturers, it was seen as the dawn of a new industrial period, in which more flexible methods of production such as just-in-time methods and teamwork were used. Taylorism and Fordism, however, were not the same things, as some small firms have used Taylorist methods of management and some large firms have used methods of flexible production. The dominance of mass production in the first half of the twentieth century has been questioned, as the continued significance of small firms in economic life and the coexistence and collaboration of small and large firms have been shown. Furthermore, mass production has not disappeared but continues to be widely used as a system of production. The examples of post-Fordist industrial districts such as Third Italy have been too few to amount to a general trend. The argument is that, rather than a radical transformation, we are witnessing a continuity of the existing trends (Kumar, 2005).

The belief in the primacy of organizational arrangements runs the danger of leading to organizational determinism. Can the changing organization of some segments of economic production be responsible for major social change? If we say yes to this question, are we not in danger of repeating the mistake of technological determinism? The methods of organization and systems of production are themselves intertwined with a large number of factors, and cannot assume a causal role in a simplistic and straightforward way. Any such determinism may underplay the differences between organizational arrangements and localities. Path dependency would mean that the organization of economic activity would depend on contextual parameters, and hence take different forms in different places. Similarly, information and communication technology, like any other technology, would yield different results if employed in different activities, firms, sectors and markets. Neither technological determinism nor organizational determinism can therefore be a reason why major changes in society and economy can take place. The interaction between the organization of economic activity and the information and communication technology shows how they influence each other (Brousseau and Rallet, 1998).

Global division of labour

The dimensions of social change that we have investigated so far only make partial sense and cannot account for the causes of change from one socio-economic formation to another. It is only when analysed within a wider context, therefore, that the perspectives that we have encountered so far begin to make sense. By investigating the supply and division of labour, we can see how some activities move from one place to another, with far-reaching consequences. In light of the changing patterns of supply and division of labour, and the changing nature of knowledge in the economy, all the other features begin to become clearer, finding a place in an overall process.

Many discussions of knowledge economy are narrowly focused on Western economies, observing the changes that have occurred in recent decades and summarizing those changes as the key features of a new post-industrial economy. But if we look at a larger, global scale, we see that these changes in the West are part of a global process of change, wherein a new global division of labour is emerging in which industrial capitalism has not disappeared but reconfigured across the globe.

Capitalism is a force for higher return and accumulation, which is achieved through searching for higher productivity and lower costs for existing activities, and through extending market exchange relations to new activities and places. The other side of this process is the urge to consume, which leads to an endless appetite for new goods, services and experiences. The combined pressure for higher returns and more consumption, both rooted in human desire to maximize power and pleasure, generates a restless process, which invents new technologies, creates new products and services, and brings new parts of the world into the marketplace. Globalization of industrial capitalism creates a new force for looking for new activities that would have exchange value. It also means looking for lower costs of production, which includes ease of access to capital through liberalization of regulatory regimes and integration of the markets through new technologies, as well as ease of access to fixed capital on cheaper land and property in peripheral locations. It also means looking for cheaper labour wherever possible: across the world for industrial production and at home for support services, which would involve a two-way process: the global flow of capital to low-cost regions and of migrant labour to the centres of command. There is, however, a sharp asymmetry between capital and labour in this factor mobility, and there are limits in the capacity of cities and regions to absorb their supply, as shown in the erection of barriers to the flow of migration or in the crisis of credit oversupply.

Large-scale societal changes, which include the emergence of knowledge economy, can therefore be partly explained by this drive for higher returns and more consumption, which transforms the division of labour across the world in an attempt to be released from the controls imposed by local regulation. Relocation of production in search of higher rewards and lower costs has led to a radical shake-up of the social and physical conditions in both old and new places of production, and to a new global division of labour. The emergence of knowledge economy indicates the dual aspects of this new phenomenon: the attempts to manage this complex organization of production, as well as the process of entry into the production networks by various sectors and localities.

From the beginning, industrial capitalism has been a global phenomenon. The European empires of the nineteenth and twentieth centuries were built to shape a global division of labour in which some regions would be forced to play a part in industrial production, either by supplying labour (initially in the form of slaves) or raw materials, by becoming a market for industrial products, or by becoming strategic points of control and command for the centres of production. While this global division of labour was established by the middle of the twentieth century, it had to face competition from the various powers' bids for hegemony, and from the democratic pressure from home and the colonized peripheries. However, as it was eventually strengthened through the collapse of the Soviet bloc and the participation of new, willing players, forceful subordination was only applied to bottlenecks in the flow of resources and to dissenting parties. What is now labelled as post-industrial, post-modern or post-Fordist, or their progression into what is known as knowledge economy or digital economy, is often a description of the local effects of the changes in the global division of labour, whereby new members have joined the process and the global map of production and consumption has been radically transformed.

At the heart of this explanation lies the notion that value is created through human effort, and so the patterns of labour supply and distribution, and its interaction with its specific contexts and processes, are significant for economic transformation. Labour scarcity can lead to technological change, as well as new gender, ethnic and spatial divisions of labour, with major social implications. The patterns of labour supply, however, are not unfolding in a void: the social and institutional context and the processes of economic transformation are both significant for the way these patterns take shape and are addressed. As it was noted at the early stages of industrialization in the West by commentators such as Adam Smith and Robert Owen, human labour was the basis for the prosperity of society. For Adam Smith, writing in 1776, value was to be classified as use value and exchange value, and labour was 'the real measure of the exchangeable value of all commodities' (Smith, 1993: 35–6). Owen wrote in 1820, 'the natural standard of value is, in principle, human labour, or the combined manual and mental powers of men called into action' (Owen, 1991: 255–6). Now at the threshold of a new wave of industrialization outside the West, the patterns of labour provision become once again a significant factor, this time in the global economy.

Value is created through human effort and judged and appreciated through social agreement. Those who see technology as the cause of economic change appear to undermine the value of human involvement in economic production. Technology, however, is a product of human endeavour and ultimately a tool to extend human capacity. It is true that human effort requires access to resources, but these resources can only be effectively created and used through human effort. So human agency, and the work performed by intelligent human beings, is the primary form and generator of social, economic and political value. The shortage, quality or cost of human labour, therefore, will have substantial consequences for economic development.

The unprecedented number of casualties in two World Wars during the twentieth century dramatically reduced the supply of labour in expanding industrialized economies. The workers, who had long struggled for better conditions, could now have the strength to demand better working conditions, higher wages and social support, which were partly met through state intervention to set up planned or mixed economies. The response to the world economic crisis of the 1930s was partly a stimulation of demand through improvements in the workers' conditions. Eventually, however, the strengthening demands of organized labour and higher costs of production led employers to think of alternative solutions to the problem of labour supply. One response by employers was to support the development of new technologies that would increase the productivity of a smaller workforce, such as automation and new transport, information and communication technologies. Another response was to look for alternative and additional supplies of labour in women, immigrants, peripheral regions and in lower-income countries.

Women took up paid work during the Second World War, filling the place left vacant by soldiers, and continued to gain an increasingly important role in the economy. Large-scale immigration to the post-war European economies was encouraged to compensate for labour shortages, substantially increasing the size of the ethnic minorities in these countries. Meanwhile, the countries that could supply low-income skilled workers within a politically low-risk environment were targeted as the destinations of choice for the relocation of labour-intensive industries. In response to their increasingly important roles, these new workers demanded equal rights, as reflected in the feminist and civil rights movements at home, and in the movement for ending colonialism overseas. The social implications of these changes included a new demographic structure, a new gender division of labour, the transformation of traditional household structure and a decline in population growth, a move towards multiculturalism to recognize ethnic and cultural minorities, and the emergence of a new global division of labour in which production and consumption of goods and services have found a new spatial configuration. Supply of labour, therefore, in interaction with the social and historic contexts and processes, has transformed the gender, ethnic and spatial division of labour.

This is a gradual process and goes beyond the short or long economic cycles. It takes account of the historic processes and social and institutional contexts, but it gives priority to human agency and effort. Technology is considered as a tool, rather than the defining feature of the age. Knowledge becomes an essential resource for human agency, and the development of knowledge and skills an essential part of expanding the productive capacity of human work. Although human effort is priced and exchanged in the market for money, it remains far more complicated than a mere price tag.

The transfer of costs to developing countries does not only include production costs in terms of labour and land, but also environmental costs. A leaked memo by Lawrence Summers, the chief economist of the World Bank, caused controversy some years ago when it suggested that the less developed countries were 'under-polluted', hence they and richer countries would benefit from the transfer of dirty industries to these countries (Ayres, 1997: 423).

The labour theory of value is, of course, not sufficient to explain all the economic processes; it needs to be complemented by an understanding of the social context in which labour is produced, the market in which its products are traded and the nature of demand. In a labour theory of value, human effort is the source of all value. If there are conditions in which share traders can earn huge sums of money by making a few phone calls or keyboard strikes, does it mean that the human source of value has been lost? It would be difficult to explain some of the complexities of value, and not all can show a direct line to labour input or output. In the property market, for example, the price of a house is not only a reflection of its construction cost, but also, and more importantly, its location. If we build two houses in two parts of the town, putting exactly the same amount of labour into building them, their cost will be different because of their location difference. The only way to explain the differences in land market is the historical process of urban development and the social geography of a place. We can see that labour theory was attractive during the labour-intensive industrial economy, but can it be the same in the knowledge-based one, where price is not a reflection of quantity of effort but perceived quality of product? Here we see a divide between manual and intellectual labour, which is at the heart of the transition in the division of labour.

Separation of conception from execution

According to Adam Smith, the fund that supplies a nation with all the necessities and conveniences that it consumes is its labour (1993: 8). The greatest improvement in the productivity and management of this fund is in the division of labour. According to his famous example, which is now even printed on British bank notes, an unskilled worker without machinery can produce one pin a day, but with the division of labour, 'One man draws out the wire, another straights it, a third cuts it, a fourth points it', and so on (p. 12). Through specialization and the division of labour, pin-making is broken into 18 distinct operations, in which skilled workers can produce about 4,800 pins a day per person. The complexity in the division of labour is an indicator of the level of advancement in society: 'what is the work of one man, in a rude state of society, being generally that of several in an improved one' (p. 13). This increase in productivity is owing to three factors: 'first, to the increase of dexterity in every particular workman; secondly, to the saving of the time which is commonly lost in passing from one species of work to another; and lastly, to the invention of a great number of machines which facilitate and abridge labour, and enable one man to do the work of many' (p. 15).

Adam Smith cannot be accused of the sort of functionalism that Plato and Aristotle held. According to these ancient thinkers, different people were suited to different functions and a happy life was one in which people did what they were good at, ranging from being a slave to being a ruler (Aristotle, 1992; Plato, 1993). Smith, in contrast, does not equate the division of labour with the in-built capacity of people to be a manual labourer or a philosopher, an inherited destiny to be an intellectual or a physical worker that would lock people into positions of privilege or disadvantage:

> The difference of natural talents in different men is, in reality, much less than we are aware of; and a very different genius which appears to distinguish men of different professions, when grown up to maturity, is not upon many occasions so much the cause, as the effect of the division of labour. The difference between the most dissimilar characters, between a philosopher and a common street porter, for example, seems to arise not so much from nature, as from habit, custom, and education.
>
> (Smith, 1993: 23–4)

Taylorism has been accused of deskilling industrial workers, but it simply applied the division of labour to their work systematically, in the way described by Adam Smith more than a century before: 'the division of labour, by reducing every man's business to some one simple operation, and by making this operation the sole employment of his life, necessarily increases very much the dexterity of the workman', which he considers an important part of improving productivity (Smith, 1993: 15).

The problem with the increased productivity that this division of labour brought about was the alienation of workers from their work, each becoming a cog in a machine. Reaction to the rule of the machine in the nineteenth century included various attempts to reunite the worker and the product, either through a rejection of the machines and mass production and a return to arts and crafts of the past, which would give an individual sense of integration and satisfaction; or through attempting to put the worker in control of the means of production, which would give the entire collective that sense of fulfilment. The twentieth-century response to this problem of alienation has been small team works in mass production, in which the team can be involved in the process of production and enjoy the result of their work; or through the expansion of consumption, as a mediated path to reunite the workers with the fruits of their work.

Taylor's scientific management changed the division of labour in fundamental ways, separating management and administration from production, which made mass production possible with its higher productivity and lower costs. Now globalization of industrial production has separated these not in the same factory but on the global scale. The manager's office in a mass-production factory is the knowledge core in the factory and the production line is where that knowledge is applied in practice. Extrapolated to a global scale, some cities and regions play the role of the manager's office in the global economy, its knowledge core, hence showing a complete change in the nature of their products, the so-called transition from material to immaterial. This is why some larger cities lie at the heart of the world economy, at the top of a hierarchy of power in which different sectors and places play different roles, which are always under pressure to conform to this global hierarchy, playing the function they are expected or else face a crisis of underinvestment.

In the same way that the division of labour created alienation for the workforce but increased its productivity, we can say the same for the new international division of labour, whereby mass production and division of labour may increase productivity and wages for some countries, but its emphasis on the division of labour, in order to keep the prevalence of Western economies in the world, may undermine the development of knowledge sectors in other economies. However, the global division of labour is more complicated than the old local mass-production systems and the result may not be de-skilling, but up-skilling in some parts of the world. The pressure to develop the full range of capacities in design and research and development is on in countries such as China, which have become known as the workshop of the world. The situation, therefore, is not static and can change rather rapidly to acquire the necessary knowledge to improve their products, rather than remaining dependent on Western innovation and expertise.

During the Industrial Revolution, the process of manufacturing was taking place on the peripheral areas inside industrializing countries, where the cost of production was low. It forced other parts of the world to supply raw materials and provide a market for industrial goods that these regions produced. In this division of labour, the tasks of conceptual development and design were performed by a relatively small group of engineers and scientists at the centre or located at these industrial regions. Now, we are witnessing an expansion of industrial production to global proportions. In this expansion, the process of manufacturing is relocated to new areas that offer lower cost of production, multiplying the productive capacity for industrial growth. There is a parallel need for the expansion of the capacity for design, research and development, which the West is currently filling and wishes to expand further. But the separation of conception from execution cannot last, as innovation comes from execution as much as from conception. The next stage of global competition, therefore, is to occupy this centre ground, where the ideas and management of the global economy are located. Some have emphasized the role of the large cities in the global economy, but the production of scientific knowledge and cultural creativity is not limited to these larger cities (Sellers, 2002). They are where parts of the creative economy may cluster, but they are not necessarily the workshops of the knowledge economy: their essential role is the command and control of the global economy.

At the early stages, the gap between conception and execution was local, between the intellectual and manual work. It distinguished the white-collar and blue-collar workers from one another. It also led to higher levels of specialization, which separated home from work, introducing gendered divisions of public and private spheres, and separating town from country. Before the age of industries, much of the productive work was in the home; from urban traders and artisans to rural farmers and workers, the places of work and home were either the same or very near one another. As cities grew and the division of labour became more complicated, the workplace and the living space were separated by large distances, giving form to the modern industrial city with its particular clusters of factories, its working-class residential neighbourhoods, and its acute segregation along functional and class lines. At the level of national space, this separation was also visible, whereby some capital cities remained the centres of command of the markets, while productive regions emerged in which goods were manufactured. The division of mental and manual work was extended to the national space, in which national economic management was separated from national economic production. London was always the command centre in the British Industrial Revolution; while northern industrial cities gained some power and influence, they never overshadowed London. These local forms of separation have now been globalized.

Now, with the globalization of industrial production, new centres of production in Asia and Latin America have gained some influence, but the traditional command centres of London and New York attempt to keep their global dominance through financial control. This would mean the same command centres that could control the economy in the national space have now globalized their reach with the help of financial globalization and the global division of labour. But in this new division of labour, sovereign states with their accumulated surplus of capital would have more political power than the regional industrial cities, hence they are able to transform the global landscape of power in significant ways.

Emergence of a global space

The globalization of industrial production has relied on the entry of new countries to the global market in a new international division of labour mediated through finance and technology. The East Asian financial crisis, which started in 1997 and soon spread to Latin America, to be followed a decade later by the global financial crisis of 2008, all were part of the construction of this global financial infrastructure, partly resulting from the speed and scale of its growth. Bloated by the oversupply of finance, itself the result of vast new supplies of labour from China and other newly industrializing countries, and in the absence of effective global governance, this fragile and unstable infrastructure has grown through trial and error, with inevitable shocks and crises. In the process, the balance of power between different countries changes, as regional power balance had once changed inside the industrial countries of the West, as reflected in the north-south relations in the US and the UK.

The knowledge economy is thought to rely on intangible outputs, as distinctive from the tangible goods of the past. As Charles Leadbeater puts it:

> Most of us [knowledge workers] make our money from thin air: we produce nothing that can be weighed, touched or easily measured. Our output is not stockpiled at harbours, stored in warehouses or shipped in railway cars. Most of us earn our livings providing service, judgement, information and analysis, whether it is a telephone call centre, a lawyer's office, a government department or a scientific laboratory. We are all in this thin-air business.
>
> (Leadbeater, 1999: viii)

And yet the presence and significance of material goods has not diminished in knowledge-based society; if anything consumer goods are more plentiful and more significant. We see the material goods all around us: harbours, warehouses and shops are full of goods, which are produced by some people somewhere. It is just that in the new international division of labour, some societies are giving up the production of these material goods, as they can be produced more cheaply elsewhere. Instead, these societies work on research, design, development, marketing and sale of these goods, and on the cultural commodities that feed into a cycle of consumption and production. The chains of production and consumption, and the diversity of roles in these chains, are interdependent and global.

The decline of manufacturing industries in the advanced industrial countries left a major hole in economic activity as well as in the identity of societies. Manufacturing was relocated to other parts of the world and many Western industrial cities became de-industrialized, a painful process associated with widespread unemployment, population loss and social crisis. The new conditions were first labelled as 'post-industrial', indicating the passing of a phase without knowing the contours of what followed. As the shape of the new economy has become clearer, some have tried to come up with new, more substantive labels that would describe the new conditions on their own, without referring back to the past. These labels have referred to the economic sectors, such as service economy, or more commonly to technological change, such as digital economy, information economy, Internet economy, etc. The label 'knowledge economy' is one of these terms and appears to sit somewhere between the extremes; it is not as wide ranging as service economy and not as narrowly defined as digital economy. It appears to be a normative and aspirational label, which is used to mobilize resources in particular directions, while describing the localized effects of change in the global division of labour. It describes the globalization of industrial economy, extending the sphere of industrial production outwards from its locations in early-industrial societies and re-establishing new locations and relations of production across the globe. Rather than new-industrial or post-industrial, which describes some parts of this system, we witness a global

The decline of manufacturing industries in the advanced industrial countries left a major hole in economic activity as well as in the identity of societies (Liverpool, UK).

economy, in which a complex division of labour has found a new geographical expression, covering much of the increasingly interconnected world.

We can see how the term knowledge economy might be applied to the de-industrialized cities and regions that attempt to adjust their position within the new international division of labour. In these countries, the spread of new technologies, the nature of the products, the social organization of production, and the social habits and cultural trends have all been in transition for adjustment. But how can we apply the term to the emerging and developing economies, in which knowledge products are not the main output and the spread of new technologies is limited?

Alongside the Janus faces of accumulation and consumption, we can see the joint forces of investors and regulators at work to expand the global economy into new areas. On the one hand, investors look for low production costs, and on the other hand, local administrations look for investment and are willing to show flexibility and offer incentives to investors. This two-way interaction distinguishes globalization from nineteenth-century imperialism, which was one way, without the willing participation of the conquered nations. The knowledge economy, therefore, becomes the interplay of these two forces and finds two different but interrelated meanings: knowledge economy as the command centre of the globalizing world, and knowledge economy as the improvement and up-skilling of localities to participate in the new global division of labour. Knowledge-based economy in this context would mean allocating a new role to the old industrial centres, consolidating and enhancing the role of the old command centres, preparing the workforce in the countries with the potential to enter the industrial capitalist production process, promoting innovation and capturing the productivity gains of new ICT.

This globalization of industrial capitalism, the global extension of modernity, continues to use violence to spread and to consolidate its grip, as seen in the wars fought in different guises. The scientific revolution of the seventeenth century was a power engine in the creation of the modern West. Ever since, the pressure has been on to extend this modernity to new parts of the world, in other words it is the process of the globalization of modernity. Rather than seeing globalization as a vague and general phenomenon, we can clearly see it as a purposeful process of modernization and industrialization, of continuous extension of industrial capitalism to new corners of the world and reconfiguring an integrating global economy accordingly. The emerging global division of labour, however, is not an absolute and final development. It can and does change, which is in line with the urge for creative destruction and restless expansion, allowing new parts of the world continually to assume new roles.

If knowledge as a form of capital tends to accumulate in particular places, it is also subject to the logic of competition for scarce resources in an increasingly globalized marketplace. Knowledge economy is a new phase in capitalist industrial economy, in which new technologies have been used for a reshaping of the world's production map. It is a new division of labour resulting from this global reshaping of production that transforms cities, rather than leaving industrial capitalism behind. Globalization is the process of intensifying interdependencies across the world, facilitated through new technologies, which enables the emergence of a new global division of labour. In this new arrangement, the location of different economic activities is adjusted to take advantage of global resources, both in terms of production and consumption, benefiting from low production costs while opening up new markets for goods and services.

There is a close parallel between intensification in globalization and the rise of the knowledge economy. Through a new global division of labour, and intensified innovation, new goods and services are produced at higher specifications, more competitive prices and in differentiated locations around the world. In this new division of labour, some low-wage regions have industrialized, while high-wage regions have been encouraged to restructure their economies by investing in high-value-added services geared towards international trade. Land and labour, the traditional factors of production, are cheaper in newly industrializing countries, which can be preferred locations for the mass production of standardized products (Simmie, 2003). The export base of advanced economies depends on competition based on quality and differentiation, rather than price, hence the significance of knowledge and innovation (Simmie, 2003: 608).

Before the global financial crisis of 2008, the UK had experienced a decade-long boom in the export of financial, computer and business services, and royalties and licence fees, which are counted as knowledge-related services. Between 1995 and 2005, these services grew from around 50% to nearly 70% of total service exports, amounting to £76 billion. Globalization, therefore, is a key driver in economic change in advanced economies. At the same time, some observers have argued that the central significance of globalization in economic change may have been overstressed. In the UK, trade is mainly conducted with other OECD countries and the share of international trade in GDP has not increased during the past 20 years. Imports from Asia have not significantly increased, the share of jobs exposed to international competition has decreased, offshoring has not caused a decline in relevant jobs such as call centres, and only 10–20% of job losses can be attributed to trade with low-wage regions. A conclusion is that the drivers of knowledge economy are primarily technological change and rising domestic demand for knowledge-based services (Brinkley, 2006: 9–11). This is why a closer look at the role of consumption in the economy is necessary, as we shall see in Chapter 9.

Unification and stratification of global space

Globalization aims to unify the global space, in which factor mobility is facilitated and consumption is expanded through opening up new markets. This unified global space builds on the world system that had emerged since the dawn of the modern age, when Western empires established a centre and pushed other countries and territories to join this system as peripheral or semi-peripheral partners (Wallerstein, 1979). There are also some clear parallels with the phase in modern history in which the nation-states evolved in the West, before the start of imperial adventures (Smith, 1996; Potter, 1995). At an earlier stage, when the nation-states were emerging, capitalism benefited from the unification of national spaces, which suppressed regional differences, establishing national markets that could go beyond the limited capacity of regional and local markets. This unified national space would facilitate the mobility of factors of production and expansion of consumption through opening up new markets, reducing the impact of local idiosyncrasies and standardizing the regulatory framework within which the market could operate. This phenomenon is repeated in the process of European integration and globalization, in which unified spaces are created out of national spaces, in which factor mobility, consumption expansion and unified regulation are being encouraged and developed. The barriers to production, regulation and consumption are being reduced in the hope of stimulating the economies of the participating countries.

The unification of global space, however, is by its nature uneven. The larger players can navigate this space much more easily than the smaller ones; they have access to more resources, more information and support from stronger governments. The impact of the context is also very significant: players from countries in which there is a tradition of mature markets are better equipped with the knowledge and institutional frameworks that are needed to thrive in a unified global space. For small firms and weaker national economies, the possibility of survival in this space is much more difficult. The proponents of globalization argue that it is beneficial for these weaker economies, as it brings in new investment and finds new markets for their products. However, improving the quality of products, marketing them effectively and finding international markets is a hard path that very few can travel, and many may lose out on the way.

Factor mobility is also not evenly applied. While the movement of capital has been eased through the use of information and communication technologies and adjustment to regulatory frameworks, the movement of labour is much more difficult to achieve and much more resisted. The social implications of migration are widely known, especially when the scale and pace of migration grows, both for the origins and destinations of the migrants. While highly skilled workers are more mobile and a very small minority can increasingly command a global level of income, the demand and the level of mobility for others is far more complicated. Meanwhile local specificities such as weather or quality of environment are not transportable and are subject to physical, historical and social circumstances. In knowledge-based economy, the mobility for knowledge as a factor of production may help further unification of economic spaces, but it is also subject to regulatory and economic conditions, such as intellectual property rights. It is also subject to the availability of other factors of production. By expanding ICT capabilities across the world, national governments and international organizations work towards opening up new markets and removing barriers to the transfer of knowledge and financial capital, creating a partially unified space for knowledge products.

New technologies, together with the globalization process, have led to a growth in the size of corporations that is unprecedented. Digital infrastructure and global division of labour have unified the global space and intensified the process of agglomeration, in which some cities are the manifestations of the socio-spatial agglomeration, and some companies the manifestations of economic accumulation. The linkage between socio-spatial and economic concentration is often strong, as large cities are better placed to attract decision-making and economic giants, becoming the nodes of a global marketplace.

The impact of the creation of a unified global space on national economies is somewhat similar to the impact of national space on regions. A new division of labour develops in which some regions emerge as command centres and others are locked in as partial suppliers of necessary input or consumers of the output from the global economy. A pattern of centres and peripheries appears that builds on the existing pattern that had been set since the rise of the modern West, with later modifications and the emergence of new command centres.

The unified global space loosens the connections between cities and regions within national economies, as they are more strongly connected to a global network of cities and regions. Nevertheless, the uneven concentration of wealth and power that characterized many national spaces does not disappear, but may be accentuated, as national centres of command are better placed to benefit from the global unified space, in the same way that larger firms are better placed to benefit from this process. The economies of scale that helped create cities in the first place continue to be the reason for the privileged position of larger agglomerations in the global space. Larger cities attract more resources, financial and human, to become larger, while some cities shrink and fade into the background of a new global landscape. New centres emerge and new hinterlands form. This is a transformation that was observed by Marx (1967: 352) at the rise of capitalist industrial cities and their relationship with their hinterland:

> the foundation of every division of labour that is well developed, and brought about by the exchange of commodities, is the separation of town and country. It may be said that the whole economic history of society is summed up in the movement of this antithesis.

While it may not be accurate to think of it as antithetical, the relationship between the centre and periphery is uneven and stratified. In the process of unification of global space, this relationship is extended to the centres and peripheries ona global scale, so that the evolving relationship between the large agglomerations and the rest of the world becomes the newest phase in the economic history of the world. The town and country relationships are detectable at all scales, from the way a town relates to its surroundings to the way the largest command centres relate to the global economy.

Unification and differentiation

In the unification of national space that took place in the nineteenth century in Europe and extended to other parts of the world in the twentieth, the dominant language and culture forced minority cultures into a corner, setting universal standards based on the majority's language, culture and history. The minority cultures and languages lost much of their regional autonomy as the evolution of capitalism and nation-state could not cope with the diversity of national territories. The unified global space, while not explicitly ruled by a global authority, is subject to pressures for cultural assimilation and linguistic unification, undermining the habits and norms that are out of tune with the dominant cultural trends. These dominant cultural trends, often characterized by the particular strands within Western culture, are themselves well adapted to working with market requirements, having lost the peculiarities that may work against general market requirements or having learned how to combine cultural diversity with the demands of the market.

The pressure for unification and stratification is in line with the pressure for social decontextualization that we noticed in the last chapter. Both are features of the restless creative destruction of modernity, which destroys existing forms to shape them in new ways in line with the new circumstances. In the new circumstances, there are continuing pressures for making all the rough edges smooth and all idiosyncrasies ironed out, so as to facilitate and standardize exchange. However, social difference does not easily disappear: it is either embedded in individuals, groups and societies through cultural practices, or acquired through liberties that they have kept or asserted through economic and institutional means. The pressure for the assertion of identity and difference may be tamed through differentiated consumption, but sometimes it looks for politics of identity that cannot always be handled through economic instruments.

The persistence of difference is one reason why economic transformation cannot explain social change, showing the limits of economic determinism. If mass production or globalized production were the ultimate word in the ways human societies arranged their lives, then unpacking these systems of production would be sufficient for explaining all that they do. But human societies are historic and complex collections of socio-biological organisms, inheriting many features from their long-distant pasts and inventing many new ones everyday. A single narrative cannot capture their complexity and resourcefulness, their limited abilities to free themselves from what has been inscribed on them or their energies and possibilities of inventing alternative futures.

Global division of labour may tend to assign single roles to regions, which could create alienation and vulnerability. In the same sense that factory towns of the past were vulnerable to the changing fortunes of their single employer, rigid division of tasks would create interdependencies that leave many regions exposed to the decisions of others. Larger cities and regions may be protected from such vulnerabilities through their sheer range of economic activities. Diverse and better placed regions would be able to benefit from a changing division of labour on the global scale, while smaller regions may either lose out or enter a new phase in which their vulnerability would increase as a trade-off with their increased prosperity, while their products meet some demand in a complex interdependent system over which they have no control. It is entering a deal to feed the whims of a giant.

Cities are compared and ranked according to their quality of life, providing information for potential investors (Vienna, Austria).

At the urban level, a number of studies have generated typologies to characterize and measure the performance of cities in moving towards a knowledge-based economy. One such study classified some cities in north-west Europe as stars, star niche-players, pearls, intellectuals, metropoles in transition and niche-players in transition (Van Winden *et al.*, 2007). Many of the factors needed to develop a cluster of innovative firms competing effectively in the global market are beyond the competencies and administrative boundaries of local and regional authorities (Simmie, 2003: 618). Therefore, it is no surprise that they focus on what is within their control: investment in the local physical and human infrastructure, to focus on the supply of more amenable conditions for innovative firms to take root (DETR/CABE, 2000). However, in an interconnected world, the success of such measures can only be partial if not complemented by finding a place in the global networks of production and exchange. One of the main reasons for investing in physical capital has been the desire to promote cities in a highly competitive global marketplace. By investment in iconic architecture and physical improvement schemes, authorities have aimed at re-imaging their cities and inviting investors and visitors.

The famous motto of modernist architecture was 'form follows function', which was an argument for a functionalist and utilitarian approach, shedding any unnecessary elements, creating an architecture that reflected its technological and functional bases (Sert, 1944). Post-modern architecture abandoned the link between form and function, voting for playfulness and ornamentation, rather than

The modernist motto of form follows function continues to hold; this time the function has changed into an external one, attracting global attention (Los Angeles, USA).

puritan functionalism (Jencks, 1991). The architecture of today has developed a synthesis of these two trends: using playful shapes towards specific functions. Now that cities and regions compete with one another in the global marketplace, branding places through architecture is a major trend. Famous architects and playful expressive shapes are employed to establish a particular image for a place, to differentiate one place from another. This may appear to some as a waste of resources on flagship projects, or an irrational appetite for playfulness, resulting in 'Disneyfication' of the urban environment, in which each building is screaming for attention, without any due regard for the rest of the city. But it is a new manifestation of the modernist motto of 'form follows function'. The function of major buildings now is to seek global attention, and the expressive shapes of many buildings perform that function very effectively. The difference between these two forms of functionalism is that the early modernists privileged the internal logic of a building, allowing it to guide the formation of its outside shape. For the late modernists of today, however, the outside shape of the building, responding to external economic imperatives, takes precedence over the internal logic of a building. Symbols are used to establish a sense of identity that would distinguish a place in the world.

Cities are treated as shops, open for business, removing regulatory barriers in tax-free areas with high-quality space and infrastructure, ready to accept investors who may give this place a function and character of their own. In this process, post-industrial cities are partly reshaped in the image of pre-industrial cities. Medieval cities and small European market towns are sometimes taken as the ideal types to which city design and planning should aspire. There are clear

Symbolic language of architecture and urban design is used to distinguish places in the global competition (Birmingham, UK).

aesthetic considerations in these preferences. But we can also detect an economic dimension: medieval cities and market towns were places of trade (Saalman, 1968), and as trade finds a stronger role in the interdependent world of global economics, cities once again are turned into nodes of trade. The city is being recreated in the image of trade, rather than industry. In the same way that all medieval cities aspired to have their own cathedrals as a symbol of status, the cities of today aspire to their own symbols, which are tall and iconic buildings and expressive architecture.

In part, this is a struggle for recognition, especially by those in weaker positions in the global economy, wishing to make a statement and make their presence noticed by others. Many of these gestures may remain on the surface, not leading to any substantial economic change, only changing the image of a place for some observers or cementing the position of local decision-makers. It is also a sign of arrival and assertion of identity by the emerging economies. Hosting international events, such as the Beijing Olympics in 2008, the Shanghai Expo in 2010, South Africa's World Cup in 2010 and India's Commonwealth Games in 2010, I have been used to make statements about their role in the world, partly expressed through new expressive buildings. Beijing's National Stadium, dubbed the Bird's Nest, captured the world's attention for its unconventional form, while the Games as a whole stamped the arrival of China as a new world power. Upon opening the largest public building in India, a new terminal at Indira Gandhi International

Cities are created as shops open for business, removing tax and regulatory barriers, with high-quality space and infrastructure, ready to accept investors (Incheon, Korea).

Airport in Delhi, built at a cost of £2billion on the eve of the Commonwealth Games, the country's civil aviation minister commented that it is 'not just a building, it's a statement'. According to the country's prime minister, 'An airport is often the first introduction to a country. A good airport will signal a new India, committed to joining the ranks of modern industrialised nations' (Burke and Jethra, 2010).

Conclusion

In addition to the changing nature of knowledge, the changing nature of products and the major contribution of new technologies, the social organization of production plays a crucial role in the development of knowledge economy. The transformation and relocation of mass production from older manufacturing regions to new low-cost areas have intensified a process of globalization, in which many global regions are joined to redraw the global map of production. As human effort

Major infrastructure projects are used as marks of distinction for cities (Paris, France).

and recognition are the source and the measure of all value, the process of globalization can be interpreted as a restless search for new supplies of labour with different skills and different levels of reward and social organization in different parts of the world. The process of specialization in the new international division of labour maintains and intensifies the gap between conception and execution, between mental and manual work, and contributes to a now globalized alienation of workers from the fruits of their work, which is sometimes hoped to be bridged through consumption of goods and imaginary lifestyles, or new methods of mass production.

The interconnected global economy creates a unified space, analogous to the unified national space that emerged in the early stages of capitalism's development but now on a global scale. Within this unified space, however, positions are uneven, giving some cities and regions priority over others. But even within this uneven geography, there is a breathtaking competition between similar regions in the hope of standing out in the increasingly homogenous global space, in which capital and information – and to a lesser degree high-skilled workers – can flow with some ease. To attract these investors, tourists and workers, cities compete with one another by resorting to a war of symbols, from tall and expressive buildings to events and festivals, searching for an image that will give them a competitive edge over their peers. The interplay of the forces of unification, homogenization and differentiation continually changes the face of cities.

Part III

Sites of production and consumption

After researching the changing nature of production in Part II, we now look at the spatial implications of the production and consumption processes in Part III. The investigation revolves around the interplay of the urban development process with the forces of augmentation, dispersion and agglomeration. While some of these forces push for further mediation of social relations through technology, others push for differentiated modes of working and living, and yet others bring the disparate parts together in the hope that agglomeration will lead to innovation and economies of scale. In Chapter 8 we concentrate on the sites of production, leaving a discussion of the sites of consumption to Chapter 9.

8 Sites of knowledge production

One of the main characteristics of capitalism has been identified as 'creative destruction' (Schumpeter, 1942), which involves 'periodic abandonment of equipment, production methods, and product designs in favour of newer and more economically performative assets' (Scott, 2006: 1). In other words, continuous adjustments are made to the physical environment and social institutions and practices to realign them with changing economic circumstances. Therefore, one way to study whether the space of knowledge economy is markedly different from the past is looking at cities or countries that were never dominated by manufacturing industries. If we compare administrative or trade cities with manufacturing ones, or compare large cities, where manufacturing industries could not dominate the scene, with the predominantly industrial cities, what significant differences do we see? Are there significant social and spatial differences? Location and type of working and living places could testify to the way these places were different: factories where people worked and mass housing where workers lived. Large-scale social organization of production, standardized agglomeration, rigid routines of life that would unify the use of time, and mass-produced spaces and consumer items were among the distinguishing features of industrial cities, which were absent from older cities in previous centuries.

If there are distinctive patterns that can be associated with manufacturing cities, what are those patterns for knowledge cities? What are the new sites of production and consumption? We start with a review of how agglomerations emerge in cities and how this plays out in the knowledge-based economy. In particular, we will investigate the new sites of production, whereby a clustering of knowledge activities takes place in universities, science and technology parks, cultural and creative economy clusters, and office clusters and their relations with home-working.

Emergence and growth of concentrations

If urban economics is about the location of firms and households, then the relationship between the knowledge economy and the city, in a narrow sense, becomes the location of firms and households that are involved in knowledge-intensive activities. Has the emergence of new knowledge-intensive activities created new locational patterns in the city? Do the processes involved with the creation of knowledge as capital and knowledge as goods and services require a new spatial organization, or do we see a continuation of the old location patterns? In a wider sense, this relationship covers not only the location, but also the context in which these new activities take place and their impact on society as a whole. Are the new knowledge-based activities using a new architectural language? Do they instigate new routines of social life? Do they create new forms of social stratification? We try to find some answers for these and many questions of this sort, which look at the variety of aspects of the wholesale rise of new economic activities.

Economists distinguish between the internal and external economies of scale that are involved in the selection of locations and the growth of urban agglomerations. Internal scale economies refer to the decisions made by the firms, showing that there is a direct link between the scale of a firm's production and the cost of its average production, so that the average cost of production decreases when the production scale increases. External scale economies refer to the decisions made outside the firm, showing how firms benefit from decisions made by other firms, which create spillovers that encourage firms to cluster in cities. The external economies are associated with rising labour productivity and higher wages, which both attract workers to cities and cover the higher costs of living in large cities (O'Sullivan, 2003).

Location and distance have also been used to explain why agglomeration takes place. If the city is defined as a permanent concentration, then an important question is how and why this concentration emerges and evolves. Alfred Marshall's answer, which singled out the role of external economies, is still widely used. Marshall analysed how in the late nineteenth century, manufacturing firms from the same industry clustered in 'industrial districts', which Marshall explained to be drawing on three factors. Such concentration would support specialized local providers of inputs; generate and draw on a pool of labour, which would be beneficial for both employers and workers; and facilitate the spread of information due to geographic proximity (Fujita *et al.*, 1999: 18). It may appear that competing firms in the same industry would do better to find different locations so as to find their own market share and geographical sphere of activity. But their clustering shows that their competition needs to be supported by some implicit sharing of resources: suppliers, labour and information.

Beyond the district, the clustering also takes place at the city level. The sharing of supplies, labour and information is not limited to the same industry, and they can link different firms and industries at the city level. The firms share intermediate inputs, so that economies of scale can be achieved in the supply of both public and private services: from roads, public transport, schools, safety and fire protection to banking, insurance, real estate, hotels, building maintenance, printing and transportation. The labour pool that a large city provides can be beneficial for workers and employers because the cost of switching from one job to another would be reduced, and the workforce of a declining industry can switch to a growing industry more easily. Sharing information and knowledge spill over is particularly significant for innovation in the products and the methods of production. Therefore, both localization and urbanization economies lead to the clustering of firms in particular localities and in urban areas in general (O'Sullivan, 2003).

The source of clustering is of course not always an economic calculation. The creation of artistic clusters, or the concentration of public sector bureaucracies, for example, may not follow an economic logic. Clusters may be interpreted as nodes that are the converging points of multiple networks, and so the density of networks and the location of such nodes in social space may explain the formation of a cluster of activities. Searching for personal development or social recognition may explain the reason why artists are attracted to some metropolitan centres, where they cluster in affordable places with supportive institutions. The location of an administrative cluster may not always be explained by the central location in a national space or a predominant location within an urban space, but also through other contextual considerations, such as the presence of some anchor points, the dynamics of land and property speculation, the policies of regional development, or the personal whims of powerful figures.

In the knowledge-based economy, where the products are intangible and communication takes place through information and communication technologies, how would distance and location be different from the past? In a 'weightless economy' in which transportation costs are close to zero, how would clusters be shaped (Quah, 2000)? Would the intangible product and the instant communication annihilate space and time, undermining the location and distance? The

Economies of scale explain the formation of clusters, but the shape of clusters may not always follow economic calculations (New York, USA).

clustering for sharing information, labour and input supplies shows that all these activities, which are vital for the development and growth of firms, depend on face-to-face communication and cannot be fragmented into isolated sites. In other words, while the new ICT and transport technologies facilitate interdependence across the world, the process of agglomeration largely continues, creating a material concentration of people and objects in time and space, which is the essence of the city.

This process of agglomeration would lead to the growth of other activities, in what is called a multiplier process. The production activities in the urban economy are divided into two types: basic and non-basic. The basic production exports the city's products, selling its goods and services to people outside the city. The so-called non-basic production, which includes everything else, from bakeries to bookstores, targets the local population. According to the multiplier process, the growth in basic production leads to a growth in non-basic production. As the export workers spend part of their income on local goods and services, an increase in export activity boosts local activity, amounting to an increase in the city's total income, which is larger than the growth in export income (O'Sullivan, 2003: 120). This analysis aims to show that a region's base production is its *raison d'etre*, on which the local production depends, expanding and contracting in parallel with the base's performance (Fujita *et al.*, 1999: 27). On this basis, the economy of a metropolitan area such as London may be partly based on its export activities of the financial institutions and cultural activities, which target the national and international markets, and upon which depend its non-base activities such as restaurants and supermarkets, etc.

The separation of the base and non-base activities may be the result of a desire for clarity in what matters most in the economy, but it undermines the structural interdependence between activities. The reason for the emergence and vibrancy of the scientific and cultural activities does not only lie in themselves, but also in the context in which they grow and are recognized. Their activities do not take place in a void and the sources of innovation are rooted in the creativity of individuals who are nurtured somewhere else. The dynamism of base activities can only exist by drawing on the resources of the so-called non-base context. The two-way relationship is also due to the fact that cities already exist as overlapping clusters of different activities. The base activities may relocate to a city for using its support infrastructure, which has been developed over decades, or even centuries, acting as the primary rationale for the location decisions of a wide range of firms. The notion that the relation is a one-way dependence of non-base on base activities is a false representation of an interdependent relationship of two-way traffic.

There is also a two-way relationship between the base production and the local market, which is considerable in larger cities. As the size of the regional economy grows, the market becomes large enough for some goods and services to be produced locally, and for the base production to grow subsequently (Pred, 1966). The multiplier process could therefore feed into the regional economy through a cumulative loop of growth, i.e., the non-base production generating new base production and so on. The problem of separating base and non-base production, however, could be avoided in an alternative explanation for the location decision of firms: to see how they may feed from the regional economy in search of reducing costs. The location of firms could be decided on the basis of market potential, for the production site to be near its market. As large urban areas are the largest concentrations of population, they offer larger markets to producers, who could locate there to reduce their transportation costs (Fujita *et al.*, 1999).

The process of agglomeration is often analysed as the outcome of independent decisions taken by firms based on an assessment of the external and internal economies of scale. However, the process can also be led by imitation and speculation by firms that see the success of similar firms and wish to replicate their success, entering a known context and hence hoping to reduce their own risk. Where other similar firms appear to do well, new firms may just join the bandwagon to benefit from an existing trend. Clustering, therefore, may be the spatial manifestation of the cumulative effects of speculative development, which can be subject to the inherent perils of the system. This speculative process creates an accumulation of productive forces in some activities in particular areas, but if successful it can also lead to over concentration of the productive forces, leading to overproduction and economic crisis.

While this crisis may be interpreted as market correction, and hence a predictable outcome of speculation, the impact of the process on the city may be devastating. Concentrations may survive for a long term, but suffer from complacency and lack of investment and innovation, which would remove their competitive advantage. Concentration of firms, therefore, is not necessarily equated with economic prosperity; it can also mean decline or oversupply, both leading to undesirable outcomes. The positive spatial effects of concentration are urban growth and expansion. But the crisis of overproduction can lead to an oversupply of built space, which would mean empty plots and buildings. In extreme cases, it can lead to abandonment, collapse of the land and property market, and decline or even disappearance of a city. As we saw in the discussion of the production of space in Chapter 3, speculative urban development may or may not overlap with the agglomeration of firms or households, owing to various gaps between the different segments of the market.

As a result of national and international connections and communications, policy initiatives as well as cultural developments have helped cities and nations learn from one another and employ similar devices in addressing their problems. Therefore, the industrial methods of construction and development may have been applied to places without industry, and mass housing schemes for non-manufacturing workers. Similarly, large-scale private corporations and bureaucratic organization of the public sector may find their way into cities in which industries had not been located. In the same manner, post-industrial features may be found in places that have never been industrialized or may never acquire knowledge-based economies. Both of these trends can be vividly seen in peripheral regions and countries, where industrial and post-industrial methods and ideas were employed without necessarily relating to the local context. Ideas and practices can travel without being sufficiently related to local conditions, and local contexts can embrace unrelated ideas and practices without sufficient connection to their circumstances. In analysing the relationship between space and society, therefore, the connections are never simplistic and narrowly causal. A space may be created for a complex array of reasons, which may not include economic or structural considerations at all.

We should be aware of the limitations of two sets of reductions: reducing spatial dimensions to location and distance, and reducing spatial relations to their monetary dimension. There is a reductive element in the models that are devised on a limited basis, removing many aspects of decision-making in order to produce neatly calculable mathematical models. These models tend to give primacy to the decisions of the households and firms, explaining the urban phenomena in the light of these decisions. However, we know that these decisions do not take place in a void, but act within an established and complex land use and property market structure, drawing a complex process of decision-making that involves many factors beyond economic exchange. Their decisions, therefore, are not necessarily based on profit-maximizing reasoning, completely free choice or full knowledge of this context. Such action could only take place within a context made of enabling and limiting frameworks, which need to be equally known for examining the relationship between the space and the economy.

For example, if we observe the current fever for tall buildings around the world, it is not, as the urban land theory suggests, the competition for the best use of expensive central location that drives the trend, but a competition for global status. Even in an earlier phase, when the famous skylines of Chicago and New York were being made, the height of many skyscrapers could not be justified by direct economic considerations. Advertising, display and prestige played as much a part as the cost of land for the companies that built or rented skyscrapers for their headquarters. The Chrysler Building was built at 77 storeys high, while calculations showed that the optimum height of an office building opposite Grand Central Station in 1930 New York was only 63 storeys. In the Woolworth Building, while the contractor was concerned about the lack of return on the client's investment, Mr Woolworth was confident that the building was going to work for him 'like a giant signboard to advertise around the world his spreading chain of five-and-ten-cent stores' (quoted in Girouard, 1985: 322).

The significance of space for knowledge economy is partly shown in the clustering of knowledge-based activities in a limited number of cities and regions. Patterns of clustering vary in different sections of the digital industries and would depend on a variety of social and institutional arrangements (Pratt *et al.*, 2007). While clustering of tacit knowledge can take place through the Internet, creating virtual clusters that are scattered around the world, other considerations, such as labour market and patterns of consumption, encourage physical clustering. Most economic activities are located in cities (Bennett *et al.*, 1999) and most of these activities in de-industrialized cities are in services (Simmie and Strambach, 2006). Parts of the two coasts in the United States and a few centres in Europe have accommodated disproportionate rates of innovation and knowledge activities. This has often been analysed through the supply-side characteristics of these regions, as well as the inter dependencies of firms in the process of knowledge acquisition. The existence of knowledge infrastructure, density of knowledge resources and investment in R&D would also contribute to the clustering of knowledge workers and firms and facilitating innovation, which is likely to be in core metropolitan regions (Simmie, 2003). The historical and social characteristics of these urban regions show how they have found a place at the centre of urban hierarchies (Simmie and Strambach, 2006).

Geographic concentration goes hand in hand with the accumulation of wealth and privilege, so that in the long run the cumulative effects of higher returns result in higher densities of people, money and power in some cities in the national and global space, and, inside the cities, in some parts as compared with other areas. The surplus of production in the countryside made it possible for the city to emerge in the ancient world, where a concentration of people lived who did not produce their own food. Here the division of labour and comparative advantage of some places and activities made trade possible, but also created a concentration that from the beginning was associated with inequality. This is why many of the egalitarian movements of the modern age have looked at cities with suspicion, as places that could only create and deepen social inequality.

Rousseau, whose ideas influenced the French revolutionaries, believed in the simplicity of the countryside, where the division of labour could be avoided. In his writing, he recalls how he was impressed by a Swiss village in his youth: this was a happy community of self-sufficient equals, where people had a variety of skills; they built and maintained their houses, without the assistance of any specialist artisans such as cabinet makers, locksmiths, glaziers or carpenters; they entertained themselves, without the help of any professionals that could be found at the urban centres (Cranston, 1968). Later revolutionaries in Russia (Bater, 1980) and China (Ma and Fu, 2005) were also suspicious of the concentrations of wealth and inequality in the city, which they saw as a site of consumption rather than production. In the emergence of the globalized map of production in the knowledge-based economies, with its deepening social inequality (OECD, 2008), however, such radical voices of anti-urbanism have not yet emerged.

Spaces of encounter

The notion of tacit knowledge advocates a transition from information to knowledge, from computers to humans, from recorded knowledge that can be transmitted through textbooks and other media to implicit knowledge, which is human beings' capacity to interpret and innovate. In its broadest sense, this is a transition from objects to humans, acknowledging the value of human capital as distinctive from other forms of capital. Both codified and tacit forms of knowledge created their own spaces, as exemplified in libraries and schools. A library is a repository of knowledge and schools prepare children for access to such a repository; the spread of public education and the construction of public libraries since the nineteenth century have aimed at spreading knowledge to a wider part of the population.

A major implication of the tacit forms of knowledge is the apparent distinction between intangible and tangible assets; at the same time, it re-emphasizes spatiality, as it shifts the focus to individual experts and to the places where they cluster, as they are subject to the labour market processes and scale economies. The accumulation of human capital, therefore, both makes the knowledge city and provides the necessary conditions for the emergence of a knowledge economy. Knowledge economy not only has a new form of capital, but also a new type of labour, the carriers of tacit knowledge who can produce and process codified knowledge. With the decline of traditional industries and the rise of automation, new forms of labour had already been emerging before the digital age (Manovich, 2001). With the arrival of the information age, it has become clear that there is a need for workers who have the knowledge to deal with, and generate, new information. As we saw in Part II, this is the result of a changing division of labour within the globalized capitalist industrial economy, rather than the emergence of a new class or a new economy, and so it is subject to the same dynamics of stratification and accumulation.

The social implications of tacitness follow from an interest in knowledge workers as the producers of knowledge and information. Some have argued that tacit knowledge refers to those areas of human intelligence that cannot be reproduced by computer programs and algorithms. An epistemic community may have a code book that is not written explicitly or is not available to others, but is known to its members, as manifested in its expert jargons and implicit assumptions. The significance of face-to-face encounters is therefore emphasized, as forums in which such uncodified knowledge can be exchanged in a conversation (Cowan *et al.*, 2000). While codified knowledge may travel well, tacit knowledge, which decodes the former, does not travel as easily. Defining tacit knowledge may be difficult and codification of some forms of knowledge very costly. So some have argued that rather than focusing on a mystified concept such as tacit knowledge, the focus should be on what can be codified, and that this codification can take place at a cost. According to this view, an alternative to covering the cost of codifying tacit knowledge may be 'a thick, active market for skilled labour as the mechanism for storing and disseminating knowledge' (Cowan *et al.*, 2000: 242).

Economic development strategies, therefore, encourage the development of such markets in their localities, hoping to create and maintain a pool of knowledge workers who carry and transmit tacit knowledge. When a high-density pool of knowledge workers exists, knowledge storage and dissemination is facilitated without the necessary cost of investing in codification. These high densities may already exist in some cities and regions, which would give them a competitive advantage, while for others much public subsidy may be invested to encourage the development of such a pool. While new technologies have facilitated communication between these experts across the world, the impact of pooling and clustering knowledge workers has also been intensified. The places that are known as nodes of knowledge economy have shown to have pools of knowledge workers and firms, which in turn attract new knowledge workers and firms.

For tacit knowledge to be transmitted, labour market mobility and social networks are essential (Simmie, 2003). The existence of social networks would enable the transmission of tacit knowledge through the development of trust in face-to-face encounters, which can only happen within space-bound contexts of cities and regions. Labour market mobility would also allow the same transmission, though on a more permanent, less flexible way. Where a high density of skilled workers exists, such as in Silicon Valley (California), flexible practices have generated a high degree of mobility, as well as insecurity, for 'itinerant professionals', who move from project to project, somewhat similar to stonemasons in medieval Europe moving from cathedral to cathedral (Barley and Kunda, 2004).

Therefore, the density of a highly skilled labour market, existence of knowledge infrastructure and resources, such as R&D expenditure, and active social networks facilitate the generation and transmission of tacit knowledge, which is primarily possible in core urban areas. But demand theories can also explain the significance of space in globalized economies.It is argued that the export of goods and services forms the primary basis for the prosperity of urban regions. The most innovative firms located in core urban regions look outwards to the global market for a market share; they show the ability to link effectively with national and international clients and customers, knowledge resources and knowledge networks. These regions operate as gateways of their local and national economies into the world market (Simmie, 2003). This also shows the ability of core urban regions to draw on their historic advantages to become the nodes of the global knowledge-based economy.

An 'incubator', it is argued, is vital in the product cycle, enabling an entrepreneur to develop a new product. These incubators are often found at the core of major urban areas, characterized by a density of infrastructure, diversity of services and abundance of rentable premises (Scott, 2006). This places an agent in interaction with a structure (Giddens, 1984), an entrepreneur in a socio-spatial context, which is 'a structure or field of entrepreneurial possibilities' (Scott, 2006: 5). Scott defines this context as a creative field, an evolving network locked into particular locations, generating an agglomeration of transaction-intensive industries of the new economy. This agglomeration can enable the development, and benefit from the existence, of technical and epistemic linkages that result from proximity and shared cultures.This descriptive historical and social analysis of the way agglomerations and creative fields emerge draws on biological metaphors of evolution, which has its own shortcomings. However, by recognizing the significance of the urban context, it can indicate the significance of space in this process.

Researchers who have argued for the significance of space in the knowledge economy often tend to stop at the regional geographical level. But it is also essential to pay attention to the more detailed features of these regions, to see how spatial expressions of knowledge economy are articulated. While the urban region is the focus of attention in these markets and networks, particular nodes within these regions are significant in the development of networks and facilitation of face-to-face encounters, through spatial and organizational places of encounter, from golf clubs to trade fairs and business parks. The attention to public space is

Following industrial decline in an inner suburb, a 22-acre (8.9 hectare) project brings arts and industry together as an incubator for future technologies (Los Angeles, USA).

perhaps one of the clearest spatial expressions of these nodes, which can act as a social and spatial support mechanism for the clustering of knowledge workers (DETR/CABE, 2000). Similarly, the development of higher densities and mixed-use areas are other factors in stimulating this clustering process. According to the British government's planning advice, 'Policies should promote mixed use developments for locations that allow the creation of linkages between different uses and can thereby create more vibrant places' (ODPM, 2005: para 27ii). There are many reasons for the development of public spaces, high densities and mixed-use developments, which include social and environmental considerations; but their linkage with the demands of economic development cannot be denied.

Is knowledge production a placeless, mental process that can happen anywhere and anytime, or is it a series of physical activities conducted by embodied individuals in specific places? It would be impossible to think of an economic process without people who are engaged in activities of production and exchange, individuals who are inevitably living in particular places and have everyday routines of life. At the local level, therefore, the significance of the physical environment remains important for the way knowledge workers conduct their work. Both at regional and local levels we see the continued significance of a spatial context, as the location of activities at the regional and local levels, as accumulating intellectual capital and facilitating the transmission of tacit knowledge.

The new sites of production

Rather than industrial districts' congregation of factories surrounded by working-class neighbourhoods, the new sites of production in the city are clusters of offices,

Public spaces are promoted as part of active social networks, which are essential in knowledge transmission (Helsinki, Finland).

cultural districts, science or business parks, universities and even homes. Knowledge that is being created and converted into an economic asset takes shape in these new sites of production, which follow the logic of economies of scale, functional and spatial specialization, processes of clustering that are intertwined with the dynamics of social stratification and spatial dispersion.

The university

Creating a critical mass for innovation requires anchor points that can attract others and build on existing strengths. The vision of a knowledge economy that draws heavily on research and development entails strengthening the existing capacities by helping them grow and creating new capacities by investing strategically in promising sectors. Two sectors of the economy seem to stand out, targeted for specialization in urban development strategies: cultural industries and high-tech industries. As both of these industries have close connections with the university, the role of this institution in urban and regional development becomes particularly significant (Benneworth, Charles and Madanipour, 2010).

The future of universities in their traditional form has come under scrutiny: on the one hand, the advent of new information and communication technologies facilitates online learning, which seems to render their physical presence less relevant than before. On the other hand, pressure on universities to be more

Old university buildings and spaces are not an obstacle for universities to be at the forefront of knowledge creation (Cambridge, UK).

entrepreneurial and engaged with economic development of their locality seems to be at odds with their traditional image and function. Both the role of technology and the market in university education, however, are open to critical questioning (Njenga and Fourie, 2010).

In the knowledge economy, universities have found a special role, as the places in which knowledge is produced and nurtured. The relationship between the university and the city, therefore, can have a new significance for urban development. In their historic form, universities were originated from monasteries and religious seminaries, where monks and priests were living a life of contemplative seclusion in their cloisters on the urban periphery or outside cities altogether. During the rise of the Industrial Revolution, universities became crucially involved in science and technology and more integrated with the social and economic life of the city. Now that knowledge is announced as the driving force of economic development, universities find an even more central role, both economically and spatially.

The relationship between the city and the university should be studied in both its institutional and physical dimensions. As a large institution, the university makes significant economic and social contributions to the city. The way this large institution finds physical form in the city influences the nature of the institution, as well as its relationship with the rest of the city, and even the character of the city as a whole. As a large landowner and sometimes developer, it can have a considerable influence on patterns of land use, access and mobility, and architecture of the city.

Depending on their mission and self-image, universities have different relationships with their regions. While teaching-oriented universities may have stronger reasons to relate to their catchment areas, research universities can be engaged in a worldwide network of communication and recruitment, remaining able to work without developing strong connections to their immediate surroundings. Some of the most prosperous and prestigious research-intensive universities in the world are located in deprived areas of industrial decline. Many universities were founded as part of the industrialization drives of the nineteenth century, to provide the necessary knowledge and expertise in the development of a new type of economy. With the decline of manufacturing industries in many such regions, the economic basis of these regions has eroded, while the university has continued to prosper through harnessing new resources, creating a mismatch that at times can be visible to any observer.

Such a mismatch was detectable in earlier periods, creating tensions between universities and the cities in which they are located, as reflected in the phrase 'town and gown'. Under these conditions, it may have been tolerable for the city authorities and populations to live with this tension in exchange for having a prestigious institution in town that would boost civic pride and local economy. However, the nature of this disjointed relationship is now beginning to change, as the nature of regional economies is changing. De-industrialized regions in search of a new economic base look to developing a niche in the global marketplace as centres of innovation through research and development. In this context, the role and significance of the university and the need for redefining its relationship with its region becomes an important focus of attention. If, the argument goes, we are to develop a new economic base, the only one seems to be innovation and knowledge, as we are unable to compete with the low-cost regions of emerging economies or with the high environmental quality of sunbelts. This would mean expecting a more active contribution by the university to this scenario, as it appears to be the most obvious nucleus in a city for knowledge production.

In addition to this shift, there is a change in the nature of governance in cities and regions. With economic liberalization after the 1980s, and the changing nature of state intervention in a number of economic and social arenas, governance arrangements in the regions have become more complicated than before, with many new agencies from the public and private sectors making decisions that would affect the region as a whole. In this context, the university as a large local institution can find a stronger voice, and is expected to play a more significant role, in urban and regional governance. As a player with ability to make decisions with potentially far-reaching impacts on the city, particularly in small to medium-sized cities, the university can find itself in a position to negotiate and even steer the course of events in new directions.

As a result of the combination of a changing economic configuration, the desire of the local and national authorities to change the economic direction towards a knowledge base, and the transformation of governance arrangements in the regions, universities are potentially in a more favourable position to influence policies and events. This change in their relative disposition inevitably has an impact on the nature of universities themselves; what they do and the way they define their role in society would be pressed to change to fit the new reality.

To perform these new roles, universities are limited by at least three sets of factors: mission, resources and organization. They are bound by their *raison d'être*, i.e., their historical mission of teaching and research, and find it difficult to contribute to the regional economy in new ways without compromising their defining mission. Any change of their relationship and role in the city may mean changing their core rationale, which would not be easy to grasp and accept. The second factor is the financial capabilities and limitations of universities as public institutions. Universities suffer from what appear to be permanent financial crises, always unable to cover their costs and perform their duties. How can they perform new roles in addition to their existing ones, while their core duties are suffering from underfunding? The third factor is the flat organization of the university, in which academics and departments have historically enjoyed a large degree of autonomy. Governments and university managers appear to have concluded that any purposeful change of direction may mean the need for a more hierarchical organization and stronger interventions by the management. This, however, would create a mismatch between the need for academic freedom, which is necessary for innovation, and the more centralized organization, which tends to limit this freedom.

Pressure for change and subsequent tensions have an impact, as well as draw, on the university as a place, as part of the urban environment. Financial pressures on universities have led to more attention being paid to their assets, which include their intellectual properties and their real estate. Both of these are seen in a new light, with major consequences for the management of the university's estate and impacts on the larger society. A knowledge economy is more than just the university; it means a network of innovative companies, groups, individuals and related activities. Pressure is mounting on universities to support spin-out companies, which can then create clusters of innovation in a region, retaining the existing and attracting new talents and energies. How a university deals with spin-out companies has spatial implications. Is there a need for on-campus provisions or off-campus investment for the promotion of these companies? When do they need support and at what point do they become larger, independent organizations? How would their location and quality of space affect their success? In high-tech industries, the quality of research space is a capital-intensive area of development. What are the spatial implications of these new types of research for universities?

Commercialization of innovation is coupled with commercial exploitation of land and property. The university is often a large landowner in the city; its land and property decisions, its policies on car parking and redevelopment of its buildings, all have consequences for urban planning and development as a whole. The built environment of universities are often the result of the accumulation of decades if not centuries of planned or ad hoc change, responding to changing needs as well as available resources. The quality of these buildings and spaces has a direct link to the nature of the university, its ability to meet its mission, how it works as an organization and how it manages its resources. Different waves of

Aalto University brings three universities together, claiming that it is 'where science and art meet technology and business' (Helsinki, Finland).

rising property prices have generated large assets in the hands of cash-strapped organizations and regions. Some see the sale of these assets as one way of getting out of their financial troubles, especially if they have difficulty repairing and maintaining their physical stock. The city and regional authorities may also see these assets as too expensive for an educational organization that can perhaps be relocated out of town and their property be used for up market housing and offices, generating new resources for public services in the process.

The way an organization's spaces and buildings are arranged has a direct impact on how it works. Its spatial configuration can make it easier or harder for the individuals and departments to deliver their teaching and research tasks. It can limit or promote collaboration among its members. Are buildings and spaces fit for purpose or outdated and unproductive? In the wave of restructuring that the British universities have experienced, whereby larger schools and faculties were created in more centralized organizations, a major factor for success or failure of these new larger units to work is their spatial arrangements. Are they located in the same space or are they spread in different buildings and in different parts of the city? Is spatial dispersion promoting or preventing the formation of new cross-disciplinary linkages?

Spatial configuration can also link the organization to its wider context, or can cut it off from this context. Depending on the location of the university, in the city centre or as an out-of-town campus, the nature of such linkage varies. While the ability for integration and linkage is greater at the centre of the town, the characteristics of streets, open spaces, access points and location of buildings, as well as the policies of the university to make its spaces available and open, or closed and monitored, all have implications for its links to the surrounding environment. Pressure is high from the city and regional authorities on the university to be present in more sites and activities across the city, to stimulate new activities and create new nuclei for economic and social development. The university is a social environment, in which thousands of staff and students communicate and share a productive part of their lives in the same place. The quality of this environment can help enhance or hinder this experience, can turn it into a more productive or a wasteful one.

Research could focus on a number of questions: what are the spatial decisions of universities, and on what bases? How can they be analysed in relation to their regional context? How can a university make optimum use of its land and property so that it maximizes its ability to perform its core duties while making positive contributions to its city and region? How are the changing nature of regional economies and the changing nature of the university's roles and challenges affecting the spatial configuration of universities? How are the physical and institutional dimensions of universities affecting one another in a situation of change in their context and nature?

The Boston area in the north-east United States has a concentration of eight research universities. The eight research universities in the Boston area are considered to be engines of economic growth, contributing a total of $7 billion annually to their regional economy (MIT, 2003). In particular, the city of Cambridge is well-known as a university city in this region, with a total of 38,000 students and 19,000 employees in its four higher education institutions: Harvard, MIT, Lesley University and Cambridge College. The city has a total population of 100,000 and is a short walk across the Charles River from Boston. Cambridge has a highly educated population (65% with bachelor's degree or higher, as compared with 39.5% in the Boston area and 24% in the United States). The universities in Cambridge contribute strongly to the life of the city, and in return benefit from its livelihood. Two world-class universities are the top employers in the city: Harvard (around 9,000 employees) and MIT (around 8,000), far ahead of the third employer, which is the city government (around 3,000), and other top employers, which include the medical and biotechnological sciences. In addition to students and scholars, the universities act as magnets for the companies that wish to be associated with their prestige and for tourists who visit part of the American cultural heritage.

The universities control 460 buildings and own 10% of the Cambridge city's area, which means their property development and transactions have a major impact on the city. However, educational establishments, like government and non-profit organizations, are exempt from paying real estate tax. In 1990, the public was particularly concerned about the universities' growing ownership and development of Cambridge's taxable real estate. As a result of these concerns for the loss of potential tax revenues, a committee was formed in 1991 to bring

The economic and cultural life of the city and the university are intertwined, but their growth and development need to be coordinated to avoid conflict over land (Cambridge, MA, USA).

together representatives from the city's neighbourhoods, city officials and the universities, resulting in a report that became known as the town-gown report (City of Cambridge, 1991). The report recommended that the city and the universities work together on their future growth, the universities pay attention to the fiscal health of the city and consider their roles as educators, economic enterprises and neighbours. Since then, the Cambridge Planning Board conducts an annual joint review, in which each university, on a voluntary basis, submits a town-gown report, providing information about its existing conditions and future plans (e.g., Harvard, 2004; MIT, 2004), followed by a presentation to the board.

Many of Cambridge's major nodes and landmarks are associated with the universities, and as such the life and identity of the city and the universities are intertwined. The city benefits from the universities' economic and cultural activities, and students and employees of the universities benefit from services provided by the city. However, there are inevitable conflicts. Universities have grown and prospered, with inevitable impact on their urban environment: higher competition for housing, higher housing densities and costs, changing mix of businesses and jobs, traffic congestion and reduced tax base for the city. House prices are high and around half of the students and two-thirds of the university employees live outside Cambridge (City of Cambridge, 2003; 2005). In addition to their tax-exempt properties, the universities own premises such as commercial and taxable housing (total 117 acres), for which they pay tax. In 2004, these higher education institutions paid the city $44 million in real estate taxes, payments in lieu of taxes, water and sewer fees and other fees and permits (City of Cambridge, 2005). Following the more active role the universities are playing in urban governance, both the universities and the city authorities are anxious to show the contribution that these very rich institutions make to the economic and social life of the city. Harvard University (2005), for example, which is the richest higher education institution in the world, announces its resources at the service of the local community, which include campus arts, sports, lectures, classes and religious services, community partnerships, programmes and planning.

Science and technology parks

In a knowledge-based economy, the new factory in which scientific knowledge is produced is the research institute and the university. The investment in human capital and the development of universities, therefore, have attracted new attention from policy-makers. Alongside this, universities are encouraged to become aware of their intellectual property rights and utilize their knowledge for economic gain. If they are not able to play this role themselves, for the lack of funds, organizational capacity and marketing skills, they are then encouraged to welcome and work with those in the market who can. Strengthening the connections between, or even co-location of, the university and industry becomes a policy objective in local economic-development circles.

Drawing on the idea that clustering would be a sign of the formation of economies of scale, some have argued that these clusters can be developed through purposeful action, which would lead to information-sharing and innovation. In his first major speech as the British minister for universities and science, David Willets (2010) stressed the role of science in economic development. He announced, 'I'm a firm believer in clusters – best defined as a low-risk environment for high-risk activity.' A longstanding strategy has been the creation of clusters of knowledge-intensive organizations, named technopolis, research parks, science parks, knowledge parks, technology parks, innovation centres, science cities, etc., where research and business organizations are located side by side and research innovation and economic application of these innovations are hoped to coincide. Research has shown that the companies that are linked with universities have higher productivity rates, higher market share, better-quality products and services and are more competitive in their costs (Malairajaa and Zawdie, 2008). The spin-off companies, business incubators, and science and technology parks are expected to generate an infrastructure for sharing information and resources necessary to develop new ideas into business success.

Different countries, therefore, promote the idea of science parks as part of their economic development strategy. UNESCO encourages governments around the world to establish partnerships, networks and innovation systems that would enhance their countries' ability to share knowledge and information. Since 2002, UNESCO has emphasized the establishment of science and technology parks in developing countries, in the hope of strengthening the ties between universities and industry (UNESCO, 2010). Research into their contribution to innovation and economic development, however, has shown different degrees of success (Ratinho and Henriques, 2010; Yang *et al.*, 2009). While firms inside the science parks generally undertake more R&D than those outside, comparisons between companies inside and outside the science park have not shown statistically different levels of engagement with universities (Squicciarini, 2008; Malairajaa and Zawdie, 2008). Studies into the effectiveness of science parks have either been inconclusive or only partly positive, unable to show the causal role they play in knowledge-based regional development (Van Geenhuizen and Soetanto, 2008). Even so, they remain popular policy tools, widely used around the world and promoted by international organizations.

The term 'park' in the title of science and technology parks betrays their suburban character and origin. The establishment of research parks in the United States, which has been the source of inspiration for other science and technology parks, has been part of the drive for suburbanization in the United States, where shops and workplaces followed houses to the suburbs. After the Second World War, the construction of a motor way network and federal subsidies helped make suburban housing affordable, encouraging the middle classes to leave the city in search of a dream for better life (Fishman, 1987; Keating and Krumholz, 1999). In concept and character, business parks and science parks were similar to shopping malls and suburban housing subdivisions. Even when their scale is large and the cluster they shape is substantial in size, the suburban character is an integral part of these parks.

There are now 700 science parks around the world, many inspired by the example of Silicon Valley in northern California, where the linkages between Stanford University and the industry created a cluster of high-tech firms and a hotbed of innovation (Malairajaa and Zawdie, 2008). Palo Alto, which was planned on a grid pattern at the turn of the last century to serve the new Stanford University on the outskirts of San Francisco, was transformed in the post-war period from a university town to a world leader in advanced technology (City of Palo Alto, 2007). Although the nearby city of San Jose is one of the largest cities in the United States, the character of Silicon Valley is essentially suburban, with wide streets, low-density suburban housing and major high-tech firms dotted around the suburban landscape.

Silicon Valley portrays a prototype for many spaces of knowledge, as a pioneer that other parts of the world envied and copied. The overall spatial configuration is one of a low-density spread of workspaces, surrounded by suburban housing, shopping strips and malls, and some town centres. Rather than a particularly knowledge-driven landscape, whatever that may be, this area may be called suburban. It is primarily following the models of suburban development that evolved after the Second World War in the United States. It belonged to a particular time and culture, and the fact that it was the centre of innovation in information communication and technology could be lost to a casual visitor, as its spatial organization and appearance could hardly suggest it. If you were not familiar with

Silicon Valley is the prototype for many spaces of knowledge, but it was built according to the style of suburban development in California, where offices joined suburban houses and shopping malls (Cupertino, CA, USA).

the names and logos of the famous companies that line the streets, you could think that you are going through yet another suburban area, where shops, offices and houses were scattered about, accessed by wide roads and large cars. This was the most cutting-edge space of knowledge, and yet it was also the most typical suburban sprawl, a model that grew on the basis of the availability of cheap fossil fuel and land, which characterized American suburban growth.

In Japan, the case of Tsukuba Science City is significant (Anttiroiko, 2004). It was established in the 1960s, when government-related research institutes and national educational institutes were relocated to a 27-square-kilometre site in Tsukuba city. It now hosts 59 educational and research institutes, in addition to 200 private organizations, and is considered to be a leading centre for research and innovation in Japan and in the world (Japan Atlas, 2010). Tsukuba Science City is a planned city, where 'the neat arrangement and straight, wide streets give the city a futuristic feel' (Japan-I, 2010), but where driving a car is necessary for moving about the town.

The idea of a science city is now widespread as a boost to universities, where their research is expected to find its development and application, hence contributing to the knowledge economy. ETH in Zurich, Switzerland, boasts about its Science City, established in 2003, that it is 'a model university for the 21st century . . . where science, business and the general public come together'; it is a 'city district for a "Thinkers' Culture" . . . where students, researchers and visitors can meet and realise new ideas' (ETH, 2010). In the UK, six cities have been designated science cities. In 2005 in Newcastle, a partnership between the university, city council and the regional development agency acquired a 24-acre site on the edge of the city centre, now called Science Central, to facilitate innovation through the collaboration of research and industry.

Development of science parks has been seen as a recipe for the regeneration of de-industrializing areas, replacing manufacturing industrial sites with knowledge

Science Central is a major project to facilitate innovation through university–industry collaboration (Newcastle, UK).

economy clusters. However, the gap in skills and housing between the two groups of workers is so wide that it creates policy dilemmas and gentrification impetus (Burfitt and Ferrari, 2008). While the logic of clustering for innovation may have been used to bring together similar and related activities to establish new relationships, the form that these new clusters have taken are still socio-spatially decontextualized and fragmentary, created at a distance from the city as part of a wider process of dispersal. Clustering is localized and functional, rather than being embedded in a city and making any contributions to strengthening the social and economic fabric of the city as a whole. The new communication and transportation technologies make it possible to be detached from the surroundings. The suburban location gives shape to this detachment. It is part of the process of segregation and fragmentation of social groups that characterizes the modern city. While the type of activities that go on in a science park may be different from previous generations of research and development, a science park is still a functional cluster, in the same vein as the functionalist land use had promoted throughout the twentieth century.

The new technologies of information and communication appear to atomize and decontextualize individuals and organizations. At the same time, there is the process of formation of economies of scale, in which similar activities cluster together and, if strong enough, attract related activities to the vicinity of this cluster. These scale economies worked for the manufacturing industries and they seem to be at work for the knowledge industries. Furthermore, the social nature of human beings brings them together, in spite of the encouragements and pressures to the contrary. The compromise between the libertarian nature of new technologies, the social nature of knowledge workers, and the logic of scale economies is the emergence of small clusters, a version of functionalist micro-urbanism that creates small residential, scientific and educational, cultural and business clusters (Madanipour, 1996). This is compounded by the effects of the functionalist planning systems, which have managed land use in separate zones. The city that emerges is a mosaic of functional pieces, connected together and to other places through transport and ICT. Integrated in the fabric of this mosaic are the spatial effects of social stratification, associated with the growing social inequality that has resulted from globalization. Social stratification is institutionalized by land and property markets, which sort people out on the basis of their ability to pay.

Creative economy clusters

If science and technology clusters are created on the stereotypical assumption that scientists in white coats are happy to be working in a secluded area on the outskirts of cities, cultural industries seem to thrive on the atmosphere of cities. Artists may at times be seeking seclusion to concentrate on their creative work, exemplified by those who are engaged in representations of the natural environment, as evidence from the history of art suggests. The image of the romantic and avant-garde solitary artist, escaping the overcrowded metropolis to find inspiration in far-away places is a strong and powerful image, which may describe some instances of some artists' lives. What this image conceals, however, are the underlying linkages and connections between these artists and metropolitan centres.

It is at urban centres that new trends emerge and paradigms of taste are created, training of new artists takes place, a cultural milieu is created to fit in or rebel against, and ideas disseminated to other places. This cultural milieu tends to emerge through social interaction and physical proximity, drawing on a dynamic social and economic context, which is often found in large urban centres. The solitude of the artist, therefore, may be a physical but not a cultural one. An artist who is completely disconnected from this milieu may remain unrecognized; education, innovation and recognition all depend on immersion in a context and a dynamic conversation with this context. Creative contexts are then essential for the development of cultural movements and their dissemination. The social context and its inherent spatiality play a significant role in the emergence and vibrancy of cultural activities.

These hotspots of creative innovation are not designed; they are complex milieus emerging out of a large number of processes. Many large urban centres may not encourage creative activities and creative clusters may be formed in unexpected places. There are many examples of how these places emerge in leftover spaces, places out of the reach or unrelated to the intentions of the public authorities or the development industry. It was indeed this lack of visibility that made such clusters possible. In de-industrializing cities, an oversupply of cheap space was a contrib-

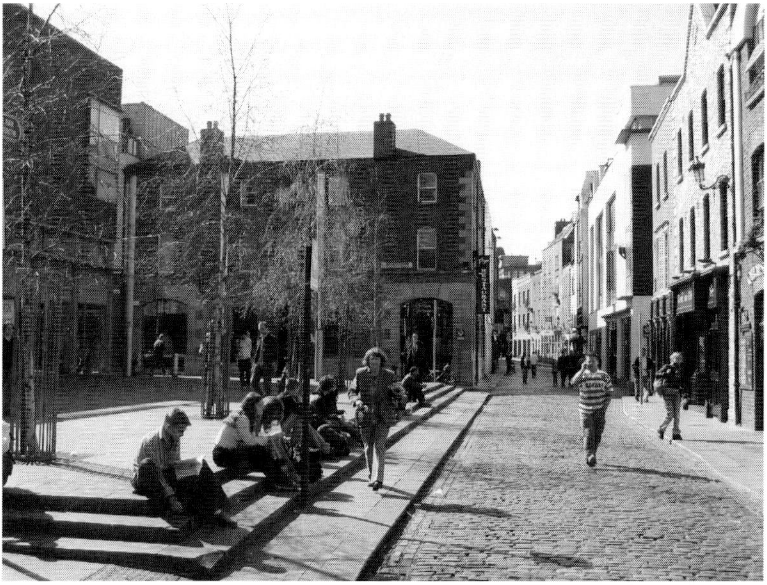

A cluster of creative activities was formed in Temple Bar, where development was delayed by planning blight (Dublin, Ireland).

uting factor, whereby old industrial buildings in low-rent parts of cities made space affordable for artists. In other cities, planning blight created spaces of invisibility, allowing a cluster of creative activities to find a breathing space. This was the case in Temple Bar in Dublin, where the area was designated for a major urban renewal scheme that was delayed for a considerable period of time.

The official regeneration efforts, however, caught up with this trend. The invisible places became visible, and in doing so lost some of their original character, becoming commercialized and turned into official destinations for policy decisions and investments. As policy-makers woke up to the fact that new sectors needed to be found for economic development, and witnessed the growth of the creative industries, it seemed only logical to pay more attention to this sector and encourage its development. Meanwhile, the transformation of demographic and economic structures brought more people to live in the city, some being attracted to the image of artists' quarters and bohemian lifestyles. These new attentions led to new investment, but also to the rising level of rents, making the place unaffordable for artists to live and work. It tended to replace a culturally minded cluster of creative and productive activities with a commercially minded cluster of firms and consumers who were attracted to and drew on the already established cultural image of the area. In some instances, these two orientations overlap, but in other instances they cannot easily co-exist, as manifest in the impact of change on rent levels.

Commercialization of creative and scientific innovation is at the heart of the knowledge-based economy. This process of commercialization finds clear spatial manifestation, as it takes over existing clusters, such as artists' quarters and university neighbourhoods, and creates new clusters in the hope of generating new hotspots of innovation.A trend in public policy is interested in creating physical proximities in the hope of generating a creative milieu. If knowledge cities are clusters of creative people, some have argued that it would make sense to attract creative people to the area, hence constructing a basis for economic revival (Florida, 2002). It is a form of reverse engineering, which may or may not work, as it is a hopeful investment in only one of the factors of production. However, this is an idea that many local authorities have embraced, deciding to help these clusters become stablished in their territories. By providing incentives and various forms of investment, they hope that they can attract footloose capital and mobile knowledge workers.

The clustering of knowledge workers is of course one element of the urban economy. Many other types of workers are also involved to work in and support these clusters, from clerical workers in offices to waiters at cafes and restaurants. So the formation of clusters should not be taken out of context, as they are part of an urban fabric in which a wide range of interdependent activities takes place. The cut-off point for what should be in a cluster is often a managerial decision, and the notion of relocating a group of such activities to a bespoke cluster would deprive them of many connections. If a cluster is well integrated into an urban fabric, its activities may benefit from adjacent activities, such as retail and entertainment, and contribute to the livelihood of the urban environment in return. If a cluster is taken out to a suburban location in search of productive seclusion, that tie is weakened, from which both sides suffer. Much of the time, however, the result, and even the intention, may not be the formation of a functional cluster but the publicity that its announcement may generate. If a city announces to have a cultural district or a science park, it is hoped that the outside image of the city has been strengthened as a place to invest or visit. The image of the place rather than its capacity for functional innovation may therefore benefit more from such 'designed clusters'. This rebranding of places, it is thought, would also contribute to the demand for space, and so the image is used to feed the development industry. In some places, the logic of the speculative production of space may be more prominent than the logic of creating a knowledge economy.

At other times, city authorities use the existing clusters of cultural activity as a city marketing tool, attempting to show that there is a critical mass of cultural institutions and activities in their city. The cities of Barcelona, New York, Berlin and London have set up cultural zones to strengthen their existing clusters and help the development of new ones. London has set up five such quarters, the largest of which is the West End, which has been a centre of the capital's cultural life for a long time, evolving around four main squares: Trafalgar Square, Leicester Square, Covent Garden and Somerset House, where a large number of theatres and restaurants are located in a vibrant cluster of cultural and recreational activities. Culture Quarter London is a partnership between eight major arts institutions

A cultural quarter has been created with the participation of eight major arts institutions (London, UK).

that are based in the area, including the National Gallery, National Portrait Gallery, English National Opera, Royal Opera House, St Martin in the Fields, Institute of Contemporary Arts, and Somerset House Trust. The partnership tries to create connections between these institutions to increase visitors and improve their experience, as a response to the government's emphasis on creative economy (Culture Quarter London, 2010).

Medium-sized cities, which are not as well placed in the global economy as compared with the largest metropolitan areas, have also been busy setting up quarters for cultural industries. The trend is strong in British cities, where the encouragement of establishment and strengthening of cultural industries has been an integral part of urban regeneration. New museums and cultural centres are built and the existing ones are refurbished as an investment in the infrastructure of a new creative economy.The principles of spatial clustering and city marketing are both paramount in these regeneration initiatives. In Sheffield, after the collapse of the manufacturing industries and witnessing the strength of popular culture, the city council in 1988 established an area of three-quarters of a square mile in the city centre as a Cultural Industries Quarter. The cultural industries associated with music, art, film and performance were recognized as 'a new growth sector for the local economy and potentially a replacement for the jobs and businesses lost in traditional industries during the 70s', which now needed to be established, legitimized and developed (CIQA, 2010). By 2006, the promotion of cultural industries was embraced more broadly by the city council, which established Creative Sheffield as the first City Development Company in the UK, which declares its areas of activity as regeneration, city marketing, investment and innovation, skills and enterprise (Creative Sheffield, 2010). Another example is the city of Leicester in England, which hopes its cultural quarter will be 'a major regional centre for the creative industries', set up with the aim of providing 'an attractive environment into which the creative business sector will want to locate' (Leicester City Council, 2010). In Lincoln, the designated cultural quarter links a group of managed workspaces to a range of cultural institutions such as theatre, library, museum and art galleries.

Creative clusters are also created by, or in partnership with, universities. Queensland University of Technology, for example, has set up a Creative Industries Precinct in Kelvin Grove Urban Village, which is on the fringe of Brisbane's central business district. The precinct is announced to be 'Australia's first site dedicated to creative experimentation and commercial development in the creative industries' (QUT, 2010). While the warmer climates may be naturally better placed to attract cultural industries, other areas promote their alternative assets.

In the middle of this small city's cultural quarter, the Terrace offers 50 serviced workshops, studios and offices 'exclusively available to the creative sector' (Lincoln, UK).

The US state of Massachusetts, for example, hopes to draw on its history, beauty and culture to draw in knowledge workers and grow its creative economy. A conference of decision-makers, private firms and academics in 2006 recommended the establishment of the Commonwealth Creative Economy Council and proposed an action plan, through which the state would be branded 'The Creative Economy State' in the United States (Salem Partnership, 2007).

The question that would apply to both science parks and creative clusters is whether spatial arrangements can be designed to have economic outcomes. The significance of space should of course be recognized, as when people are physically near one another the possibility for interaction is likely to increase. A long utopian tradition in garden cities and new towns has advocated the possibility of creating communities through spatial design and planning. Indeed, the father of garden cities, Ebenezer Howard, was highly influenced by Alfred Marshall's work (Howard, 1960). Can the same be applied to the creation of innovation and economic development? By clustering related activities, whether in science and technology or in arts and culture, can there be an added value that can be

With its blend of history, beauty and culture, Massachusetts hopes to be branded The Creative Economy State in the United States (Cambridge, MA, USA).

generated through spatial arrangements? If so, the space of the knowledge city would be the space of such clusters, in which groups of scientists or artists are joined by groups of entrepreneurs and industrialists, to create new products and services. However, we know of the limits and perils of social engineering and physical determinism, whereby spatial reorganization is taken to be the primary tool with which to change social and economic organization of a society, with unavoidable failures. These policies of providing spatial knowledge clusters are based on the idea of commercialization of science and culture, and of being located in designated places, two conditions to which not all practitioners may subscribe. In contrast to this trend of 'designed clusters', there is the idea of the death of geography and the workplace, in which flexible working practices made possible by new technologies remove the need for any form of physical presence or clustering.

Office clusters and home-working

The advent of new technologies brought about the idea that offices are no longer needed, and even cities may no longer survive, as the need for proximity evaporates through heightened mobility and communication. Would flexible working practices of a networked worker create a new urban form? The manufacturing industrial economy had reshaped cities in its own image: clusters of large factories accessible through transport networks for the import of raw materials and export of manufactured goods, flanked by mass housing for industrial workers. As the industrial economy took over from the agricultural economy, industrial cities replaced market towns as the nodes of the new economy. With the decline of manufacturing industries, and relaxation of their strict routines in time and space, a new spatial order is expected to emerge in response. In the past, streets, waterways, railways and motor ways (as well as airways), one after the other, became the backbone of urban physical infrastructure, raising the expectation that the new communication infrastructure would somehow become the backbone of the new economy.

The decline of manufacturing industries, the emergence of new information and communication technologies, labour market deregulation, privatization and outsourcing, decentralization of activities for regional development and the large-scale entry of women into the workforce have promoted flexible working patterns (Dahlström and Hermelin, 2007). Public and private organizations have introduced flexible practices in response to the concerns about work–life balance (Kelliher and Anderson, 2008; O'Brien and Hayden, 2008). Where firms have promoted a more flexible organization of work, through employee involvement, flatter hierarchies and teamwork, productivity has been higher (OECD, 2000). These practices are most common in the industries that are considered to be part of the knowledge economy, in firms that are concerned with quality, depend on highly skilled workers and compete in international markets (Powell and Snellman, 2004).

These new practices have brought about a higher degree of autonomy for workers, as well as new constraints and risks, though these vary widely among different groups and tend to reflect the conditions of the workers (Haddon and Brynin, 2005). Flexible working practices are thought to be driven by ICT and be about 'working in real time', allowing workers 'to work anytime, anywhere, using any device', which would facilitate flexible access to information and applications across the organization (Ashton, 2005: 12). More widely, flexible working practices, which have direct implications for the temporal and spatial organization of the city, include tele working, home-based working, flexitime, part-time, job-share, compressed working week, annualized hours, temporary and casual work and fixed-term contracts (Williams, 2005).

These practices are not yet the main form of working, and their impact on urban space, therefore, may still be limited. They have, however, the potential to change the temporal routines of the city: the barriers between home and work have become more blurred, shops and services are available for longer hours, even round the clock, and people travel to work at different times, which is a major shift from the harmonized and mass scale of work routines in manufacturing cities. Routines and destinations to work are also differentiated, so the predominant pattern of journey from the periphery to the centre has become supplemented by many different journey patterns between many different locations. The decline of standard mass journeys, however, could undermine the rationale of public transport provision, stimulating a more intensive reliance on private cars, fuelling further suburban sprawl and subsequent socio-spatial segregation.

Differentiated routines may transform the social life of the city, but they cannot easily transform its physical infrastructure. Once developed, the physical environment lasts for a long time, surviving social and economic changes, as exemplified by some of today's historic buildings and streets that were developed before the advent of the Industrial Revolution. While streets may survive even for millennia, buildings are far more perishable in comparison, though still lasting much longer than the social and economic conditions that may be behind their development. Land use, however, is the element of urban form that is most susceptible to change (Whitehand, 1992). It is here that pressure for flexibility can make its highest impact.

Modernist city planning, which worked as a means of reorganizing urban space for industrial economy, had argued in favour of zoning and land use regulation (Cullingworth and Caves, 2003). The Charter of Athens had identified four primary functions for the city (working, housing, transport, recreation), and had argued that these functions should be well ordered and kept apart (Sert, 1944). With the decline of traditional industrial production, however, this organization needed to change. Rather than strict separation of land uses, the new conventions of land use promote mixed use (Urban Task Force, 1999), a primary sign of introducing flexibility into spatial organization. The British Government's White Paper on planning, for example, asks for mixed-use developments that allow for 'greater flexibility of landuse' (HM Government, 2007: 113). Most regeneration proposals for cities now include mixed-use areas. On the one hand, in an uncertain atmosphere of economic change, this flexibility provides for a more entrepreneurial approach to urban development, as it is not clearly predictable what

Differentiated routines may transform the social life of the city, but they cannot easily transform its physical infrastructure (Tokyo, Japan).

activities may be attracted to a place. On the other hand, this flexibility would help a more diverse pattern of activities, hence a more vibrant environment, which could be used at different times of the day and week.

The result is a more mobile workforce and a higher degree of flexibility. There are, however, limits to flexibility in working arrangements and spatial behaviour, as workers still need to anchor themselves in particular places and temporal routines (Brown and O'Hara, 2003). The other side of flexibility is risk, and flexible working practices could also involve more precarious conditions for workers (Lipietz, 2003). The question remains as to who benefits from such gains: teams that make it possible or people at the top? Critics have argued that flexible working methods have intensified the demands on workers and reinforced managerial control at the cost of informal work cultures and formal union powers (Powell and Snellman, 2004). Concerns have also been raised about the negative impacts of flexible work on innovation (Michie and Sheehan, 2003), about the quality of these jobs and the limits on long-term opportunities for workers, despite a higher degree of job satisfaction associated with flexible working (Kelliher and Anderson, 2008).

Has flexible and home-working overcome the historic divide between home and work, between conception and execution? Work may be done at home, which affords the worker with some more control over the place and time of work, but it transfers pressures to workers; in a sense work conquers home, invading the private sphere of households to take control. While some types of work may benefit from this flexibility, the overall pattern is that individual contribution is a fragment of a larger process of work, and so the control exerted by the worker is limited, perhaps not much more than it would be in the office. The home and work may be integrated, but in a way that home becomes an extension of the office. Furthermore, it does not necessarily offer the worker the possibility of conception, it may be mainly execution that has been outsourced to a private home, transferring costs and anxieties to the individual worker, who now has to manage the balance.

Meanwhile, offices have continued to be built and cluster in particular parts of cities, from city centres to suburban business parks. Expectations from office buildings are higher, so new specifications are required from office space, new types of activities emerge and new management practices develop, all needing new office space. The economies of scale, as well as the firms' bid for status, bring them together in existing and new office districts. Security threats in cities, traffic congestion and high rental levels may deter offices from clustering in the centres

New clusters of offices emerge, displaying the continued significance of physical proximity for the assertion of status and benefiting from economies of scale (Paris, France).

of large metropolitan areas, but the larger firms cannot afford to be away from the dense agglomerations in which the fortunes of their trade may be made.

Conclusion

Agglomeration of firms and activities continues to shape cities, and as the basis of the urban economy changes from manufacturing to services, new patterns in the clustering of these activities are emerging, either by public policy or by the decisions of individuals and firms. The new sites of production in the knowledge economy include universities, science and technology parks and creative economy clusters, as well as homes and office clusters. The pressure for specialization and suburbanization has created fragmented specialist sites, while the nature of some sectors makes it undesirable for them to be separated from the life of the city. The economies of scale and the pressure for agglomeration are produced either through the market or the public policy to create new clusters, in the hope that innovation will result. The core of these ideas is that clustering will generate innovation and economic development. A subtext is that clustering, which is often clearly badged and well advertised, will generate a positive image for city marketing and global competition between cities. The relationship between the cluster and the rest of the city, both in terms of the sectors of economy and the type of workers employed, and in the spatial relations of proximity and integration or decontextualization and segregation, is often undermined in this process. 'Designed clusters' may not lead to functional innovation or new investment in the city, and if they are not a part of the city's economy and society, their success, if it materializes at all, will be limited. The production of space may be only partly connected to the need for clusters, responding to the demands of the development industry rather than knowledge economy.

9 Sites of differentiated consumption

Much of the discussion about knowledge society revolves around production and how to boost the prerequisites for its development and growth. What are the consumption patterns in knowledge society and in what ways are these patterns reflected in space? Do knowledge products lead to new forms and spaces of consumption? Where the economy is driven by consumption, what are the role and shape of space in facilitating and promoting consumption? Within the context of growing social inequality, how does the knowledge-based economy fare in addressing spatial fragmentation and divide? How are the pressures to control the social consequences of growing inequality handled? Are raising spatial barriers and introducing new forms of surveillance and control a part of the knowledge-based economy? Answers to these and similar questions can be found in the changing nature of consumption, the role of consumption in the economy and the differential forms of consumption, which create new spatial patterns of dispersion and agglomeration, new signs and symbols of status and power, all linked with new challenges for cities.

Changing patterns of consumption

We have seen how the nature of products in the knowledge economy is considered to be intangible, no longer physical objects but 'weightless' representations that can be sent and received by information and communication technologies. Would this mean that the nature of consumption has essentially changed, whereby the consumption of material goods has dwindled? It is in fact quite the opposite: affluent societies of today have accumulated goods at unprecedented rates. According to the director of the Design Museum in London, 'Never have more of us had more possessions than we do now, even as we make less and less use of them' (Sudjic, 2009: 5).

The emergence of the knowledge economy is often associated with the changing configuration of production, in which alterations in technology and organization are facilitated for higher returns on investment. Much of the literature on the subject is written from a producer's perspective, to show how and why a knowledge economy can be developed and how the necessary elements for its growth should be put in place, such as the skills and the technical infrastructure needed.

Consumption of material goods has grown rather than dwindled (Paris, France).

The rise of the knowledge economy, however, should also be associated with the changing patterns of consumption, in which the demand for new goods and services drives the changes in the patterns of supply. If the demand is for things to be 'better, faster, cheaper' (Advisory Committee, 2008: ix), the result would be pressure on the systems of production to innovate and produce these goods and services in new ways. This is closely related to market pressures to generate demand through advertising and entertainment, facilitated by new media. If demand diminishes or stops, the cycle of production comes to a halt. It becomes therefore necessary for the producers both to offer new products and to create demand for these products.

To analyse demand, we come across the longstanding problem of need. What is the threshold of the need, and where can we say that we have had enough of something? We know that a large number of people in the world live in poverty, deprived of their basic needs such as food, drinking water, shelter, healthcare and education. But beyond these essential needs, which are easier to meet for the better off, how can we distinguish between need and desire? Is there a need for many of the products in the market, or is the need induced in the consumers to seek out new products? Advertising and marketing agencies work hard with luring images and stories to instil in their potential segments of the market the desire for their products (Berger, 1977). In these circumstances, it is the production that encourages consumption, rather than the other way round. Rather than meeting an existing need, the task of some producers and their advertising agencies is to

Demand for products is created by advertising (Tokyo, Japan).

create the impression of a need, to which their product appears to be a response. The proliferation of products and the reach of the media, however, is such that there is no way a person can arrive at a point in which these needs are fully met, especially as the famous brands and celebrity lifestyles are used to generate these images and desires. The result is a never-ending sense of shortcoming, which no amount of consumption can overcome.

An intensified chain of 'creative destruction' would then be generated, in which faster, shorter cycles of production and consumption would be coupled with a higher frequency of obsolescence and disposability of goods and services. The entry of low-cost production regions into the global marketplace has intensified the disposable attitude, as exemplified in the way everyday consumer items are bought and used in rich societies. A focus on the production side of this process would evaluate it to signify an innovative and vibrant economy, while a focus on the consumption side would show a wealthy society engaged in ever expanding consumption. Consumption, therefore, could be seen as the engine of the economy, being stimulated by the producers, generating demands for a continually regenerating chain of new goods and services, which would fuel economic growth.

This chain of producer-driven, advertising-generated sense of need can be visibly found in the urban space, whereby larger flats and houses and new retail and entertainment areas are produced for the well off, luring them to change their attitude to spatial consumption in search of a better sense of themselves. Luring images of the city glamorize the urban lifestyle, popular songs sing the praises of

Urban areas go through radical transformation through 'creative destruction' (Nottingham, UK).

big cities, and even the word 'urban' becomes a brand that is attached to many unrelated goods and services. Part of the drive for urban living can therefore be attributed to the triumph of advertising, which works hard to help the development industry inject exchange value into the obsolete parts of the city.

An associated problem is that of identity and social status, in which people can feel happy when feeling secure in comparing themselves with their peers in their habits of consumption. The construction of cultural meaning through the consumption of goods and services has long been noted by sociologists and anthropologists. Cultural categories that generate patterns of distinction in society find material form through goods and services, which materialize and visualize the existing cultural order. Advertising, fashion systems and consumer rituals help transfer meaning between the general cultural context, consumer goods and individual consumers (McCracken, 1986; Sudjic, 2009).

In a globalized economy, where information and cultural products can easily travel, and where goods and services can be visible everywhere through information and communication technologies, the problem of distinction becomes ever more complex. On the one hand, the problem of homogenization emerges, in which large corporations with their distinctive visual appearance and standardized goods and services are present everywhere (Townshend and Madanipour, 2008). On the other hand, as the cases from the Soviet-dominated lands show, homogenization of cultural forms was not merely enforced through market mechanisms of capitalism, but also through political processes of imperial powers (Adams, 2008). The forms of consumption contribute to the development of subcultures that help their members construct meaning and a sense of the self in fluid cultural contexts (Kozinets, 2001; Maffesoli, 1996).

As the patterns of consumption become embedded in society, they put pressure on individuals to match their peers, to secure their sense of identity and social status, or merely to satisfy their never-ending desires. The resources that are necessary to feed these habits, however, are not available for most people. The result has been the enormously high levels of personal debt, as became widely noticed in the credit crisis of 2008. In the UK, two-thirds of the GDP is consumer-related, which means, 'consumer spending drives the economy and much of this is funded by debt' (Cockerill and Black, 2009). The accumulation of this debt, which was induced by the suppliers of credit, and the inability to pay it back by those on lower incomes, was at the centre of the financial crisis, the so-called subprime mortgages that pulled the leg from under the luxury table of the global financial system.

Debt has also been accumulated by governments, through the fiscal stimulus that has injected vast amounts of money into the global economy. However,

Consumer-driven economy was funded by personal and public debt (Birmingham, UK).

when a government, such as Dubai in 2009 or Greece in 2010, appears unable to repay its debt, the world's financial system is once again shaken, showing the extent of interdependence in the global economy (Hughes *et al.*, 2009). Most problematic of all perhaps now is the impact of the growth in consumption, and associated economic growth, on the earth's resources. Consumer products that are shipped around the world, waste mountains that pile up owing to faster cycles of use and disposal, and the extent to which the extraction of natural resources go, from drilling the depth of seas to waging wars, all driven by embedded modes of consumption and among the primary causes of environmental degradation. There is a clear parallel here between the environmental and financial crisis, both built on debt, one financial and the other environmental, both very hard to pay back.

What, then, is the aim and shape of the knowledge economy in this context? If the chain of production and consumption is so tightly intertwined, creating a successful knowledge-based economy would inevitably mean a more vibrant model of production and a more intensified form of consumption. But if consumption is not satisfying a need, cannot be a reliable source of identity, is not equally accessible and can have adverse effects on the earth's resources, how can the knowledge economy, or for that matter any economy, succeed? In advocating the rise of the knowledge economy, therefore, it is not enough to focus on how it is produced, as many international organizations and governments do, but also what it leads to and how the results are managed.

Social and philosophical context of diversity

A cultural approach to historic periodization has held the advent of knowledge economy to be a radical break, mapping, as well as advocating, the end of the modernism that dominated the twentieth century, or even the modern period that started in the eighteenth century with the age of the Enlightenment. Rather than post-industrial or post-Fordist, the term post-modern became perhaps the most widely used form of the term 'post-'. Here the historic sequence was considered to be a transition from traditional to modern societies, which in turn was now moving into post-modernity. This transition has sometimes been depicted as a progress, changing from a less advanced economic condition to a more advanced one. It is based on a linear and progressive interpretation of time, which has been doubted by post-modern critics as fictional. Rather than temporal and causal linkages, they have insisted on spatial, simultaneous and disconnected orders (Foucault, 2002). The term 'post-modern' has been widely used to denote an epochal change, which is a cultural reading of a series of social transformations and ideologies, without any direct engagement with technological, organizational or economic change. While modernism was the cultural face of industrial mass production, post-modernism was interpreted as that of flexible production (Harvey, 1989) and differentiated consumption. The knowledge economy, however, appears also to refer to an even later phase, in which technological interpretations were reinvigorated (Castells, 1996) and globalized economic relations have replaced the older local tensions between the organized industrial workers and their employers (Aglietta, 2008).

For Lyotard, one of its key advocates, post-modernism is the cultural dimension of the post-industrial society. The transition into this society and culture started at the end of reconstruction in Europe in the 1950s, turning knowledge into the key force of production in the 'computerized societies' of the developed countries (Lyotard, 1984: 3). This strand brought about a cultural turn in social analysis, as distinctive from, and in contrast to, the political economic turn that had characterized the previous generation. This cultural turn was characterized by political disillusionment, philosophical scepticism, celebration of subjectivity and assertion of social and aesthetic diversity.

The modern attitude draws on a sense of confidence in human abilities, the belief in progress and a disregard for the past. An early formulation of this approach is made by Descartes, who started by doubting what he had learned before and looked for certainty through the application of a systematic method of reasoning based on mathematics. Descartes (1968: 39) was 'convinced that our beliefs are based on custom and example', which needed to be dismantled and rebuilt in the light of reason. It was good to know about the past, but 'when one is too interested in what went on in past centuries, one usually remains extremely ignorant of what is happening in this century' (Descartes, 1968: 31). This attitude transferred the focus of attention to the present, which was no longer tied to the past; and moved the centre of gravity to the human subject, who was no longer bound by tradition or context. Whereas the medieval mind looked to traditions, scriptures and heavens for guidance, the modern mind had to resort to itself for solutions. As Western civilization grew in confidence, armed by industrial technology, complex organization, modern nation-state, accumulated wealth and conquered territories around the world, the faith in human subjects and their scientific knowledge seemed to have paid off. To advocate the modern attitude, modernism emerged in the nineteenth-century revolutionary and romantic movements, and reached the twentieth century as a recipe for a radical break with the past, as continuously redefined, and optimism in a future shaped by science and technology. The end of the post-war boom, however, heralded the rise of a new approach, which criticized the modern outlook, hence known as a post-modern attitude.

Philosophical scepticism is best exemplified in Lyotard's famous definition of post-modern as 'incredulity toward metanarratives', which he attributes to 'progress in the sciences' (1984: xxiv). All the grand ideas and universal values that the modern age had advocated were now being questioned. The notions of truth, progress and justice had been used to force people into a consensus that would undermine their diversity and heterogeneity. This resistance to 'grand narratives' is a resistance to the dominance of instrumental reason, which tends to justify particular power relations in accordance with some established norms. But if these norms are themselves questioned, or the ability of the instrumental reason to deliver them, then the critics hope to have performed an act of defiance. Lyotard predicts that future society will be less based on general systems such as structuralism or systems theory, but on many different language games. The result would be 'a heterogeneity of elements', 'institutions in patches' and 'local determinism' (Lyotard, 1984: xxiv).

Lyotard's notion of language games draws on Wittgenstein, but scepticism towards modern culture and society is often traced back to Nietzsche, who described his main task as 'revaluation of all values' (Nietzsche, 2007: 60). Nietzsche questioned the lofty ideas of philosophy as dogmatic, seeing them as 'some folk superstition . . . some play on words perhaps, some seductive aspect of grammar, or a daring generalization from very limited, very personal, very human, all-too-human facts' (Nietzsche, 1998: 3). He explicitly describes this work as '*a critique of modernity*, not excluding the modern sciences, the modern arts, even modern politics' (Nietzsche, 2007: 77).

Post-modern scepticism appears to be the result of a huge disillusionment with the twentieth-century promises of modernism, and more broadly with the promises of the Enlightenment. Modernity had failed to deliver its promises of reason and progress, as evidenced by the largest death toll in human history in two world wars, which was made possible by the industrialization and globalization of violence. The post-war Keynesianism appeared to reduce social inequalities, but leaving many other deficiencies and gaps that needed addressing. The cultural turn to post-modernism was also a reaction against orthodox Marxism, which had placed the primary emphasis on political economy, but its implementation in socialist countries had disappointed Western intellectuals. Now post-modern thinkers questioned the notions of progress, hierarchy and stratification and focused their attention on social diversity.

In the absence of grand ideas and universal values, what remain are fragmented trajectories and localized and overlapping patterns of meaning. The celebration of diversity and ambiguity, therefore, becomes the primary feature of post-modern thinking. For the post-modern thinkers, and their inspiration Nietzsche, this focus on fragmentation and diversity has been a normative agenda, a critique of the accepted ideas of their time. Fragmentation, however, has become a reality in society, as the size and complexity of the cities, the collapse of old certainties and mass beliefs, and the plurality of lifestyles and perspectives have been an integral part of social life.

More than a critique, recognition of fragmentation means coming to terms with the existing and growing diversity of society. Complexity and diversity had already emerged in the nineteenth-century industrial city, as it grew through immigration from the countryside, a process now taking place in many developing countries. It continues to be the case in globalized industrial societies, where international migration has fuelled urban growth and diversity, particularly in larger cities. In the nineteenth century, religion and class became the weapons of choice against this emerging diversity. In the twentieth century, some mourn the emergence of fragmentation as a symptom of atomization, arguing for recognition as a route to overcome fragmentation (Honneth, 1995), for a return to communitarian (Etzioni, 1995) or liberal universal (Barry, 2001) ideals. Post-modernists, however, accept this fragmentation and see it even as an internal feature of the

Ethnic diversity is only one facet of the wider phenomenon of the assertion of difference (Toronto, Canada).

individual's mind (hence the notion of decentred humans) and the social realm (as expressed through tribalism), which some see as a source of renewal and rejuvenation (Maffesoli, 1996).

The social movements that emerged in the 1960s reflected disillusionment with the post-war settlement and led simultaneously to an optimistic fight for gender and racial equality, with considerable advances, and to a pessimistic post-modern outlook that denied the possibility of any major improvements. One of the major figures that displays both these dimensions is Michel Foucault, who revealed some of the power imbalances inherent in everyday life, the disadvantages suffered by those who did not fit the established norms, and therefore questioning modern society's capacity to deliver a more just settlement (Gutting, 1994).

History is a selective narrative of events after they have unfolded (Badiou, 2005), and many have attempted to package their accounts as changing epochs with a degree of internal consistency (Savage, 2009). At all times, lines of continuity and disruption can be detected in the sequence of events. The way historians decide to develop a coherent story out of a sea of different events and processes depends much on their situation and the attitude of others. Some stories find popularity as they are found to reflect the events more accurately or interestingly, or more relevant to the story-tellers and their audiences. These interpretations of historical change all seemed to need the use of the prefix post-, as they were all rooted in observing what went on before, anchoring their observations on 'change from' and not yet being able to see the conditions of 'change to'. They were all sure about the advent of substantial change in society, but they could hardly see the destinations, only the point of departure and some of the scenery on the way. Furthermore, they all seemed to think in terms of linear time and essentialist change (even by the post-modern deniers of linearity and essentialism) so that a new phase appeared fully to remove the previous phase and create somewhat more positive conditions. The lines of continuity between modern and post-modern are far more visible than the patterns of discontinuity and rupture. In other words, the attitude of modernity has resumed in full force, in all areas of economy, politics and culture.

The post-modernist writers often reacted to, and at times encouraged, the transition from Fordism to post-Fordism, or in other words from one form of social organization of work to another. Radical and critical thinkers criticized the rigid routines of mass-production society as signs of an oppressive mass society (Arendt, 1958), the domination of systems of money and power (Habermas, 1984), reflections of a mode of production that oppressed everyday life (Lefebvre, 1991), the structures that dominated individuals (Althusser, 2005; Sturrock, 1979). The twentieth century was the century of large organizations, evident in state bureaucracies and large private corporations. It was against the grip of large organizations that many artists and social critics revolted. In this revolt, they shared a direction with the critics of state bureaucracies, also advocating a reorganization of the large private corporation. Different shades of political spectrum, both in intellectuals and analysts as well as politicians and employers, seemed to share the notion that the existing social organization was not working, being too oppressive if you looked from below or too rigid if you looked from above. The critique of modernism, therefore, was not being generated outside the systems of production and consumption; it was part of a general attempt to dislodge one settlement, so that another can be created. The vision of this alternative may have been different for the different shades of opinion. But the deconstructivist effect of their critique seems to have been a shared one. Some critics of Fordism, however, ended up mourning its passing, seeing it as a progressive compromise, rather than an oppressive conspiracy as it was once thought to be. How can we distinguish between the representations used in dismantling the old manufacturing industrial order and those used in the establishment of a new one based on knowledge? Some features of society and economy may be merely acts of 'creative destruction', in which the obsolete physical objects and social attitudes are dismantled to open the way for new ones to emerge. Is there a sufficiently distinguishable difference between these two rhetorics?

Differentiated consumption

The overall story seems to be a mass-production system that required mass consumption of standardized products, which in time was turned into mass consumption of differentiated products. We might, however, question this change from standardization to differentiation. What is the extent of differentiation? A myth of affluent societies is that the forms of consumption are very diverse to respond to differentiated lifestyles and demands. There is no doubt some truth in this myth, when compared with the past and with poorer places, but the ubiquity of difference turns it into a commonplace, a context, a background, rather than an exception.

A long line of writers have emphasized the significance of status (Bourdieu, 2000; Weber, 1978) and the role of recognition in social life (Honneth, 2007; Riceour, 1995), which is indeed a key theme in Hegel's philosophy (Hegel, 1967). The driving force for economic activity, Thorstein Veblen (2007) argued, is the acquisition and display of status, rather than production of utility, as the neoclassical economics holds. Therefore, conspicuous consumption, a term used widely after Veblen, would be the manifestation and driving force for capitalism, maintained by a leisure class who does not produce goods and services but enjoys an elite position in society. So, differentiated consumption is a means to the assertion of status and identity, a form of standing out in the crowd. However, in a crowd where everyone is using the same methods of crying for attention, the result is an undifferentiated difference, whereby diversity is the primary social condition rather than describing occasional circumstances. The knowledge economy is based on responding to, and encouraging, continuous demand for differentiated products. Diversity of these products is partly a reflection of the fundamental differences between consumers, and partly induced as an aesthetic category to help people seek recognition through consumption.

Consumption of fashion items influences the sense of identity and the need for recognition (Paris, France).

In parallel with the competition for differentiation between cities, which we discussed earlier, there is also competition for differentiation within cities. The social geography of the city is a map that overlays social status and economic condition as translated into land and property markets. This map, which is captured by estate agents as 'location, location, location', shows how each place finds an exchange value, a position in the marketplace and an image. Images may have a temporal gap with property values, but ultimately they are in tune: as a place finds a positive image, its property prices rise to reflect that change, and, vice versa, the stigmatization of a place becomes an incentive for people to try to escape if they can, even leading to the collapse of the property market in that area. Image becomes a forerunner for change, a tool for regeneration of declining areas, and an instrument of marketing for buildings and neighbourhoods. The architectural styles that emerged from the 1970s onwards used colourful and playful appearances, in time to be replaced by expressive forms and tall buildings, all as markers of distinction for places, activities and cities. The model of land use that emerged in this period was also an encouragement for diversity: whereas modernist urban design and planning promoted strict segregation of land use, creating large blocks of unified land use, the post-modern approach was to mix uses, so as to create vibrant and diversified scenes, rejecting a pure functionalist attitude in favour of eclectic and playful aesthetics.

The attempts to stand out in the marketplace find visual manifestation in the urban space: using all possible surfaces for advertising places, commodities, events, etc. Furthermore, the urban space is used for all sorts of instructions given to drivers and pedestrians, creating a flurry of signs that clutter the city. The use of colour, form, sound and even smell to attract the attention of potential consumers, and the development of institutionalized forms of publicity via fashion, sport and entertainment, all turn the urban environment into a giant advertising board for thousands of different products competing for attention. The boundary between art and advertising become blurred, as artists and architects seem to act as brand managers and directors of marketing companies (Sudjic, 2009). The products come from everywhere around the world, and it would be hard to distinguish what is a knowledge product from others. Knowledge economy appears to lie at all stages of making the product, creating a luring image of that product and in presenting it to its potential market. Some workers in this sense are not producing knowledge or creating new ideas and practices, but playing on other people's weaknesses to make money. This is not productive or creative knowledge but manipulative knowledge. Gambling in the stock market or selling dubious financial products makes huge earnings for the workers and their institutions at the cost of huge losses for a large number of people, raising the question: is manipulative knowledge the main form of knowledge in the knowledge economy?

A key feature of post-modernism, inherited from structuralists and ultimately a feature of philosophical scepticism, is the separation of representation from reality, leading to a critique of representation, in which the relationship between signifier and signified is problematized. This gap is used by some to analyse the relationship between production and consumption (Debord, 1994). The industrial methods of mass production created a gap between production and consumption,

Fashion encourages consumption and transforms the urban space (Seoul, Korea).

which was the source of alienation for workers, as they became cogs in production machines, out of touch with what they produced. With the globalization of production, this gap has widened for many products, which may be produced in different pieces around the world, assembled in a location and consumed in other places. Consumption of goods and services becomes fully detached from the processes of production, leaving consumers ignorant about the conditions in which they were produced and production workers disconnected from the products and the conditions in which they are consumed. Overlaid on this gap between production and consumption, there is a gap between representation and reality.

Following Marx, who had analysed the production–consumption gap as a source of alienation, whereby workers are denied the fruits of their work, Debord (1994) identifies a gap between image and reality, which lies at the heart of modern society, where social relations between people are mediated through images, making it a society of spectacle. The production becomes the accumulation of spectacles, and the life of society becomes consumption of representations. Spectacle, which takes specific form in news, propaganda, advertising or entertainment, 'is the very heart of society's real unreality' and not merely a decorative element added to the real world (Debord, 1994: 13). The rise of the new mass media was, therefore, closely linked to the development of new forms of production and consumption, one in which the product was a commodified image, dominating the everyday life of people who were involved in consuming these images, which were now taking over from real life.

The urban space is turned into a giant board to advertise consumer products (Barcelona, Spain).

For Baudrillard, the nature of meaning under the conditions of mass media and the Internet has completely changed, becoming only an illusion linked to a desire. In a consumer society, it is the image that is being consumed as advertised: 'If we consume the product as product, we consume its meaning through advertising' (Poster, 2001: 13). The image becomes reality, rather than representing it: 'Simulation . . . is the generation by models of a real without origin or reality: a hyperreal. The territory no longer precedes the map, nor survives it. Henceforth, it is the map that precedes the territory – precession of simulacra' (Poster, 2001: 167). This focus on simulation and simulacra as a replacement for reality, however, attributes undue power to the media and to the technology that makes them possible, and allocates only a passive, or at best resisting, role to the audience. Baudrillard acknowledges McLuhan for 'the true revolution which he brought about in media analysis' (Poster, 2001: 211), and so follows him in finding a determinant role for technology, even though from a more critical, less optimistic standpoint. He even uses simulacra to periodize Western civilization after the Renaissance into stages characterized by their technological development, moving from simple automata to factories, and then on to computers and mass media in consumer society, and eventually to the information age with its particularity and fragmentation (Baudrillard, 2004).

The emphasis on the gap between representation and reality, however, can take on a reductionist character. Representation produces abstract concepts of reality, which analysts and decision-makers tend to use instead of engaging directly with the material and social conditions of society. Attempts to give primacy to mental representation over the social and physical space, which the philosophy of language analysed, were highly criticized by Lefebvre (1991). He argued that the gap between scientific and artistic representations, and between representation and reality, should be addressed through social practice and reclaiming everyday life. However, the possibility of an integrated domain of everyday life that is free from abstract thought, from the intrusion of spectacle and the globalized division of labour may be merely a romantic and nostalgic idea.

The consumer city

The spatial division of labour has led to the notion of consumer and producer cities, a division that has a long history. For Max Weber (1978; 1998), the prime example of the producer city was the medieval city, where new institutions, ideas and social classes emerged as part of a division of labour with the countryside, in which both were engaged in production and exchange. In contrast to this positive image of the medieval city stood the image of the ancient city, especially Rome: there was no political distinction between the ancient city and the countryside, both ruled by the same elite, in which the city consumed what the countryside produced, suggesting a parasitic role for the city at the expense of the countryside. Historians of ancient cities, however, have rejected this characterization, arguing that the relationships between the town and the countryside in ancient Rome should be put in a broader context, concentrating on the role of households, rather than on the geographical separation between town and country. The relationships between town and country were two-way, both being parts of the economy, with a level of investment by the landed aristocracy in the productive capacity of the urban economy. Indeed, the argument goes, the dystopian characterization of the ancient metropolis, exemplified in the influential work of Mumford (1961) and the city-planning tradition, draws on the twentieth-century approaches to the city, in which the metropolis was equated with unhealthy and chaotic conditions, as opposed to the planned order of smaller cities (Parkins, 1997).

With the passing of manufacturing industry in some cities, the idea of consumer cities has now been applied to the contemporary city. De-industrialized cities and those dominated by services are called consumer cities, a term that carries a pejorative undertone, implying that these cities no longer earn their living out of hard work, but consume what others produce, and to do so these cities resort to various tricks. The opposite to these consumer cities, it is thought, are producer cities, as exemplified by the centres of manufacturing industry, where useful objects were produced by honest, diligent people. Engagement in services, it has been argued by the critics of de-industrialization, is not productive work, but only a soft form of economic activity that is not reliable enough or sustainable. To counter this accusation, the idea of knowledge economy appears to be offering a positive label for services, acknowledging their productive force and economic value.

In this positive portrayal, the knowledge city's relation to the manufacturing city is similar to the medieval city's relation to the countryside: two forms of

Modern anxieties have been transposed into ancient Rome, calling it a consumer city now echoed in the modern cities (Rome, Italy).

production incorporated in an interdependent spatial division of labour within integrated economies. Knowledge and information are the products of this city, which are exchanged for agricultural and manufacturing goods produced elsewhere. This description of the new roles for de-industrializing economies moves away from the idea of consumer city and leads to an assertive role for the intangible products of the services that prevail in the knowledge economy. Inherent in this integration, however, there is a hierarchical representation of a tension, which is ultimately addressed through changing positions in the hierarchy.

The range of intangible goods and services produced in the knowledge city, therefore, could be economically productive work, generating income and employment for the city, enabling it to earn its living. However, as the global financial crisis of 2008 showed, intangible products are precarious, potentially fictitious and ultimately dependent on persuading consumers that they need these products. When the new Coalition Government came to power in the UK in 2010, their diagnosis was that the country was too dependent on the finance industry and it now needed to find alternative ways of earning a living, while learning to live within its means (Onanuga, 2010).

Growing social inequality

The chains of production and consumption that have evolved in recent decades, heralding the dawn of a new economy, have shown a dark side, with many consequences that are widely discussed. The overall size of consumption in the US has been phenomenal, to the extent that the US economy in recent decades has been driven by consumption, accounting for 70% of the $14 trillion GDP in the country, although this figure is not entirely formed of personal household consumption. The consumption, however, is not equally spread. 'Since 1975, practically all the gains in household income have gone to the top 20% of households' (CIA, 2009). This inequality in the distribution of resources would lead to unequal patterns of consumption.

Social change in globalizing cities has been substantial, fuelling international migration and a growing, diverse population (Buzar *et al.*, 2007; Champion, 2001; Glasmeier, 2005). In recent decades, cities have undergone dramatic social, economic and cultural changes, triggering new tensions and debates about the production and use of urban space (Atkinson and Bridge, 2005). An overall trend of urban growth has occurred in the largest US cities (US Census Bureau, 2009). In 2007–08, 64 out of the 75 largest US cities (with populations larger than 200,000) grew, and in some cities, such as Washington, DC, and Atlanta, the central area outpaced the suburbs and reversed a longstanding trend (Frey, 2009). In the past two decades, New York has once again led the population growth in the US for the first time since the 1930s (National Atlas, 2009). In Europe, while shrinking cities in former manufacturing and socialist areas continue to lose population, a process of re-urbanization is also at work, partially turning the tide of the 1970s' counter-urbanization (Buzar *et al.*, 2007; Champion, 2001). In the last three decades in the UK, London and smaller cities in the south and east have grown rapidly, while large northern and western cities show some demographic recovery after long periods of decline, which is modestly evident in their central areas (Parkinson, 2006; Pointer, 2005; Urban Task Force, 1999). In parallel with these demographic changes, a series of economic, political and social changes and their associated spatial transformation is also visible in these cities. The ascendancy of market-based solutions to economic and social problems is a major characteristic of these changes, leading to a growth in social inequality.

Social inequality has intensified through marketization and globalization. Through increased reliance on the markets and intensified flows of capital, goods and services across the world, inequality has deepened. The economic and social landscape of European cities is undergoing dramatic changes, through centrifugal forces of differential access to resources and opportunities, technological change and a new international division of labour. The rapid decline of manufacturing industries, emergence of new forms of economic activity, radical transformation of Eastern European countries, European enlargement and integration, changing role of the state in the economy, globalization and intensified flow of international migration have all created new conditions in European societies. As evident in the spread and impact of the global financial crisis in 2008, intensified interdependencies have created completely new frameworks for the life of societies around the world.

Social inequality is multi-dimensional. Inequality is often studied in its economic dimension, measured through income inequality and how it has been rising. Others have studied welfare inequality and how access to health, education and other public services has varied across different sections of the population.

However, inequality is also manifest in other areas, which include access to social recognition, political participation, quality of life and perceptions of well-being (Bourdieu, 2000; Honneth, 2007). Inequality, therefore, is multi-dimensional, including economic, social, political and cultural dimensions (Madanipour, 2007b). A study of inequality that focuses only on income disparity would miss the complexity of the phenomenon.

Three forms of support are instrumental in addressing inequality: welfare support, social networks and family support. Welfare regimes have redistributed resources to provide different forms of support for those at the bottom of the social hierarchy, hence helping to reduce inequality in income and use of public services (Esping-Andersen, 1999). These provisions had decommodified some services and needs, even though the level of decommodification varied across different countries. Meanwhile, social networks, from the organized unions to the informal circles of civil society organizations, have been active in helping individuals and groups be protected from the worst impacts of social inequality. Recent attention to social capital is one of the manifestations of seeing social networks as an effective replacement for state-led redistribution. The third pillar of support, provided by family and friends, is the historical form of support, which is still very important, particularly in countries where state provision of welfare or civil society organizations have not been strong. Conservatives have historically advocated the family as the primary support mechanism in society.

As the welfare state, social networks and family relations have weakened, the mechanisms for social support have become less effective in addressing social inequality. Smaller households, weakened unions and a less engaged state have reduced the opportunities for more equal and cohesive social relations. As market operations have been extended to new areas of policy and practice, the logic of efficiency, rather than need, has become the primary justification for public action. As a result, the paths of education and redistribution, which have historically enabled social mobility, have been more difficult to travel.

Social inequality generates social and spatial fragmentation. The multiple dimensions of inequality lead to a complex process of social inequality, which finds long-term and large-scale impacts through their spatial manifestation in the concentrations of multiple disadvantage in deprived urban neighbourhoods (Madanipour *et al.*, 2003; Maloutas, 2004). The significance of the local context on the life trajectories of individuals and groups cannot be underestimated (Cars *et al.*, 2002). The shape of the urban system has changed: while some cities have prospered, others have declined and lost their population and economic base. Inside cities, a dramatic transformation has taken place. As the industrial working class has dwindled and international migration has intensified, public housing areas have lost much of their popularity and status, becoming areas of decline and deprivation. Meanwhile, the rise of services and the new European and global economies have created new layers of prosperity. The pressures on the public purse and ideological debates have transformed welfare support for deprived sections of the population, creating increased social and spatial polarization in cities.

Unequal access to knowledge

A considerable proportion of new employment opportunities are associated with new information and communication technologies, which favour the high-skilled over low-skilled, young over old workers, and regions that have access to leading research institutions, venture capital and a large supply of educated workers. The result is unequal distribution of opportunities and rewards for individuals, regions and nations (Powell and Snellman, 2004). These rewards tend to generate cumulative advantages for individuals and regions to which others can only aspire. Such inequality is added to the traditional forms of inequality engendered by gender, age, income and ethnicity, creating stronger forces of social polarization, which find spatial manifestation in a fragmented and segregated social geography.

A centralized and hierarchical world order has been in the making since the advent of mercantile and industrial capitalist economies in Europe, creating centres and peripheries and distributing power and resources accordingly (Wallerstein, 1974). The current globalization process has created a new spatial division of labour, in which new centres have emerged, somewhat reshaping this map of the world. It has also intensified existing forms of inequality through linking new areas and processes to the historical world system, inevitably changing its nature and morphology on the way. A minority of key metropolitan regions tend to attract innovative firms (Simmie, 2003), and the headquarters of multinational organizations have clustered in a few world cities, which are the centres of command and control of the global economy (Hall, 1988). This generates a widening gap between these centres and their national and international hinterlands. Meanwhile, as some argue (Sellers, 2002), much knowledge production goes on in medium-sized cities, and not necessarily in world cities.

The 'knowledge divide' that already exists between the developed and developing countries can grow wider in the global economy. Much new knowledge is produced by developed countries, which remains beyond the reach of developing countries, owing to their limited access, inadequate economic frameworks and weak institutions. Furthermore, through intensified competition that has followed trade liberalization, these countries lose their low labour cost advantage and suffer from the erosion of their natural resources (World Bank, 2008a). Nevertheless, they are encouraged to improve their information infrastructure, educate their workforce, encourage innovation and provide the necessary economic and institutional frameworks that would enable them to benefit from joining the global economy.

Digital divide can lead to knowledge divide, both within societies and across different countries. Knowledge divide, according to UNESCO (2005: 22), is the real challenge that is facing the development of knowledge societies. It is rooted in the intensification of existing unequal patterns of access to knowledge, through access to information, education, scientific research, and cultural and linguistic diversity. It is also rooted in the unequal values that knowledge economy places on different forms of knowledge. Knowledge becomes exchangeable through codification and commodification, which can undermine different forms of knowledge, such as local and indigenous heritage, as well as lead to unequal access to privilege (UNESCO, 2005). When treated as a commodity, tensions arise over the ownership and control of knowledge, where it is argued, through intellectual property rights, public funds are used to guarantee returns on private investment by powerful players (Drahos and Braithwaite, 2002).

The emphasis on information, triggered by new information and communication technologies, at times slides into technological determinism, or privileges information over knowledge. But the growth of networks alone, even if they overcome the partial and fragmented access, cannot lead to a knowledge society. Rather than a narrow focus on information society, some argue in favour of creating a knowledge society, which is nurtured by its diversity and its capacities, 'connecting the forms of knowledge that societies already possess' (UNESCO, 2005: 17). Such a knowledge society treats knowledge as a public good, rather than a commodity, and shares it openly, rather than setting up barriers and exclusionary practices (UNESCO, 2005).

In the economic transition, the production of material wealth has shifted from industrial workers to service workers, from blue-collar to white-collar workers. But the opportunities for entering the workforce for the children of blue-collar workers are limited, as they are less likely to enter universities and gain high-level training and education. They are then forced to move into servicing the highly skilled workforce, which is the engine of the knowledge economy. The pathway to cross this social divide is sometimes seen through the creative industries, as exemplified by the popularity of the popular music industry, which is so popular with many young people as a shortcut to fame and fortune. The shift of wealth creation from blue- to white-collar workers, therefore, can create a two-tier society in which the opportunities for social mobility are reduced, hence the problem of the widening gap and increased social inequality.

Can we separate a phase of transition from a phase of consolidation? If we are moving into a knowledge-based economy, can we merely attribute the rise in social inequality to be a symptom of a transitional period? In transition, or creative destruction, many of the previous features are dismantled. Here we may see the rise of inequality and polarization, but can we then hope that there is a phase of consolidation, in which a better distribution of resources is possible, where more and more people benefit from the growth of knowledge economy? If knowledge is a new form of capital, then unequal access to this capital would generate a new form of inequality. However, differential access to this new form of capital is not taking place in a void; it is growing out of, and often intensifying, the historic patterns of inequality, both at inter-city and intra-city levels.

Inequality, dispersion and segregation

The growth of social inequality has intensified the existing patterns of social and spatial stratification, unleashing centrifugal and dividing forces that have created new tensions around urban space, manifest primarily in the rise of new agglomerations, further fragmentation of urban space, segregation and gentrification

Knowledge divide can be bridged through education and treatment of knowledge as a public good (Dublin, Ireland).

(Madanipour, 2010a). The segregated space of the capitalist industrial city reflected the separation of the rich and poor in urban space, gathering large numbers of workers living in dense working-class neighbourhoods near industrial workplaces, living according to the rigid tempo of manufacturing processes.

As these cities grew, two simultaneous trends evolved to adjust the outcome of their hasty, *laissez-faire* development. There was a gradual market-led process of suburbanization, in which the middle classes fled the city in search of more space and tranquillity (Fishman, 1987). An associated process, the garden city movement (Howard, 1960), with its follow-up new towns and new urbanism movements, advocated a tidying-up and rationalization of suburban development. Another adjustment was the state-led process of urban renewal, advocating a reorganization of the central areas (Le Corbusier, 1971), which took the form of new motorways cutting through the city centres and housing redevelopment projects that partially transformed the urban social geography. These two processes of outward expansion and inward redevelopment of cities reshaped cities throughout the twentieth century. The picture may have been different in continental Europe and the Anglophone world, whereby affluent groups kept the centre in one while evacuating the other. Their social consequences in both cases, however, were creating segregated spaces, in which the centre and periphery of the city were torn apart along income and social status. The decline of manufacturing industries entailed the regeneration of their sites, which marked a new phase in urban development. However, even after the decline of manufacturing industries and through the new readjustment of urban space, these twin processes of outward and inward spatial transformation continue to shape cities, segregating social groups further and gentrifying some areas. In the knowledge economy, the nature of products and the production processes may have changed, but the deep-seated trends of social stratification and inequality have continued to shape society and space.

In some US cities with small black populations, there has been some evidence of a reduction in segregation, but the underlying structure of racial segregation has hardly changed (Glasmeier, 2005; Smelser *et al.*, 2001). In European cities, the growth of migration and ethnic minorities alongside the processes of economic restructuring, pressures on public budgets and demands for welfare reform have found a social exclusionary effect (Madanipour *et al.*, 2003). Coupled with the advent of international terrorism, the overall rise in crime rates (Bureau of Justice Statistics, 2010; Kershaw *et al.*, 2008) and the fear of crime, the space of the city has become a place to avoid or make secure, which only intensifies its fragmentation. The presence of strangers partly leads to fear, resulting in withdrawal from public spaces and creation of exclusive spaces (Blakely and Snyder, 1999), and partly to pressures for the celebration of difference and the promotion of tolerance.

Whenever the pace of social diversification has risen, the fear of strangers and the loss of control have taken centre stage, a condition that characterized the

Concentrations of multiple forms of exclusion stigmatize some parts of the city, setting them apart from others (Vienna, Austria).

Growing social inequality has been evident in urban space (Washington, DC, USA).

nineteenth-century advent of the industrial city, which now seems to have returned in the globalized cities of the knowledge economy. The nineteenth-century city was a source of pride, but also fear and alienation, in which the rich and poor lived in different worlds and their inequality and segregation kept the city on the edge of revolt (Briggs, 1968; Engels, 1993). As people congregated in large cities, uprooted from their villages and small towns, and freed from their locality's social norms and controls, they entered a world that was characterized by heterogeneity (Wirth, 1964), a society rather than a community (Tönnies, 1957), where a withdrawal into an indifferent attitude was the only weapon to cope with the overload of information and emotion (Simmel, 1950). In the globalized city of the twenty-first century, with its new *laissez-faire* attitude where people come from around the world, the degree of difference is heightened, the pace of differentiation is fast, the frameworks of socialization multiplied and hence weakened, and information and emotional overload is greater than ever. The lines of continuity with the early industrial city are unmistakeable, which the dimensions and rhythms of urban life made faster and more complex.

Intensified inequality is either reflected in further suburban sprawl, or the renaissance of the centres. The fragmentary effects of sprawl are well known: different social groups are located separately, connected only through transport and communication networks (Fishman, 1987). When places of work, shopping and home are located in widely different parts of urban space, the possibility of social segregation and polarization intensifies. Different groups can live and work in completely separate worlds. Meanwhile, suburbs continue to grow, and people who live in city centres only do so at some stage of their life. British city centres are dominated by retail and leisure activities, around which a number of other functions are woven. The entertainment and property development sectors, rather than the knowledge sector, may be more responsible for fuelling the growth of attention to city centres. In other words, consumption of leisure and the production of space, rather than the production of knowledge products, is a driving force of city centre remodelling. As far as individuals are concerned, the more flexible patterns of work, higher disposable incomes and higher personal debt may be responsible for a major part of these changes. At the government level, public investment in the built environment circulates resources into the economy, establishing a framework for bringing land and labour back to the market.

Diversity and inequality in the city have been managed through spatial arrangement, placing barriers between different social groups so as to keep them apart. Two primary forms of spatial management have been walls and distance. In the compact cities of the past, where the city could only expand to a limited extent within the city walls, physical barriers were frequently used, keeping entire areas within walls and protected by gates. Walls appeared to be a crude device for segregation, and so many walls have come down in the modern Western city. This was a time in which new transport technologies would enable the horizontal expansion of the city, hence allowing the use of distance as a partitioning device. With the rise of fear, however, the wall has now come back in the form of gated neighbourhoods and exclusive enclaves. Horizontal expansion facilitated a move away from others, fragmenting the urban society into smaller, more homogenous groups living together in suburban and central neighbourhoods, using distance to keep them apart. The social geography that was so created was fixed and institutionalized through the land and property markets and land use regulations (Cullingworth and Caves, 2003; Keating and Krumholz, 1999). Distance alone, however, seemed unable to cope with the growing social inequality of the de-industrializing cities, and the deepening sense of insecurity that goes with it; therefore there was a return to a much older, cruder spatial device: the wall and gate.

The partitioning of the city, whether through 'defensible space' or through ghettoization, creates a mosaic of unrelated fragments. The idea of defensible space was developed as a critique of low-income, public housing schemes, arguing for private control over space. According to Oscar Newman (1996: 9), 'All Defensible Space programs have a common purpose: They restructure the physical layout of communities to allow residents to control the areas around their homes.' The result for the minority who are inside may be markedly different from those on the outside. For the most vulnerable, ghettoization may be the outcome, which is a spatial manifestation of social exclusion (Madanipour, 2011; Spear, 1967; Vergara, 1999). The multi-dimensional social exclusion is worst for those who suffer from a combined lack of access to resources, decision-making and cultural exchange, often finding spatial expression in deprived neighbourhoods (Madanipour, 2007b).

The idea of partitioning the city into distinctive neighbourhoods has been a longstanding trend in urban design and planning, as neighbourhoods are seen as a necessary building block of an urban society (Park *et al.*, 1984; Mumford, 1954; Lynch, 1979). Communitarians have argued in favour of neighbourhoods as a mechanism for togetherness, a defence against the individualizing forces of liberal thinking, and large-scale urban developers have shown their preference for neighbourhood-scale development projects, reflecting the structure of the construction industry. The property markets have also shown interest in the idea, as it allows a clear demarcation of the market and a vehicle of branding and status assertion for some consumers of space (Madanipour, 2001). Meanwhile, encouraging these patterns of differentiation, which reflect market forces, political pressures and individual preferences, could be the creation of parallel worlds, in which different groups live in their separate enclaves without knowledge of, and tolerance for, others. Some have portrayed this fragmentation as inevitable and even desirable. But the question is whether it is socially sustainable, and whether people who live under these conditions do so out of choice or in response to some force. Would they live in the same place if they were free from these pressures, especially of discrimination, poverty and fear?

If the early signs of a knowledge economy is the intensification of social inequality, should we conclude that the cities built on knowledge economy are inherently more unequal than their predecessors? If the past is an indicator, however, there may be some hope that the phase of growing inequality may be followed by a period of pressure for more equality. This follow-up, however, is by no means guaranteed, and it needs huge efforts to take place. An apparent effort, which attempts to work against segregation, is social mixing. But it may not be as straightforward as it seems.

Social mixing, gentrification and displacement

Social mixing has been promoted as an alternative response to the challenges of diversity; welcoming, rather than excluding, strangers through mixing populations to promote tolerance and coexistence. The importance of diversity and the role of strangers in urban society have long been acknowledged by sociologists (Simmel, 1950; Schutz, 1970), which is reflected in the design of cities, whereby the mixture of different populations is facilitated through spatial arrangements (Jacobs, 1961; Sennett, 1993; Hillier and Hanson, 1984). Overlap, accessibility and openness, rather than segregation and separation, are advocated to address stratification and social conflict. Public space becomes a key theme in the way a society can address its social diversity (Madanipour, 1999; 2003; 2010b). This approach, however, is not without its own problems, which may include displacement and gentrification.

There is a strong trend in urban design and planning that advocates mixed land uses, mixed-tenure housing and mixed neighbourhoods. The argument is that vibrant and integrative urban areas can confront social exclusion and segregation. Mixing different income and cultural groups, it is thought, would help create an integrated society, rather than one that is partitioned along the various fault lines of diversity. Planning and design of the city sees its role as social mixing, as a response to the decline of public housing areas and the ghettoization of deprived neighbourhoods. Within the framework of strong centrifugal trends of social inequality, however, social mixing may not work as intended, leading to further social conflict rather than integrative spaces.

Through gentrification, the control and use of space is shifted from lower-income to higher-income social groups, resulting from a competition for land, which is a finite resource. It is shaped by the demand for prime space by higher earners, profit-seeking by land and property markets, and public sector urban regeneration policies and initiatives that aim to improve the conditions of an area. When gentrification happens at the level of a neighbourhood, the character of the area changes in terms of its resident population and its land use.

Gentrification is partly driven by the logic of production: the operations of the land and property markets, which constantly looks for opportunities for profitable investment (Lefebvre, 1991; Smith, 1996). Investors who may have abandoned

Gentrification, which replaces one social group with a higher income group, is sometimes the declared aim of urban development projects (Tokyo, Japan).

the declining and de-industrializing city have returned to the city, thereby reigniting the tensions between exchange and use values (Boyer, 1990; Logan and Molotch, 1987). As understood from early on by Adam Smith, these two types of value may not always coincide, and at times they come into conflict: investors and dealers in land and property are concerned about the return on their investment and all other considerations may become marginal issues. The markets allow investors to invest in abstract products, separated from their social use and meaning, and so land and property may be bought and sold like any other commodity, with the sole aim of financial reward. This is in sharp contrast with the residents and users of a place, who may not have any financial stake, but evaluate it primarily for its social use, such as a playground or a park. In many instances, these values may overlap and coexist peacefully, but in other circumstances, especially through the process of urban development, they can come into conflict. This conflict between an existing condition and the challenge of development can also be seen in the conservation of historic areas, the use of natural resources, and the provision and delivery of common goods.

The dynamics of speculative development may create an urban landscape that is not directly addressing the needs of economic development (Toronto, Canada).

Gentrification is also the result of demand, responding to the new patterns of demography, lifestyle and work, which ask for new types of spaces. As some workers in the new economic sectors are based in city centres, they expect to live nearer their workplaces, competing with working classes who live in these neighbourhoods, causing displacement and gentrification (Ley, 1996; Hamnett, 2003). This process is supported by public policy (Cameron, 2003; Punter, 2010). In the regeneration of declining areas, associated with manufacturing industries and their workers, governments are actively engaged in the supply of spaces that are fit for new consumers of space. The economic and social significance of cities is now widely recognized, and regenerating these areas would simultaneously increase their tax base and improve their political legitimacy. Involved in partnership with the private sector, public sector agencies think and act in a similar way, seeking profit from the rise in land value and financial rewards resulting from speculative development. Eradicating the signs of poverty from the urban scene would also mean displacing the poor, and so the concept of gentrification is used as an integral part of regenerating cities.

The argument by public and private sector organizations is that cities need investment, which is only available by higher earners who can spend their money buying land and property and spend it for the range of services they need. Urban regeneration is thought to be attracting higher income earners, the so-called creative class. First, the arrival of higher income groups cannot be guaranteed, as the necessary services and lifestyle images may not be present, leading to hesitation and avoidance. But when the regeneration schemes are successful in attracting these groups, their arrival is not necessarily leading to social harmony and coexistence with lower earners. At best, their mixture may be superficial and physical, but not social and cultural, and they may continue to live in their different worlds. At worst, their mixture may result in resentment and alienation, as the juxtaposition of different and incompatible models of unfair consumption may collide. At the least, new investment in urban development would lead to a rise in land and property prices, pricing out local inhabitants, who will then need public subsidies for their survival. The likely outcome for low-earners is displacement, which runs counter to the idea of mixing social groups. The good intentions of social mixing, therefore, may not be achieved in the absence of public support and under the conditions of growing social inequality.

Gentrification can be both an engine and an outcome of urban transformation. Examples of such change are everywhere. In the UK, the cases of Covent Garden and the Docklands in London, and many similar cases in almost all major cities (Punter, 2010), created new spaces for new activities to replace the old, obsolete spaces. Many city centres were empty of a resident population and so the process of regeneration was less controversial in these cities. When it involved a resident population, however, it caused much pain and controversy, and the gains have often favoured the more powerful voices (Slater, 2006; Lees and Ley, 2008). New York, which has once again started to lead urban population growth in the United States, has been involved in major gentrification processes, as exemplified in the controversial case of Times Square (Smith, 1998; Makagon, 2004; Miller, 2007;

The controversial gentrification of Times Square changed an iconic urban space (New York, USA).

Berman, 2009). When the issue was intertwined with race, the problems became even more heated, as exemplified in the process of gentrification and displacement resulting from urban redevelopment schemes such as HOPE VI in the United States, which has led to organized resistance by those who have suffered from the process (Right to the City, 2009).

The general trend in de-industrialized UK cities has been an attempt to learn lessons from southern European cities, characterized by a mixture of land uses and attention to the quality of public environment. This is against a background of faster growth in the knowledge economy in northern and western Europe, as compared with Mediterranean countries. While 48% of the workforce in the Netherlands and 40% in the UK are classified as knowledge workers, only about 30% of the workforce are in this category in Spain and Italy (Brinkley, 2006: 20), countries that are admired for their quality of urban environment. If the quality of urban environment in Mediterranean countries is what the northern and western countries aspire to, then linking the knowledge economy and the urban environment may become somewhat problematic. At the same time, as the centres of successful Mediterranean cities, such as Barcelona, have prospered, the city has suffered from the same problems of sprawl and segregation (Marshall, 2004).

In parallel, there is a new attention to city living, a return of the capital to the city. It is possible to see the positive impact of city centres on social cohesion: if the centre of the settlement is abandoned and different groups and functions are dispersed in all directions, social fragmentation will intensify and long-term viability of a society may be undermined through factionalism and strife. If the centre holds, the sustainability of society has a better chance to be ensured, as exemplified by the European city model, in which the city centre is kept alive as a hub of social life. Even in the American city, the centre is still the most important hub of economic activity, despite significant suburbanization and dispersion (Loukaitou-Sideris and Banerjee, 1998).

At the same time, the nature of this society is hierarchical and stratified along access to resources. Reviving the centre means injecting new life into a hierarchical system in which rich and poor have been growing apart. If the centre is enhanced and revitalized, it may appear to be in favour of the powerful groups who are already in control. Whether it is middle-class residential areas in European cities, or corporate offices in American cities, the centre is occupied by the more powerful players. Investment in the centre may appear to be reinforcing their position in the social hierarchy, rather than creating spaces for all, inevitably leading to gentrification and displacement. The British urban renaissance has primarily been taking place in the centre, without similar attention to the inner city or peripheral areas (Punter, 2010; Madanipour, 2010c).

One of the reasons for investment in city centres has been the attraction of knowledge workers, investors and visitors. This is a basis on which much investment has been made in cities, turning city centres into points of attraction for work, pleasure, shopping and living functions. There are modest levels of growth

The British urban renaissance has primarily taken place in city centres, without similar attention to the inner city or peripheral areas (Nottingham, UK).

in urban populations, which are taken to show that the two phenomena are related, that cities attract knowledge workers and that knowledge workers are served by an army of service providers, who work in restaurants, domestic services, etc.

Is gentrification a necessary part of the transition from an industrial economy to a knowledge economy? Can urban improvement be equated with gentrification? These trends show a process of re-adjustment to urban space, clearing the traces of manufacturing industries and preparing the way for new economic activities of office work, consumption and the associated support services. In this transition, those who used to work in the old sectors have suffered from the pain of transition, falling from the peak of being productive and well-looked-after workers to the trough of being surplus to requirement and abandoned. The so-called creative destruction has been fully applied to the sectors of the economy, the life of the workers and the spaces of the city. Displacement and gentrification, however, are not the only solutions, as this process of transition can be managed in different, fairer ways.

Conclusion

Within a changing context, the prevalence of manufacturing industries in the urban economy has given way to services, associated with a change in the nature of work and technology, the acceptance of market solutions that have changed the balance of relations between the public and private sectors, diversification and growing social inequality. Knowledge products are not weightless and immaterial, and consumption of material goods and services is a primary engine for the economy. Consumption in the knowledge economy, therefore, intensifies and globalizes the features of capitalist economies: encouragement of social differentiation to facilitate the spread of consumption and the reorganization of space to cater for the sense of status that comes from differentiated consumption. Alongside this differentiation is an intensified stratification, in which social inequality grows to unprecedented levels, finding spatial manifestation in partitioned cities and parallel tribes.

The city is the largest site of economic production and a change in the economic life of the city would be accompanied by a change in its social relations and physical spaces. To understand how a city with a knowledge-based economy is organized, we might look at how the manufacturing city was organized. In the manufacturing city, blue-collar workers worked in factories in large numbers and in rigid temporal routines; in the service city people work in smaller, white-collar units (even if sometimes in larger companies) with more flexible working hours, so the size and location of the workplace appears to have changed. Workers produced material objects, whereas now they produce services and intangible products. Workers in the industrializing cities were uprooted and unrelated, so labour organization and religious advocacy plus strict moral codes were developed to try to order their social coexistence. Now these forces have declined and the pressure for individualization has intensified, as reflected in the changing patterns of households, the ageing population and the decline of collective narratives. Therefore, the communication media and the consumption of goods and services offer a new public infrastructure of meaning to keep the social order, by displaying what is desirable: fame, fortune and personal pleasure. Another code is reference to science, which competes with religion as an alternative framework of belief for society. In both periods, some form of violence was needed to avoid the imagined chaos of the crowds, in response to the arrival of new workers: in the industrial city from the local and national countryside, and in the service city from the global countryside, which are the countries on the fringes of the global centres of economic activity. In the manufacturing city, working people were living in poor conditions and social segregation defined the social geography, so there were some efforts to decommodify space by public provisions such as housing. Now inequality and segregation have intensified and gentrification is the key instrument of displacement and replacement of the declining industrial working class by the white-collar knowledge workers. Will this phase of growing social inequality be followed by a fairer distribution of resources and opportunities and a reduction of social inequality?

10 Spaces of knowledge?

Knowledge economy refers to the economic application of knowledge, whereby highly skilled workers use information and communication technologies to produce marketable innovations. While knowledge has always been a basis for the activities of human societies, now it finds an added economic significance, a pathway to innovation that would make things 'better, faster, cheaper'. International organizations, national governments and local authorities see knowledge as a basis for economic growth and they produce indices and scoreboards to measure innovation and compare the performance and conditions of different societies in the knowledge economy. These measurements tend to see the prerequisites for the emergence of the knowledge economy to lie in the governance of innovation: spread of ICT, development of science and technology, support for innovation, and growth of knowledge and skills through research and education, encouraged by an efficient legal and administrative framework. Knowledge economy, however, is not entirely based on science and technology; it also includes cultural and creative industries, the economic significance of which is increasingly recognized. Arts and culture as well as science and technology are both seen as the engines of future economic growth. Symbols and experiences, aesthetic as well as scientific, find functional roles through design and technology, are proliferated and transmitted with the help of ICT, and turned into commodities, helping the development of new relations of production, exchange and consumption.

Knowledge economy is an umbrella term that brings together a number of different trends in economic production, which we have identified under four themes: the nature of economic products, the function of knowledge, the role of technology and the social organization of production. As we have seen in this book, none of these trends can be on its own credited with structural economic and social change. Furthermore, it is doubtful whether there is sufficient consistency inside these themes, whether together they amount to a coherent whole and whether this whole is radically different from the past. There are as many lines of continuity as there are discontinuities between the knowledge economy and what went before.

The term knowledge economy, and similar terms such as information or digital economy, has been used as much to describe the current conditions as to foresee the future orientations, with which to mobilize forces and advocate particular courses of action. These policies, on the one hand, promote expansion of digital infrastructure, development of science and technology, training a highly skilled workforce and the emergence of new creative and cultural industries. On the other hand, however, they point towards an unsustainable pattern of consumption, an unfair distribution of resources, the export of environmental degradation and industrial disputes, the loss of key skills, the decline of many cities and regions, and the suppression of many different forms of knowledge and ways of life.

In analysing the spaces of knowledge economy, we have used the theoretical framework of dynamic multiplicity, which acknowledges the embedded and embodied nature of the perspectives that we use to analyse society and space, attempting to go beyond limited perspectives and a frozen time scale. By studying the phenomena in their movement and transformation and in their material and social contexts, dynamic multiplicity provides the ability to see things in their place, through their change, and from more than one perspective. Rather than an aesthetic pleasure from the diverse landscape that is opened up in this way, however, this dynamic perspective is anchored in a critical viewpoint, which evaluates this landscape with social and environmental concerns in mind. By combining political, economic and cultural analysis, it can help gain a better understanding of the socio-spatial phenomena.

Knowledge economy has clear spatial implications, which we can group under the subheadings of four spatial processes: dispersion, differentiation, connection and concentration.

Spatiality of knowledge economy

Rather than the widely held view that it is immaterial and aspatial, knowledge economy is indeed both material and spatial. The spatiality of knowledge economy is manifest in at least three dimensions: embeddedness, embodiment and commodification.

The metaphysical notion of an abstract space that exists independently and formlessly, a notion that was systematized by Euclid, held by Descartes and Newton, but doubted by Liebniz and ultimately shattered by Einstein, is no longer tenable. The notion of relational space and time as independent of their material and social context is equally untenable. Space and time are indeed collections of ever-changing animate and inanimate objects engaged in ever-changing relationships with one another. The material and the social dimensions of these objects and relationships are tightly intertwined.

The changing nature of products is one of the key features of the knowledge economy. As agrarian and industrial economies were identified with foodstuffs and manufactured goods, the knowledge economy is now being identified with producing knowledge and information. Rather than accumulating physical capital and producing physical objects, it is now called an immaterial, weightless economy, producing intangible products, such as the digital streams that are transmitted through global networks of communication, and so benefiting from lower transaction costs, as compared with the bulky items that need to go from one place to another through physical transportation. It is considered to be an immaterial culture involved in symbolic production, as distinctive from the material culture of the past; thought to be involved in the creation of a parallel electromagnetic world, a cyber space in which sounds, images and ideas are present, while the norms and conditions of the material world seem to desist. Rather than scarcity, which ruled the production and consumption of physical goods, knowledge products are non-rival and non-finite; they can be consumed simultaneously by many people. Sounding the death knell of the material world, however, is premature, as knowledge products, their producers, the material objects in which they are embedded, the conditions of production, and the ways of exchange and consumption are all material processes, performed by embodied and embedded individuals. Knowledge products are about the material world and part of that world, and as such are not mere mental events detached from the physical reality. Rather than an immaterial economy, knowledge economy is a segment of a larger, global process of material production, exchange and consumption.

As a result of the apparent transition from the production of manufactured goods to services, from tangible to intangible products, knowledge economy has been interpreted as a post-industrial economy. The notion of a radical transformation into a new type of post-industrial society has been advocated by a series of writers wishing to mark the dawn of a new era. Production of goods, however, is closely related to services, and the production and consumption of goods and services are interdependent. Rather than post-industrialization, we have witnessed global industrialization, in which a new map of production of goods and services across the world has emerged, allowing the high-cost regions to move up the value chain. Competition from emerging economies could successfully supply some products at lower costs, while relocation to low-cost regions and automation were pursued by industrialists in search of higher returns and lower expenses, avoiding expensive industrial relations at home and exporting environmental costs. The life story of a manufactured item now runs through many cities and countries around the world, each making a contribution, from inception and design to the manufacturing of its component parts, assembly, marketing and consumption, a thread that links the local components of a global capitalist industrial economy.

The intangible becomes tangible through finding economic value, facilitated through intellectual property rights, which have become a cornerstone of the knowledge economy. The conversion of knowledge and information into commodity takes place through intellectual property rights, within a framework set by a series of international treaties, which go as far back as the late nineteenth century and are now strengthened and expanded through the World Trade Organization. Alongside the growth of knowledge products, there have been pressures on states to regulate access to these products, adopting measures to protect the economic and moral rights of creators and inventors, as well as promoting creativity and encouraging fair trade. Industrial property and copyright are the two main forms of intellectual property rights, which protect an idea or the form of expression of ideas. Critics, however, argue that these international treaties are in the interest of the more advanced economies and the more powerful players in the marketplace, rewarding the vested interests and undermining others, limiting access to natural resources and weakening local cultures. They argue that knowledge products are public goods, which can help with health and education, among others, and joining the international property rights regime would deprive the developing countries of their ability to provide this public good for their populations. The reduced public access to knowledge is detrimental to its further development, as patents and copyrights are at odds with the need to share and collaborate, which fuels innovation and creativity. In response, some have argued for the development of intellectual commons that would avoid the dominance of monopolies over knowledge.

While knowledge economy may appear to break free from any particular context (spatial, temporal, social), it is important to recognize the contextual nature of knowledge. Knowledge is embedded in a context formed by history and culture, in which social conventions and practices shape the conditions for the development, recognition and transmission of knowledge. While structural changes in this context can lead to epistemic ruptures and the transformation of how knowledge is evaluated, the change from one perspective to another is always gradual, told by the traditions made available in the existing tradition. The nature of knowledge in knowledge economy, therefore, shows as much continuity as disjunction from the past.

Knowledge is also embodied in intelligent humans, who have the capacity to produce, exchange and interpret knowledge and information. In the definitions of knowledge economy, the theoretical and scientific aspects of knowledge are emphasized, and codified knowledge is given priority. In response, the notion of tacit knowledge has been advocated, in which knowledge is contextualized in shared exemplars, rather than rules and laws, in personal capacities of knowledge workers rather than explicit instructions written in code books. As a result of emphasis on scientific knowledge, the practical and productive forms of knowledge are undermined, from the local and traditional knowledge that is essential to making life in society possible to the artistic and creative knowledge that interprets the world in alternative ways. Knowledge takes the local, informal and everyday forms, which are essential to support the development of scientific and cultural forms of knowledge. Without these other forms of knowledge, the possibility of developing a scientific and cultural flourishing is not imaginable. In the same way that the workers in knowledge-intensive sectors need the presence and support of a wide range of other skills, the knowledge that is used in the knowledge economy needs to be supplemented by these other types of knowledge.

Understanding knowledge as embodied and embedded goes beyond a dichotomous relationship between structure and agency, recognizing the various forms of knowledge, as well as the social and psychological contexts in which they are located. In this way, the spatial implications of knowledge become apparent, as the practices of individuals and societies take place within, and help transform, a spatial framework, rather than in an immaterial virtual world. What is indeed taking place is the formation of new contexts, rather than the disappearance of all contexts. The emphasis on personal knowledge is a shift of emphasis from fixed places to mobile individuals, who are encouraged to go on a journey through partly connected contexts, establishing new links and reshaping the existing ones. The fluidity of the contexts, however, brings forward doubt as the measure of all knowledge, challenging those who are involved in the supply and assessment of information to search for new parameters for judgement.

Knowledge economy, broadly defined as a collection of different knowledge-intensive activities, appears interested in whatever passes as knowledge in society, as long as it can be turned into a commodity. The instrumental use of knowledge and focus on the types of knowledge that can be converted into economic value have challenged the notion of knowledge as an end in itself, which is satisfying the need to know, providing an account of the world, helping us find our place and guiding us how to act. Education, which opens up the doors to such knowledge, is also defined in instrumental terms, as a preparation for economic activities. When accumulated and used towards economic ends, knowledge is turned into a new form of capital. In both embedded and embodied forms, the accumulation of this capital finds spatial implications, turning some agglomerations into knowledge hubs.

Economy is the collection of goods and services and the processes of their production, exchange and use. In the knowledge economy, knowledge finds three important roles: knowledge as instrument of producing goods and services, knowledge as goods and services, and knowledge as capital. In all three aspects, knowledge economy is intensifying the roles that have been historically set: humans have always used knowledge as an instrument, a product and a capacity for production. In knowledge economy, the growth of knowledge as epistemic capital has found a central place, encouraging its accumulation through education, training and research, through meeting of minds and innovation, and through the physical co-presence of knowledge workers. The knowledge economy is a phase in capitalist economy in which knowledge is a key factor of production, a new form of capital. As such, it is subject to the dynamics of capitalism, including commodification, competition, accumulation, creative destruction and unequal distribution, all finding spatial manifestations. The way epistemic capital works, however, is through conversion into money, as money is the most liquid and mobile form of value and can be converted back into many other products and capacities.

By virtue of being embedded and embodied, knowledge cannot reach the level of abstraction that money does. Money and information can both be carried as physical objects in boxes or symbols in computer networks. But the accumulation of knowledge does not automatically entitle its owner to exchange it with any privilege or even with everyday necessities; it needs to be converted into money first and for that conversion it needs to be marketable and marketed. Money continues to be the medium of exchange, and accumulation of knowledge in the knowledge-based economy considered beneficial only if it can help the accumulation of wealth. Knowledge can be interpreted as a new form of capital, as compared with the physical capital used in manufacturing, but both are mediums for a higher level of abstraction and transferability, which is money.

Space is an embodiment of social processes, shaping and framing the conditions within which those activities can take place, and becoming a commodity, the production of which is an important part of any economy. The functional evaluation of space encourages us to ask what spaces are distinctively serving the knowledge economy needs, while the logic of production asks what role the production of space plays in the knowledge economy. The production of space has an internal dynamic that may or may not relate to the problem of need. The development industry does not necessarily follow the line of needs and demand; it also attempts to generate demand for space. As evident from the global financial crisis, the production of space lies at the heart of the global economy, expected to help absorb and reproduce the oversupply of credit produced by the financial industry. What appear to be spaces of knowledge economy might actually be spaces of speculation and market-making.

1 Dispersion

Attempts to overcome the limitations of space and time are the engines of economic growth. As time and space are turned into assets, their use is maximized through the changing organization of work and the development of new technologies, with which a faster pace of life round the clock and round the world is made possible, filling up every possible package of time and space. The globalized capitalist economy transforms space and time, using space to overcome the limitations of time, through the use of new technologies that would facilitate a new global division of labour and accelerate the speed of life within localities. Spatial dispersion is made possible by organizational and technological innovation, expanding the global workforce and facilitating a more condensed use of time that is internalized by knowledge workers through emotional attachment to their gadgets and the partial sense of liberty that comes from flexible working.

Knowledge economy has been associated with a transition from Fordism to post-Fordism, from mass production to flexible production; one allied with the large-scale availability of unskilled workers and demand for standardized goods, the other with the supply of skilled workers and differentiated demand. While the transition is visible in some cities and regions, the two forms of production have co-existed for a long time, and they are now in the process of integration into a new global division of labour. The separation of conception from execution which characterized the industrial economy and was the cause of workers' alienation, and which had once separated home from work and town from countryside, has now become globalized, with some cities and regions involved in intellectual labour, now labelled knowledge economy, while others perform the physical production. The globalized separation creates its own form of alienation, which is attempted to be bridged by consumption of goods and imaginary lifestyles or new methods of production.

The restless energies of capitalism, which through the post-war compromise were tamed to improve workers' living conditions, now freed themselves from some of these bonds, as they looked for new outlets elsewhere. Rather than disappearing, industrial capitalism has spread around the world through globalization. Capitalism is a force for higher returns and accumulation, searching for higher productivity and lower costs, innovating through extending economic exchange relations to new activities and places, and developing markets for the consumption of its products. Drawing on the human desire to assert status and seek pleasure, it generates a restless process of production and consumption, generating new productive capacities, inventing new technologies, creating new products and bringing new parts of society into the marketplace.

As human work is the source of all value, scarcity in the quantity and quality of labour has been significant in economic change, bringing about a new gender, ethnic and spatial division of labour. At home, the roles of women, ethnic minorities and the elderly are recognized as important sources of value in the economic process; elsewhere, the seemingly endless supply of labour in populous countries has been another source. Knowledge economy is characterized by innovation, which results from an intensive and instrumental cultivation and use of knowledge, facilitated by the spread of new technologies and a supportive institutional and regulatory framework, and applied by a high-skilled and differentiated workforce. As a segment of the global economy, it can only be fully understood in the context of the globalization processes.

Globalization is a spatial solution to the problems of economic production, dispersing the production to lower-cost places, where the factors of production, in particular labour supplies, are cheaper and less complicated. Globalization is also a solution to the problems of consumption, stimulating demand and searching for new markets everywhere. Knowledge economy is the high end of this global division of labour, where high value-added products are produced; where conception, as distinction from execution, of the global industrial production is performed; located in a wide range of places, which are coordinated and managed from the core of a global space.

Nation-states had unified national spaces, going beyond the limited capacities of regional and local markets. Now globalization aims to unify a global space, going beyond the limitations of these national territories. This process is made possible by transport and communication technologies that make better connections between the different segments of the production process, intensify the removal of national barriers to the free movement of capital, free trade and some flexibility for the movement of labour, all linked through finance and guarded and enforced through political agreement and military engagement. Despite their best efforts, however, nation-states could not remove much of the local and regional differences; globalization is even more unlikely to be able to rule out national and local differences. In the national space, knowledge was distributed through the education system, but it was still concentrated in some areas; at the global level, the absence of such universal systems of education, and the embodied and embedded nature of knowledge, make its free movement and the ability of local contexts to benefit from it more limited. Information may flow more easily, but knowledge may not. Globalization of modernity, through creative destruction and restless expansion, is the cultural dimension of the emergence of a global industrial capitalism, but it may not be able to win over the deep-seated patterns of diversity that are inscribed on societies and their members.

This global space is by nature uneven: the capacities of the players are widely different, where natural and social contexts vary widely and where large corporations and powerful states can shape the rules of the game and benefit most from sailing its waters. Built on the existing systems of stratification, but always challenging it, there is a system of centres and peripheries in the global economy, the more privileged parts of which lay claim to, or work towards developing, knowledge economy. These centres treat the global space as their hinterland, in a somewhat similar fashion to the relationship between the town and the country. Similar cities in this uneven landscape compete for attracting resources, acting like firms in a marketplace, engaged in a war of symbols to assert their desirability for investors and visitors, seeking any appearance that could give them a competitive edge over others, from flagship projects and iconic buildings to works of art, events and festivals, all at the service of image-making and rebranding cities.

Dispersion can also be seen at work at the urban level. Cities are concentrations of different people. The location of people within a city is a pattern of dispersion that reflects this diversity, manifest in stratification, producing centrifugal forces that separate them according to their access to resources, power and status, bringing them back again together in localized concentrations. Location and distance become instruments of spatial configuration, with which to manage and shape social relationships, protect hierarchies and keep the unfamiliar away. Location and distance are institutionalized through the cost of land and transport, which in turn generates the social geography of the city. The choices that are made in the trade-off between land rent/use and transport costs are subject to contextual limitations, a diverse set of motivations that go well beyond a simple calculation of monetary costs and benefits, but including the expression of emotions, reflection of biological urges, following social norms and the desire to assert status and seek recognition.

The advent of ICT has brought about speculations about the annihilation of space and time, death of geography and even the death of the city as a permanent concentration. Would flexible working practices of a networked worker create a new urban form? Labour market deregulation, privatization and outsourcing, decentralization of activities and large-scale entry of women into the workforce have created more flexible working patterns, which include teleworking, home-based working, flexitime, part-time, job-share, compressed working week, annualized hours, temporary and casual work and fixed-term contracts. Office buildings became known as dinosaurs, expecting that knowledge workers who were freed from the constraints of space would now be able to work anywhere and anytime with any device. Flatter hierarchies, teamwork and employee involvement, especially in knowledge-intensive activities, led to higher degrees of autonomy for workers and higher productivity. Conception and execution seemed to have been integrated once again, removing the alienation that industrial workers suffered from; but a more detailed real picture shows the conquest of the home by work, in which the worker may be involved in execution that is outsourced to a private home. The impact of flexible working on urban space is still limited, but it has blurred the boundaries between home and work, generated a more flexible pattern of travel to work, temporal routines of shops and offices, mixture of land use and a more entrepreneurial approach to urban development. Workers, however, still need to anchor themselves in particular places and temporal routines, are exposed to higher uncertainty, carry some of the costs of the workplace, are deprived of the social atmosphere of the workplace and struggle to balance the demands of their home and work. Meanwhile, taller office buildings continue to be built, asserting the status and ambitions of the companies, and cities, in their global competition.

Information and communication technologies are developed within a libertarian frame of mind, hoping to maximize individual freedoms on where to locate, how to live and who to communicate with. As such, they are accused of being a threat to society, detaching individuals from their contexts and undermining their contacts and commitment to the surrounding environment. These technologies, however, are the last in a long line of inventions that have facilitated individual liberties at the cost of their social contexts: trains that uprooted people from the countryside, cars that would increase individual mobility and living away from the city, telegraph and telephone that allowed them a wider communicative reach, while central heating and low prices of radios and televisions had dispersed the members of the household from the bonds of the living room. As such, they all show how technologies are developed in response to, or facilitating, the demand for individualization, which is at the heart of modern urban life, a manifestation of the idea of the autonomous individual that has evolved for centuries and has been widely accepted, and challenged, in culture.

2 Differentiation

The investigation about production in the knowledge economy needs to be accompanied by inquiry into consumption, which after all is the primary target of production. Innovation and higher productivity, through which things become 'better, faster, cheaper', would inevitably rely on expansion and acceleration of consumption. The other side of the coin from the proliferation of new products is a larger scale and faster pace of consumption, either by finding new markets or expanding the existing ones. Consumption becomes the driving force for the economy, and growing it a vital need for the restless process of production. Rather than responding to existing need and thus striking a balance between supply and demand, supply makes new demand, in a continuous cycle in which producers and advertisers induce in the potential customers a desire for their products. Creative destruction is intensified, generating higher rates of obsolescence, and faster and shorter cycles of production and consumption.

Encouraging consumption is primarily through differentiation between products and between consumers. Product and consumer differentiation takes many forms, but it essentially draws on a desire for status, in which individuals identify with particular products, the consumption of which might distinguish them in comparison with their peers. The sense of identity and the cultural meaning that are created through the consumption of goods and services may be crystallized in lifestyles, which work with brands and images as the lens through which individuals see themselves. Selling products to a mass society under the guise of differentiation is a delicate trade-off, giving the impression that each individual is different and has the possibility of developing and exploring that difference, while at the same time, each individual is part of a mass society with largely limited possibilities in its everyday experiences. Digital technologies help achieve this balance to some extent, while expanding the boundaries of mass society beyond national territories to global proportions. However, when diversity becomes the norm, rather than exception, it loses its power of making distinctions.

The push for differentiation was partly a revolt against large-scale organization, which was a central feature of the twentieth century. Social and philosophical implications of a drive for differentiation could be seen in the post-modern attitude, characterized by political disillusionment, philosophical scepticism, celebration of subjectivity and assertion of social and aesthetic diversity – an attitude that could be seen as the cultural face of creative destruction, rejecting the ideas and practices of mass industrial society to pave the way for the emergence of a revised version of the modern attitude. The lines of continuity, however, are as strong as the lines of disruption, and so the practices of cultural creative destruction can only partially work in some fields.

Growth in consumption relies on limitless desires that are never possible fully to satisfy, and so it could lead to a permanent sense of shortcoming and a mountain of personal and collective financial and environmental debt. While obsolescence and renewal in intangible products may seem to create little physical waste, the process of consumption is not limited to intangibles, as evidenced by the amount of material waste produced everywhere. These consequences of expanded consumption would entail that the knowledge economy be always studied in association with a clear idea of what it leads to and how the results are managed.

The spatial implications of differentiation seek distinction and recognition between different parts of the city or between different cities, consolidating it through social geography of the city, which institutionalizes an overlay of social status and economic conditions as translated into land and property market. This differentiation is encouraged by mixing land use and tenure, drawing on a range of symbols and images mobilized for seeking attention and marketing, including expressive architecture, differentiated townscape and visual messages that occupy the public space. The use of colour, form, sound and smell, and the institutionalized forms of publicity in fashion, sport and entertainment, turn the urban environment into a giant board, advertising thousands of products, a space of spectacle in which the production and consumption of image is an end in itself. The inhabitants of this city, however, are not necessarily passive spectators and consumers, but producers of knowledge-rich goods and services that have positive social and economic value for the city and contribute to a global process of production.

Can knowledge economy be associated with new social configurations, changing the existing forms of diversification and stratification into new ones? It cannot be distinguished from its predecessors by the rise of a new social class, in the same way that industrial capitalist economy had generated new social classes.

Although the existence of these classes may no longer be clear-cut and obvious, they were powerful indicators of social change for a long time. While some have heralded the emergence of a new so-called creative class, there is little evidence to distinguish this new class from the middle classes of the industrial society. The key social phenomenon in the emergence of the knowledge economy is the growth of consumption, which diversifies society into different consumption patterns, and the growth of social inequality, which widens social divisions according to households' access to resources.

The high productivity brought about by knowledge and innovation has led to new wealth for some; consumption has grown but not been equally distributed, benefitting a highly skilled and well-placed elite but being out of reach for those who have not been able to join the knowledge economy. Marketization and globalization have opened up new avenues, which are not easy to travel for those with weaker positions in the social space, deepening social inequality. Social inequality is a multi-dimensional phenomenon that includes access to economic resources, social recognition, political participation, quality of life and perceptions of well-being, but inequality can be exacerbated by the weakening of welfare support, social networks and family support. Social mobility, which could be seen as a remedy, also suffers when its pathways of education and redistribution are blocked. The shift of wealth creation from blue-collar to white-collar work, and the limits to the educational attainment of the younger generations in low-income families, can create a two-tier society. Unequal access to knowledge would mean a large proportion of the population may not be able to join the knowledge economy as an equal partner. Pressures for differentiation are combined with the pressures for stratification, resulting in a fragmented society with a partitioned space.

Differential access to knowledge does not take place in a void, but in a historic pattern of inequality, both at inter-city and intra-city levels. At the inter-city level, at the global and national scales, the traditional centres of the economy with their access to leading research institutions, venture capital and educated workforce have kept and consolidated their positions of power *vis-à-vis* their national and global hinterlands. While new partners have joined these traditional centres, global inequality has not been addressed, with clear spatial manifestations in the growth of large metropolitan areas and the shrinkage of the smaller peripheral regions. Knowledge divide is overlaid on the other forms of divide that already characterized stratified societies and international relations. Knowledge divide is a serious challenge for developing countries, preventing them from joining the knowledge economy. If knowledge is treated as a public good and is shared openly, this divide at the global and national levels may be bridged, creating knowledge societies that draw on different forms of existing knowledge and develop new ones.

3 Connection

Knowledge is the capacity to make sense of information, sensory inputs and cognitive processes, made possible by producing, sharing and making active and dynamic connections between different pieces of information, a capacity that has been considerably magnified with the help of information and communication technologies.

Knowledge economy is widely equated with the phenomenal growth of information and communication technologies, which have revolutionized the way information is produced, stored, transmitted and exchanged, with far-reaching implications for innovation and productivity, and hence for economic development. National and international organizations look for ways of spreading their application even further. An information age has been identified, in which digital technologies penetrate into and shape every sphere of life, with the Internet reaching a quarter of the world's population. Such phenomenal growth continually amazes observers, who search for the impact of these technologies on society, some even embracing technological determinism, giving these technologies a causal role in social change, using them to define our age. The rise of digital technologies has been associated with a cyclical, techno-economic change in capitalism since the late eighteenth century, in which the productive apparatus is rejuvenated through a succession of innovation and creative destruction, manifest in a series of long and short cycles. Every 50 years or so, a new technology emerges that spearheads a new industrial revolution, with innovations in steam-powered transport, steel, fossil-fuel energy and microelectronics each causing the crisis and structural adjustment of social and institutional spheres. In a down swing of a long wave, a new technology emerges, which promises to reduce costs and open new possibilities for the most efficient organization of production. The adoption of this new technology signals a new wave, which grows widely and intensively until the point of saturation, followed by inertia and decline, and eventually the start of a new wave.

This model provides a sense of clarity and regularity for historical change, looking for patterns in a sea of diverse events and weaving together a number of trends and themes to produce epochal paradigms with which everything else can be explained and the future can be predicted. Such modelling, however, by nature would be selective and reductionist, inherently endorsing the dominance of structure over agency, of new over old, of technology over society. Accordingly, it designates some ideas, objects and practices as progressive and innovative, while condemning others as obsolete and ready for creative destruction. While it offers a neat explanation for the advent of knowledge economy as caused by the emergence of a new technology, its evidence and reasoning are not fully convincing. It narrows the range of innovation to technological change, while innovation could be in the development of new forms of organization, new sources of supply, new markets, etc.It selects some technological innovations to characterize an age, ignoring a sequence of ground-breaking developments, such as the nuclear, space and genetic technologies, or how ICT itself has been in the making for almost two centuries. More importantly, technology is only one factor among others, and while it is an important factor of economic activity, it is produced and used within a complex social context, in which no single source can be credited with causing dramatic change. Organizational or technological change cannot lead to major social and economic changes on their own or without due regard for the context in which they emerge and are deployed.

In the past, the backbones of urban space were formed, one after the other, by streets, waterways, railways, motorways as well as airways; would information and communication technology be the new backbone to the urban space in the knowledge economy? Information and communication technologies have abridged human work and extended human capacities, thus augmenting functions and expanding the scope of possibilities to unprecedented and unimagined levels. The application of ICT has penetrated widely and deeply into many spheres of urban life, as reflected in the terms e-business, e-government, e-learning, e-museum, etc., in what amounts to a mediated city. These technologies are used to exert and challenge political power and social control, conduct cultural and economic exchange, and enhance representation by adding a virtual layer to the experiences of the physical world.

Since the end of the medieval period, three technological metaphors have been used to shape and reshape cities. First, the invention of mechanical clocks inspired the Renaissance and early modern periods, thinking of the universe as a mechanical clock and organizing urban space accordingly in the manner of a mechanical machine with interlocking parts. The universe had unchanging rules and absolute principles, which could be translated into a city with a static Euclidean geometry, superimposing a system of nodes, axes and networks on the apparently disorderly medieval cities. Second, the invention of engines facilitated mobility and connectivity; and in the form of trains, cars and airplanes it opened up cities, transformed their relationships with one another and with the countryside. Cities grew horizontally and vertically, shaped in a dynamic and fragmented geometry, adopting the aesthetics of the machine age that had been developed by a technologically determinist school of thought. Third, the invention of computers turned these new machines into a dominant symbol, which, together with a large number of other inventions, changed the city into an increasingly technologically mediated one.

In the political field, digital technologies are used as a weapon of social and political control, as well as a vehicle of free expression and democratic struggle. They are used by governments, providing online services and establishing interactive relationships between governments and citizens, as well as facilitating surveillance regarding traffic management and crime prevention. However, the boundaries between public and private spheres are blurred, and what appears to be free movement in physical or virtual spaces becomes monitored and recorded by some machines somewhere, with or without the knowledge and consent of the person involved. While many local communities welcome the installation of security cameras and Internet users seem unworried about the traces they leave from their virtual tours, the extent of this surveillance raises concerns about the collection, storage and application of such data, which can be used for security or commercial purposes, and their implication for privacy and human rights. Meanwhile, these technologies are also used by activists for grassroots mass mobilization, helping political protesters to coordinate their activities, spread information and stage events.

In the economic field, digital technologies are used for increasing productivity and economic development, which is a linchpin of the idea of knowledge economy. The possibilities of innovation in developing new products, expansion of trade and exchange, articulation of the division of labour, transforming organization of production and access to new markets are enhanced through the application of these technologies. Here the interface between the businesses and their clients echoes some of the concerns in the political field between the government and citizens, regarding the relations of power and control of information – how the information is collected, stored and used. The interface is subject to experimentation in search of ways to charge customers for online services and content that would benefit the producers and distributors but not deter the users.

In the cultural field, the development of online universities, libraries, museums, art galleries, music and movies have provided new forms of access to cultural products. While proliferating the possibilities of access to these cultural assets, digital technologies challenge some of the traditional formats and spatial configurations, asking whether many of these institutions can survive in their current form. There is, however, always a distinction between a functional delivery of a service or a product, and the social environment that is shaped around that service. A clear example is a university, which is not only a place for the development of knowledge, but also a place of sociability, and while digital technologies might offer the former they cannot compete with the latter.

Augmentation may challenge the existing depositories of knowledge, such as the library, now that knowledge and information are readily available through a digital infrastructure upon which theoretically anyone can draw. The relationship between digital technologies and existing physical transactions has been subject to trial and error, looking for a balance between bricks and clicks, bridging the real and virtual spaces by mixing computer-generated stimuli with direct experience, with the aim of helping user interaction in real time.The virtual forms of representation are used to augment the way physical processes function, with applications in health, education, engineering, entertainment, etc. An invisible digital infrastructure is emerging that through its ubiquity can enhance urban space, augmenting the city's functions. Meanwhile, by aiming to replace direct contacts, digital mediation in the city could also undermine the development of multi-sensual relations with the surrounding physical and social environment.

One of the foundations of social relations is recognition, which offers individuals a sense of themselves and others. Our sense of identity relies on how we think others perceive us, and so recognition is a socially mediated process. As the normative models are conveyed through this process of recognition, we think of ourselves in comparison with those implicit or explicit social norms, adjusting our behaviour accordingly. When social processes are themselves mediated through technologies of mass media and telecommunication, our social recognition and identity will be doubly mediated, relying now on what we think society as a whole perceives to be good, as presented through the media. The adoration of celebrity comes partly from this sense of mediated normative models, in which social aspirations are shaped by comparing ourselves with the images of fame and fortune, of success and perfection, as portrayed in the media, which are inevitably doctored, unreal images.

4 Concentration

Alongside the patterns of dispersion and differentiation there is a pattern of agglomeration, which brings people together to work and socialize, partly in response to the social nature of human beings, and partly owing to the logic of scale economies and mutual interdependence for everyday needs. Cities are magnets that attract more and more people, while depopulating some areas in the countryside and in peripheral and declining cities. Cities grow, rather than disappear, which at first appears to be a paradox of the globalized knowledge economies, combining centrifugal and centripetal forces. Individualization, and its spatial manifestation dispersion, however, does not take place endlessly to create a thinly scattered population on the earth's surface. It is part of a process of creative destruction, which dislocates people from one context to graft them onto another, a process of destroying one set of relationships to replace it with another. In the formation of new agglomerations, older ones may be condemned to decline if they are not recreated or not adjusted to the new circumstances.

Spatial concentrations consolidate particular social relationships, and any attempt to change these relationships, as in the periods of economic change, ends up pushing for dispersion, through the so-called creative destruction, and re-concentration in new ways. The social and economic map of a city is often a map of *dispersed meso-agglomerations*, which accounts for a combination of centrifugal and centripetal forces, one driven by a desire to abandon restrictions and acquire distinction and the other by the necessity and the desire to congregate and relate to others. Both of these forces operate within a framework set by a combination of the drive for financial reward, social status and decision-making power.

Cities are permanent concentrations of people, who gather other life forms and objects around them, at densities that facilitate the economies of scale in production and exchange of goods and services, with complex instrumental and expressive relationships that make their co-existence possible. Whether marking a crossroad or the edge of a territory, cities emerge as nodes within a larger spatial division of labour, which is increasingly global. Concentrations are closely associated with innovation; agglomeration creates economies of scale, reduces the consequences of failure in experimentation and facilitates collaboration among the different parties involved in economic production, which in turn can trigger innovation.

A schematic characterization of the cities dominated by manufacturing industries shows clusters of factories and working-class neighbourhoods, working and living in large numbers according to standardized routines, using a network for the transportation of manufactured goods and labour. Mass production and mass consumption shaped the city, with large-scale social organization of production, rigid routines of life that standardized the use of time, a social geography that standardized the use of space and methods of governance that reflected the ontology of social classes. In cities dominated by knowledge-based services, this social and spatial organization is somewhat different. Work takes place in clusters of offices and other white-collar workspaces, engaged in more flexible organization of production, producing intangible products, according to more flexible temporal routines, accompanied by more differentiated patterns of consumption, blurring the lines of distinction between social classes but introducing new and deeper patterns of social inequality. In cities that have gone through a transition from the first model to the second, spatial organization is gradually reflecting these changes in city centres and suburbs, by removing the traces of the manufacturing city's ways of working and living, or reusing some of its spaces where possible but devoid of their original meaning, and replacing them with new offices and white-collar housing, with the supporting retail and entertainment spaces. Spatial change, accompanied by social inequality, however, sometimes leads to overt conflict over space, gentrification and displacement, as the forces of 'creative destruction' replace one activity with another, one group with another, one way of life with another, demolishing one cluster to make way for the formation of another.

Knowledge economy draws on innovation, which is made possible through the meeting of minds, in turn made possible through clustering. Cyber-clustering is enabled through the use of information and communication technologies, linking people to one another from across time and space. Spatial clustering, however, is still the key to the process of innovation. Spatial clustering may be a concentration of firms looking for higher productivity, benefiting from the external economies of scale, drawing on spillovers that encourage them to cluster, using the infrastructure of transport, health, education and other services available in a city, while implicitly or explicitly sharing suppliers, labour, information and markets with their competitor firms. Clustering may result from the speculative imitation of successful firms, manifesting a herd mentality rather than a clear calculation of risks and rewards. Clustering may also be a concentration of administrative units shaped by political decisions, institutions gathering around an anchor point, artists inhabiting the affordable in-between spaces, or a grouping of individuals with similar interests, who are in search of higher wages, social recognition, information or pleasure.

Knowledge workers are the embodiments of tacit knowledge, a notion that shows a transition from information to knowledge, from objects to humans, reflecting the human capacity to interpret and codify information and innovate. Their clustering is the material and spatial indications of, and necessary conditions for, the knowledge economy, which will be subject to labour market processes and economies of scale. Economic development strategies, therefore, encourage the growth of substantial, active labour markets for skilled knowledge workers who can carry and transmit tacit knowledge.

Clusters are the nodes that signify the converging points of multiple networks, concentrating productive forces and subsequently accumulating wealth and privilege for those who are centrally located within these forces. In clustering, the so-called base activities are given priority, as exporting their products can become the source of a city's prosperity, which in the knowledge economy would be the production of knowledge-intensive, high value-added products. Through a multiplier process, all other activities, also forming clusters of their own, are thought to group around these base production clusters, in interdependent relations of exchange, competition and collaboration. However, this one-way dependence of non-base on base is hardly accurate, for the urban context, with its infrastructure of support, from both public and private sectors, and its large and diversified market of consumers, could be the primary reason for the location decisions of a firm, showing a two-way interaction between the firm and the urban context. In the same way, the clustering of knowledge workers cannot be credited with being the sole basis for a city's prosperity; while the city's range of human effort and infrastructure provision may not be included in the knowledge-intensive sectors, they are an essential ground upon which any new activity may thrive. This is why the larger cities are often better placed to benefit from the development of knowledge-intensive sectors, both as rich contexts in themselves and as gateways to their national hinterlands.

While some clusters are formed by the decisions of firms and individuals, others are induced by public policy, encouraged by decision-makers hoping that reverse engineering in economic development could be performed, and then cultivating seeds that might grow and develop into strong crops. This is why office quarters, cultural districts, science or business parks, universities and research institutes are set up by public policy. These clusters may be the concentration of new spaces and support for new activities; they may also be the result of repackaging and rebranding existing activities, marketing them in the hope of attracting investment. An essential part of this rebranding is architecture and urban design, taken to be image-makers and image-changers, companions to advertising campaigns and marketing strategies, used at the service of the battle for differentiation in the marketplace. Some of the rebranding and repackaging inevitably serves the public authorities' bid for legitimacy, hoping to show the electorate the politicians' effectiveness in laying the foundations of a new economy.

The clustering, imaginary or real, may also be an infrastructure upon which the property market could thrive and the public consumption of goods and services be encouraged, which is an underlying engine for the economy. What appears to be a search for a new economic base, around which support activities could flourish, may end up being a device for the circulation of resources within an economy. The features of urban space are diverse and overlapping, reflecting different historical periods, economic sectors, social habits and cultural preferences. In particular, the production of space may or may not coincide with the needs of the knowledge economy, as producers of space may target some functional and social segments of the market, where they think speculative development may lead to higher rewards, without showing any interest to equally significant but less profitable segments. The result may be a crisis of overproduction and under provision, which reflects the dynamics of the development industry rather than the knowledge economy. This is why the public authorities have an important role to play in providing the necessary infrastructure that profit-seekers will not provide.

Clusters are stepping stones towards the formation of the economies of scale, where the cost of experimentation for innovation could be reduced through the number and density of such experiments. Clusters provide a critical mass for innovation, with the necessary ingredients in the development of knowledge economy: the density of a highly skilled labour market, the existence of knowledge infrastructure and resources, resulted from education and R&D expenditure, and active social networks that facilitate the generation and transmission of knowledge. At times, there seems to be a naïve belief that mere co-presence of relevant stakeholders would automatically lead to innovation, while it requires a range of contextual conditions as a prerequisite. The clusters work on the basis of facilitating direct or indirect relationships between the agencies involved and the relationships between them and their urban context. The spatial implication of this process would be the need for the spaces of encounter, places for developing knowledge and skills and various forums where different firms and individuals can become aware of one another and of what the urban context can offer. For businesses, knowledge workers and creative individuals, the spaces of encounter are significant places for social networks to develop through face-to-face meetings. These spaces of encounter can be developed in a range of spatial and organizational nodes, which include public spaces, mixed-use areas and high-density developments.

While knowledge and innovation may take place in the scientists' laboratory or the artists' workshop, knowledge economy is interested in the conversion of this innovation into economic value; hence it is in the marketplace that innovation finds expression. Knowledge economy takes shape at the meeting point of knowledge producers and the private enterprise, the intersection of the laboratory, workshop, library, office, cyberspace and other spaces of innovation with the virtual and physical spaces of product development and economic exchange. Economic development strategies may push for the proliferation of these intersections, as the cultivating grounds for the growth of new activities. If these crossroads of knowledge and commerce prosper, their impact on the city could be considerable.

If these 'designed' clusters are located within cities, they sometimes work as alien implants, with a wide gap with the locality's character and patterns of working and living. Their impacts could include higher competition for housing and support services, higher rents, changing mix of businesses and jobs, and traffic congestion, which can have adverse effects on the local population, especially those who are not party to this new prosperity. If these intersections are developed outside the urban areas, in suburban science and technology parks, they create new single-use specialist areas, which may help further spatial fragmentation, with negative social and environmental consequences; they may even fail to attract workers, and their effectiveness in being a crossroad between knowledge and industry has so far been inconclusive. In the case of cultural districts, the impacts may be reverse, as the coexistence of creative activities and cultural industries may not be easy; when commercial considerations are brought in, cultural innovations may step back, or may change their character in ways that are not acceptable to the creative community. The idea of creating clusters, then, may fail on the grounds of the failure of social engineering and physical determinism: the clusters induced by public policy could fail in meeting two basic requirements: commercialization of science and culture, and locating these activities in designated places, as the practitioners in these fields may not always subscribe to these requirements. For the implant to take root and work effectively, they need to be embedded more closely in their urban contexts, rather than being imposed as a new reality on an unwilling and ill-prepared context, in the manner of gentrification, creating new social and economic clusters, as one group of people are replaced by another, at substantial social and political costs.

The challenge is to combat and reduce social inequality in the knowledge economy. In the manufacturing economy, the collaboration between workers, employers and the state had a positive impact on reducing inequalities. Now, with the global organization of industrial production, the quest for equality and fairness becomes global, generating pressure from the new industrializing economies, which are increasingly able to play a stronger role in the global balance of power. In this process, the conditions of local inequalities may exacerbate, as local actors have limited access to global processes, while the pressures move across borders and hence go through the gate-keepers of the state and large corporations.

Bibliography

Abramovitz, M. and P. A. David (1996) Technological change and the rise of intangible investments: The US economy's growth-path in the twentieth century, in *Employment and Growth in the Knowledge-Based Economy*, pp. 35–60. Paris: Organization for Economic Cooperation and Development.

Adams, L. (2008) Globalization, universalism, and cultural form. *Comparative Studies in Society and History*. Vol. 50, No. 3, pp. 614–40.

Advisory Committee on Measuring Innovation in the 21st Century Economy (2008) *Innovation Measurement: Tracking the state of innovation in the American economy*. Washington, DC: US Department of Commerce. http://www.innovationmetrics.gov/Innovation%20Measurement%2001-08%20rev%20040908.pdf, accessed 16 October 2009.

Aglietta, M. (2000) *A Theory of Capitalist Regulation: The US experience*. New edition. London: Verso.

Aglietta, M. (2008) Into a new growth regime. *New Left Review*. Nov–Dec, No. 54, pp. 61–74.

Alberti, L. B. (1988) *On the Art of Building in Ten Books*. Cambridge, MA: MIT Press.

Allen, J. and D. Dillman (1994) *Against All Odds: Rural community in the information age*. Boulder, CO: Westview Press.

Alonso, W. (1971) A theory of the urban land market, in L. S. Bourne (ed.) *Internal Structure of the City*, pp. 154–9. New York: Oxford University Press.

Althusser, L. (2005) *For Marx*. London: Verso.

Amin, A. (ed.) (1994) *Post-Fordism: A reader*. Oxford: Blackwell.

Angeles, L. (2009) An alternative test of Kuznets' hypothesis. *Journal of Economic Inequality*. http://www.springerlink.com/content/0q4v0813002525tm/?p=cc4f40c777734582b905497a58260f18&pi=19, accessed 1 July 2010.

Anttiroiko, A. V. (2004) Science Cities: Their characteristics and future challenges. *International Journal of Technology Management*. Vol. 28, No. 3–6, pp. 395–418.

Arendt, H. (1958) *The Human Condition*. Chicago, IL: University of Chicago Press.

Aristotle. (1992) *The Politics*. London: Penguin.

Aristotle. (1998) *The Nicomachean Ethics*. Oxford: Oxford University Press.

Arpaci, I. (2010) E-government and technological innovation in Turkey: Case studies on governmental organizations. *Transforming Government: People, process and policy*. Vol. 4, No. 1, pp. 37–53.

Ashton, P. (2005) Flexible working: The way forward? *IT NOW*. May, pp. 12–13.

Atkinson, R. and G. Bridge (eds) (2005) *Gentrification in a Global Context: The new urban colonialism*. London: Routledge.

Audi, R. (ed.) (1995) *The Cambridge Dictionary of Philosophy*. Cambridge: Cambridge University Press.

Aurigi, A. (2006) New technologies, same dilemmas: Policy and design issues for the augmented city. *Journal of Urban Technology*. Vol. 13, No. 3, pp. 5–28.

Aurigi, A. (2008) What you don't see is (also) what you get: Invisible flows and the shaping of media-rich cities. *Journal of Architectural and Planning Research*. Vol. 25, No. 2, June, pp. 106–17.

Aveni, A. (2000) *Empires of Time: Calendars, clocks and cultures*. London: TaurisParke Paperbacks.

Avery, V., E. Chamberlain, C. Summerfield and L. Zealey (eds) (2007) *Focus on the Digital Age*. Office for National Statistics. London: Palgrave Macmillan.

Ayres, R. (1997) The Kuznets curve and the life cycle analogy. *Structural Change and Economic Dynamics*. Vol. 8, pp. 413–26.

Badiou, A. (2005) *Being and Event*. London: Continuum.

Bannock, G., E. E. Baxter and E. Davis (2003) *The Penguin Dictionary of Economics*. 7th edition. London: Penguin Books.

Barber, L. (2009) Capitalism redrawn. *Financial Times: The future of capitalism*. 12 May, p. 3.

Barley, S. and G. Kunda (2004) *Gurus, Hired Guns and Warm Bodies: Itinerant experts in a knowledge economy*. Princeton, NJ: Princeton University Press.

Barrera, A. (2007) *Globalization and Economic Ethics: Distributive justice in the knowledge economy*. Basingstoke: Palgrave Macmillan.

Barry, B. (2001) *Culture and Equality*. Cambridge: Polity Press.

Bater, J. H. (1980) *The Soviet City*. London: Edward Arnold.

Baudrillard, J. (2004) *Fragments*. London: Routledge.

BBC (2009a) Government 'ineffectual' and 'panic stricken'. *The Andrew Marr Show*. 25 January. http://news.bbc.co.uk/1/hi/programmes/andrew_marr_show/7849830.stm, accessed 26 November 2009.

BBC (2009b) Q and A: Iran and the nuclear issue. http://news.bbc.co.uk/1/hi/world/middle_east/4031603.stm, accessed 17 August 2009.

BBC (2010) Profile: G8. http://news.bbc.co.uk/1/hi/world/americas/country_profiles/3777557.stm, accessed 30 June 2010.

Beetham, H. and R. Sharpe (2007) *Rethinking Pedagogy for a Digital Age: Designing and delivering e-learning*. London: Routledge.

Bell, D. (1973) *The Coming of Post-Industrial Society: A venture in social forecasting*. New York: Basic Books.

Benjafield, J. (2007) *Cognition*. 3rd edition. Oxford: Oxford University Press.

Bennett, R. J., D. J. Graham and W. Bratton (1999) The location and concentration of business clusters, business services, market coverage and local economic development. *Transactions of the Institute of British Geographers*. No. 24, pp. 393–420.

Benneworth, P., D. Charles and A. Madanipour (2010) Building localised interactions between universities and cities through university spatial development. *European Planning Studies*.

Berger, J. (1977) *Ways of Seeing*. London: British Broadcasting Corporation.

Berger, P. and T. Luckmann (1991) *The Social Construction of Reality: A treatise in the sociology of knowledge*. London: Penguin.

Berman, M. (2009) *On the Town: One hundred years of spectacle in Times Square*. London: Verso.

Berry, J. (ed.) (2004) *Contemporary Newspaper Design: Shaping the news in the digital age*. West New York, NJ: Mark Batty Publisher.

Best, K. (2010) Living in the control society: Surveillance, users and digital screen technologies. *International Journal of Cultural Studies*. Vol. 13, No. 1, January, pp. 5–24.

Billinghurst, M. and H. Kato (2002) Collaborative augmented reality. *Communications of the ACM*. Vol. 45, No. 7, pp. 64–70.

Blackburn, S. (1996) *The Oxford Dictionary of Philosophy*. Oxford: Oxford University Press.

Blake, N., J. Croot and J. Hastings (2004) *Measuring the Competitiveness of the UK Construction Industry, Volume 2*. London: Department for Trade and Industry.

Blakely, E. J. and M. G. Snyder (1999) *Fortress America: Gated Communities in the United States*. Washington, DC: Brookings Institution Press.

BonJour, L. and E. Sosa (2003) *Epistemic Justification: Internalism vs externalism, foundations vs virtues*. Oxford: Blackwell.

Bottéro, J., C. Herrenschmidt and J.-P. Vernant (2000) *Ancestor of the West*. Chicago, IL: University of Chicago Press.

Bourdieu, P. (2000) *Pascalian Meditations*. Cambridge: Polity Press.

Bourdieu, P. (2004) *Sketch for a Self-Analysis*. Cambridge: Polity Press.

Bourdieu, P. and J. S. Coleman (eds) (1991) *Social Theory for a Changing Society*. Boulder, CO: Westview Press.

Bowie, M. (1979) Jacque Lacan, in J. Sturrock (ed.) *Structuralism and Since*. Oxford: Oxford University Press, pp. 116–53.

Boyer, M. C. (1990) The return of aesthetics to city planning, in D. Crow (ed.) *Philosophical Streets: New approaches to urbanism*. Washington, DC: Maisonneuve Press. pp. 93–112.

Bradshaw, J. (1997) *Human Evolution: A neuropsychological perspective*. Hove: Psychology Press.

Briggs, A. (1968) *Victorian Cities*. Harmondsworth: Penguin.

Brinkley, I. (2006) *Defining the Knowledge Economy*. London: The Work Foundation.

Brophy, P. (2001) *The Library in the Twenty-first Century: New services for the information age*. London: Library Association.

Brousseau, E. and A. Rallet (1998) Beyond technological or organisational determinism: A framework to understand the link between information technologies and organisational changes, in S. MacDonald and G. Madden (eds) *Telecommunications and Socio-economic Development*. North Holland: Elsevier Science, pp. 245–62.

Brown, B. and K. O'Hara (2003) Place as a practical concern for mobile workers. *Environment and Planning*. Vol. 35, pp. 1565–87.

Brown, M. (2003) *Who Owns Native Culture?* Cambridge, MA: Harvard University Press.

Brusco, S. (1982) The Emilian model: Productive decentralization and social integration. *Cambridge Journal of Economics*. No. 6, pp. 167–84.

Buiter, W. (2008) The end of American capitalism (as we know it). *Open Democracy*. 20 September. http://www.opendemocracy.Net/article/the-end-of-american-capitalism, accessed 25 May 2010.

Bunyan, T. (2010) Just over the horizon – the surveillance society and the state in the EU. *Race and Class*. Vol. 51, No. 3, January, pp. 1–12.

Bureau of Economic Analysis (2008) *Bureau of Economic Analysis Strategic Plan 2008–2012*. Bureau of Economic Analysis, US Department of Commerce, https://www.bea.gov/about/pdf/strategic_plan_matrix_2008-2012.pdf, accessed on 16 October 2009.

Bureau of Justice Statistics (2010) *Crime – State Level State-by-State and National Trends*. http://bjsdata.ojp.usdoj.gov/dataonline/Search/Crime/State/RunCrimeStatebyState.cfm, accessed 19 May 2010.

Burfitt, A. and E. Ferrari (2008) The housing and neighbourhood impacts of knowledge-based economic development following industrial closure. *Policy Studies*. Vol. 29, No. 3, September 2008, pp. 293–304.

Burke, J. and A. Jethra (2010) £2bn Delhi airport terminal signals a new India, says PM. *The Guardian*. 4 July. http://www.guardian.co.uk/world/2010/jul/04/delhi-india-airport-terminal/print

Burke, P. (2000) *A Social History of Knowledge: From Gutenberg to Diderot*. Cambridge: Polity Press.

Buzar, S., P. Ogden, R. Hall, A. Haase, S. Kabisch and A. Steinfuhrer (2007) Splintering urban populations: emergent landscapes of reurbanization in four European cities. *Urban Studies*. Vol. 44, No. 4, pp. 651–77.

Cabinet Office (2007) *E-Government Unit*. http://archive.cabinetoffice.gov.uk/e-government/, accessed 29 March 2010.

Cameron, S. (2003) Gentrification, housing re-differentiation and urban regeneration: ‘going for growth’ in Newcastle upon Tyne. *Urban Studies*. Vol. 40, No. 12, pp. 2367–82.

Canguilhem, G. (1994) The death of man, or the exhaustion of the cogito? In G. Gutting (ed.) *The Cambridge Companion to Foucault*. Cambridge: Cambridge University Press, pp. 71–91.

Capron, H. L. (1996) *Computers: Tools for an information age*. 4th edition. Menlo Park, CA: Benajmin/Cummings Publishing Co.

Carr, J. and N. Kutty (eds) (2008) *Segregation: The rising cost for America*. New York: Routledge.

Cars, G., P. Healey, A. Madanipour and C. de Magalhaes (eds) (2002) *Urban Governance, Institutional Capacity and Social Milieux*. Aldershot: Ashgate.

Castells, M. (1996) *The Rise of the Network Society*. Oxford: Blackwell.

Cavanagh, A. (2007) *Sociology in the Age of the Internet*. Maidenhead: McGraw-Hill/Open University Press.

Caves, R. (ed.) (2005) *Encyclopedia of the City*. London: Routledge.

Champion, A. G. (2001) A changing demographic regime and evolving polycentric urban regions: consequences for the size, composition and distribution of city populations. *Urban Studies*. Vol. 38, No. 4, pp. 657–77.

Chen, D. and C. Dahlman (2005) *The Knowledge Economy, the KAM methodology and World Bank Options*. Washington, DC: The World Bank.

Christaller, W. (1966) *Central Places in Southern Germany*. London: Prentice Hall.

CIA (2009) *The World Factbook: United States*. https://www.cia.gov/library/publications/the-world-factbook/geos/us.html, accessed 30 November 2009.

CIQA (Cultural Industries Quarter Agency) (2010) *Building the Creative and Digital Economy in South Yorkshire and Beyond*. http://www.ciq.org.uk/about-us/, accessed 21 April 2010.

City of Cambridge (1991) *Report of the Mayor's Committee on University-Community Relationships*. City of Cambridge, MA, 9 December.

City of Cambridge (2003) *Demographics and Socioeconomic Profile*. Cambridge Community Development Department, City of Cambridge, MA, August 22.

City of Cambridge (2005) *2003 Cambridge Town Gown Annual Report Data*. City of Cambridge, MA.

City of Palo Alto (2007) *Palo Alto Comprehensive Plan*. http://www.cityofpaloalto.org/civica/filebank/blobdload.asp?BlobID=8170, accessed 9 April 2010.

Clark, J. and M. Diani (eds) (1996) *Alain Touraine*. London: Falmer Press.

Cockerill, T. and D. Black (2009) Should there be a cap on personal debt? *The Observer*. 20 September. http://www.guardian.co.uk/money/2009/sep/20/caps-on-personal-debt, accessed 30 November 2009.

Coleman, J. (1996) Preface, in J. Coleman (ed.) *The Individual in Political Theory and Practice*. Oxford: Clarendon Press, pp. ix–xix.

Collins, J. (1995) *Architecture of Excess: Cultural life in the information age*. London: Routledge.

Cooke, P. and A. Piccaluga (2006) *Regional Development in the Knowledge Economy*. London: Routledge.

Cooper, D. (ed.) (1999) *Epistemology: The classic readings*. Oxford: Blackwell.

Cope, B. and A. Phillips (2006) *The Future of the Book in the Digital Age*. Oxford: Chandos.

Corey, K. and M. Wilson (2006) *Urban and Regional Technology Planning: Planning practice in the global knowledge economy*. London: Routledge.

Corner House (2004) *Who Owns the Knowledge Economy? Political organising behind TRIPS*. Briefing 32, Dorset: Corner House.

Cornford, F. M. (1976) The invention of space, in M. Čapek (ed.) *The Concepts of Space and Time*, Boston Studies in the Philosophy of Science, Vol. XXII, Dordrecht and Boston: D. Reidel Publishing, pp. 3–16.

Cottingham, J. (1992) Cartesian dualism: theology, metaphysics, and science, in J. Cottingham (ed.) *The Cambridge Companion to Descartes*. Cambridge: Cambridge University Press, pp. 236–57.

Coveney, R. and R. Highfield (1991) *The Arrow of Time: The quest to solve the science's greatest mystery*. London: Flamingo.

Cowan, R., P. David and D. Foray (2000) The explicit economics of knowledge codification and tacitness. *Industrial and Corporate Change*. Vol. 9, No. 2, pp. 211–53.

Cranston, M. (1968) Introduction, in Jean-Jacques Rousseau, *The Social Contract*. London: Penguin, pp. 9–43.

Creative Sheffield (2010) *Creative Sheffield: Transforming Sheffield's economy*. http://www.creativesheffield.co.uk/, accessed 21 April 2010.

Cullingworth, B. and R. Caves (2003) *Planning in the USA: Policies, issues and processes*. 2nd edition. London: Routledge.

Culture Quarter London (2010) *Culture Quarter London*. http://culturequarterlondon.org/index.html, accessed 21 April 2010.

Cunningham, P., M. Cunningham and P. Fatelnig (eds) (2003) *Building the Knowledge Economy: Issues, applications, case studies*. Amsterdam: IOS Press.

Dahlman, C., J. T. Routti and P. Ylä-Anttila (2007) *Finland as a Knowledge Economy: Elements of success and lessons learned*. Washington, DC: World Bank.

Dahlström, M. and B. Hermelin (2007) Creative industries, spatiality and flexibility: The example of film production. *Norsk Geografisk Tidsskrift – Norwegian Journal of Geography*. Vol. 61, pp. 111–21.

Damodaran, L., W. Olphert and P. Balatsoukas (2008) Democratizing local e-government: The role of virtual dialogue. *ACM International Conference Proceeding Series*. Vol. 351, pp. 388–93.

DCLG. (2010) *Local e-Government*. http://www.communities.gov.uk/localgovernment/efficiencybetter/localegovernment/, accessed 29 March 2010.

DCMS (2008) *Creative Britain: New talents for the new economy*. London: Department for Culture, Media and Sport. http://www.culture.gov.uk/images/publications/CEPFeb2008.pdf, accessed 26 November 2009.

DCMS (2009) *Creative Industries*. http://www.culture.gov.uk/about_us/creative_industries/default.aspx, accessed 26 November 2009.

De Freitas, S., G. Rebolledo-Mendez, F. Liarokapis, G. Magoulas and A. Poulovassilis (2010) Learning as immersive experiences: Using the four-dimensional framework for designing and evaluating immersive learning experiences in a virtual world. *British Journal of Educational Technology*. Vol. 41, No. 1, pp. 69–85.

De la Blache, V. (1926) *Principles of Human Geography*. London: Constable Publishers.

Debord, G. (1994) *The Society of the Spectacle*. New York: Zone Books.

Delong, B. and L. Summers (1991) Equipment investment and economic growth. *Quart. J. Econ*. Vol. 106, pp. 445–502.

Department for Constitutional Affairs (2002) *Grant of City Status*. http://www.dca.gov.uk/constitution/city/citygj.htm, accessed 16 December 2009.

Descartes, R. (1968) *Discourse on Method and the Meditations*. London: Penguin.

DETR/CABE (2000) *By Design: Urban design in the planning system: Towards better practice*. London: Department for the Environment, Transport and the Regions.

Diani, M. (ed.) (1992) *The Immaterial Society: Design, culture and technology in the postmodern world*. London: Prentice Hall.

Dicken, P. and P. Lloyd (1990) *Location in Space: Theoretical perspectives in economic geography*. 3rd edition. New York: Harper Collins.

DirectGov (2009) *Government Outlines Plans for UK's Digital Future*. http://www.direct.gov.uk/en/Nl1/Newsroom/DG_174468, accessed 8 July 2009.

Dosi, G. (1988) *Technical Change and Industrial Organization*. London: McMillan.

Drahos, P. (2004) The regulation of public good., *Journal of International Economic Law*. Vol. 7, No. 2, pp. 321–39.

Drahos, P. (2006a) A defence of the intellectual commons. *Consumer Policy Review*. May/June, Vol. 16, No. 3, pp. 101–4.

Drahos, P. (2006b) Cities of planning and cities of non-planning: A geography of intellectual property. *Cultural Intelligence*. http://world-information.org/wio/readme/992003309, accessed 25 February 2010.

Drahos, P. and J. Braithwaite (2002) *Information Feudalism: Who owns the knowledge economy?* London: Earthscan.

Dunning, J. (2000) *Regions, Globalization, and the Knowledge-Based Economy*. Oxford: Oxford University Press.

Dutton, W. (1999) *Society on the Line: Information politics in the digital age*. Oxford: Oxford University Press.

Dutton, W. (2005) *Transforming Enterprise: The economic and social implications of information technology*. Cambridge, MA: MIT Press.

Dye, J. and J. Sosimi (2009) *United Kingdom National Accounts: The Blue Book*. Newport: Office for National Statistics/Palgrave Macmillan.

EC (2009a) *Consultation on the Future 'EU 2020' Strategy*, COM (2009) 647 final (24.11.2009, Brussels: European Commission, http://ec.europa.eu/eu2020/pdf/eu2020_en.pdf, accessed 27 November 2009.

EC (2009b) *Europe's Information Society: Thematic portal*. http://ec.europa.eu/information_society/services/ncg/en/index_en.htm, accessed 24 November 2009.

EC (2009c) *European Innovation Scoreboard 2008: Comparative analysis of innovation performance*. Luxembourg: European Commission Enterprise and Industry.

http://www.proinno-europe.eu/admin/uploaded_documents/EIS2008_Final_report-pv.pdf, accessed 17 October 2009.

EC (2010) *Green Paper: Unlocking the potential of cultural and creative industries*, COM (2010) 183, Brussels: European Commission, http://ec.europa.eu/culture/our-policy-development/doc/GreenPaper_creative_industries_en.pdf, accessed 16 July 2010.

Einstein, A. (1954) Foreword, in M. Jammer, *Concepts of Space: The history of theories of space in physics*. Cambridge, MA: Harvard University Press, pp. xi–xvi.

Eisner, C. and M. Vicinus (eds) (2008) *Originality, Imitation, and Plagiarism: Teaching writing in the digital age*. Ann Arbor, MI: University of Michigan Press.

Eldridge, N. (1997) Evolution in the marketplace. *Structural Change and Economic Dynamics*. Vol. 8, pp. 385–98.

Engels, F. (1993) *The Condition of the Working Class in England.* Oxford: Oxford University Press.

Epstein, R. (1998) *Principles for a Free Society: Reconciling individual liberty with the common good.* Reading, MA: Perseus Books.

Eriksson, J. and G. Giacomello (eds) (2007) *International Relations and Security in the Digital Age*. London: Routledge.

ESA (2009) http://www.esa.int/esaCP/index.html, European Space Agency, accessed 17 August 2009.

Esping-Andersen, G. (1999) *Social Foundations of Postindustrial Economies*. Oxford: Oxford University Press.

ETH (2010) *ETH Science City Campus*. http://www.sciencecity.ethz.ch/index_EN, accessed 11 June 2010.

Etzioni, A. (1995) *The Spirit of Community: Rights, responsibilities and the communitarian agenda*. London: Fontana Press.

EU (2009) *Information Society*. Brussels: European Commission, http://europa.eu/pol/infso/overview_en.htm, accessed 17 August 2009.

European Policy Centre (2009) *Background Note*. 1st Brussels Debate. http://create2009.europa.eu/fileadmin/Content/Downloads/PDF/Events/background_paper_1st_brussels_debate.pdf, accessed 26 November 2009.

Eurostat (2009) *Europe in Figures: Eurostat yearbook 2009*. Luxembourg: European Communities. http://eppeurostat.ec.europa.eu/cache/ITY_OFFPUB/KS-CD-09-001/EN/KS-CD-09-001-EN.pdf, accessed 24 November 2009.

Fishman, R. (1977) *Urban Utopias in the Twentieth Century: Ebenezer Howard, Frank Lloyd Wright, and Le Corbusier*. New York: Basic Books.

Fishman, R. (1987) *Bourgeois Utopia: The rise and fall of suburbia*. New York: Basic Books.

Florida, R. (2002) *The Rise of the Creative Class*. New York: Basic Books.

Florida, R. and J. Goodnight (2008) Managing for creativity, in Harvard Business Review (ed.) *Leading Creative People*. 2nd edition. Cambridge, MA: Harvard Business School, pp. 37–43.

Flynn, T. (1994) Foucault's mapping of history, in G. Gutting (ed.) *The Cambridge Companion to Foucault*. Cambridge: Cambridge University Press, pp. 28–46.

Folkestad, G. (1996) *Computer Based Creative Music Making: Young people's music in the digital age*. Göteborg, Sweden: ACTA Universitatis Gothoburgensis.

Foucault, M. (1989) *The Archaeology of Knowledge*. Abingdon: Routledge.

Foucault, M. (2002) *The Order of Things*. London: Routledge.

Fraser, N. and A. Honneth (2003) *Redistribution or Recognition: A political-philosophical exchange*. London: Verso.

Freeman, L. (2006) *There Goes the 'Hood: Gentrification from the ground up*. Philadelphia, PA: Temple University Press.
Frey, W. (2009) *Big City Populations Survive the Housing Crunch*. The Brookings Institution, accessed 27 July 2009.
Fujita, M., P. Krugman and A. Venebles (1999) *The Spatial Economy: Cities, regions and the international trade*. Cambridge, MA: MIT Press.
Fuller, S. (2003) *Kuhn vs Popper*. Cambridge: Icon Books.
Gallagher, T. (ed.) (2007) *Intellectual Property*. Aldershot: Ashgate.
Gershuny, J. and I. Miles (1983) *The New Service Economy: The transformation of employment in industrial societies*. New York: Praeger Publishers.
Gershuny, J. (1978) *After Industrial Society? The emerging self-service economy*. London: Macmillan.
Gershuny, J. (2000) *Changing Times: Work and leisure in postindustrial society*. Oxford: Oxford University Press.
Gibson, J. (2008) *Patenting Lives: Life patents, culture and development*. Aldershot: Ashgate.
Giddens, A. (1984) *The Constitution of Society: Outline of the theory of structuration*. Cambridge: Polity Press.
Giedion, S. (1967) *Space, Time and Architecture: The growth of a tradition*. 5th edition. Cambridge, MA: Harvard University Press.
Girouard, M. (1985) *Cities and People: A social and architectural history*. New Haven, CT: Yale University Press.
Given, L. M. and L. McTavish (2010) What's old is new again: The reconvergence of libraries, archives, and museums in the digital age. *Library Quarterly*. Vol. 80, No. 1, pp. 7–32.
Glasmeier, A. (2005) *An Atlas of Poverty in America: One nation, pulling apart, 1960–2003*. University Park, PA: Pennsylvania State University.
Godwin, M. (1998) *Cyber Rights: Defending free speech in the digital age*. New York: Times Books.
Goodwyn, A. (ed.) (2000) *English in the Digital Age: Information and communications technology (ICT) and the teaching of English*. London: Cassell.
Gottdiener, M and L. Budd (2005) *Key Concepts in Urban Studies*. London: Sage.
Gowdy, J. (1997) Introduction: biology and economics. *Structural Change and Economic Dynamics*. No. 8, pp. 377–83.
Grabosky, P. and R. Smith (1998) *Crime in the Digital Age: Controlling telecommunications and cyberspace illegalities*. New Brunswick, NJ: Transaction Publishers.
Graham, S. and S. Marvin (1996) *Telecommunications and the City*. London: Routledge.
Graham, S. and S. Marvin (2001) *Splintering Urbanism*. London: Routledge.
Gray, J. (1989) *Ideas of Space: Euclidean, Non-Euclidean and Relativistic*. Second edition. Oxford Science Publications. Oxford: Clarendon Press.
Greenpeace (2009) *Nuclear Power*. http://www.greenpeace.org.uk/nuclear, accessed 17 August 2009.
Gulati, R. and J. Garino (2000) Get the right mix of bricks and clicks. *Harvard Business Review*. May–June, pp. 107–14.
Gutting, G. (1980) Introduction, in G. Gutting (ed.) *Paradigms and Revolutions: Appraisals and applications of Thomas Kun's philosophy of science*. Notre Dame: University of Notre Dame Press, pp. 1–21.
Gutting, G. (ed.) (1994) *The Cambridge Companion to Foucault*. Cambridge: Cambridge University Press.

Habermas, J. (1984) *The Theory of Communicative Action*. London: Heinemann.

Haddon, L. and M. Brynin (2005) The character of telework and the characteristics of teleworkers. *New Technology, Work and Employment*. Vol. 20, No. 1, pp. 34–46.

Hale, C. (1996) *Wired Style: Principles of English usage in the digital age*. San Francisco: HardWired.

Hall, P. (1988) *Cities of Tomorrow: An intellectual history of urban planning and design in the twentieth century*. Oxford: Blackwell.

Hamil, S. (ed.) (2000) *Football in the Digital Age: Whose game is it anyway?* Edinburgh: Mainstream.

Hamnett, C. (2003) *Unequal City: London in the global arena*. London: Routledge.

Hansen, C., J. Wieferich, F. Ritter, C. Rieder and H.-O. Peitgen (2010) Illustrative visualization of 3D planning models for augmented reality in liver surgery. *International Journal of Computer-Assisted Radiology and Surgery*. Vol. 5, No. 2, pp. 133–41.

Hardt, M. and A. Negri (2000) *Empire*. Cambridge, MA: Harvard University Press.

Harrison, C. E. (2005) The bourgeois after the bourgeois revolution: Recent approaches to the middle class in European cities. *Journal of Urban History*. Vol. 31, No. 3, March, pp. 382–92.

Harvard University. (2004) *Harvard University's Town Gown Report*. Harvard Planning and Allston Initiative. Cambridge, MA: Harvard University Press.

Harvard University. (2005) *Neighbors and visitors*. Harvard University website, http://www.harvard.edu/community/

Harvey, D. (1985) *The Urbanization of Capital*. Oxford: Blackwell.

Harvey, D. (1989) *The Condition of Postmodernity*. Oxford: Blackwell.

Hass, C. (2009) *'On the Frontline' with the Nation's Mayors*. http://my.barackobama.com/page/community/post/obamaforamerica/gGxhGL, accessed 7 July 2009.

Hayman, A. (2008) Mandelson – Create knowledge jobs. *Regeneration and Renewal*. 31 October. http://www.regen.Net/news/858317/Mandelson-create-knowledge-jobs/, accessed 26 November 2009.

Hegel, F. (1967) *Hegel's Philosophy of Right*. Oxford: Oxford University Press.

Hepworth, M. and K. Ducatel (1992) *Transport in the Information Age: Wheels and wires*. London: Belhaven Press.

Hill, J. (2006) *Immaterial Architecture*. London: Routledge.

Hillier, B. and J. Hanson (1984) *The Social Logic of Space*. Cambridge: Cambridge University Press.

Hilmola, O.-P. (2007) Stock market performance and manufacturing capability of the fifth long-cycle industries. *Futures*. No. 39, pp. 393–407.

HM Government (2007) *Planning for a Sustainable Future: White Paper*. London: HMSO.

HM Government (2010) *The Coalition: Our programme for government*. London: Cabinet Office, May 2010.

Hollaar, L. (2002) *Legal Protection of Digital Information*. Arlington, VA: BNA Books.

Hollanders, H. and A. Van Cruysen (2009) *Design, Creativity and Innovation: A scoreboard approach*. February 2009, Pro Inno Europe Inno Metrics. http://www.proinno-europe.eu/admin/uploaded_documents/EIS_2008_Creativity_and_Design.pdf, accessed 27 November 2009.

Höller, N., A. Geven, M. Tscheligi, L. Paletta, K. Amlacher, P. Luley and D. Omercevic (2009) Exploring the urban environment with a camera phone: Lessons from a user study. *MobileHCI09 – The 11th International Conference on Human-Computer Interaction with Mobile Devices and Services*. Article number 67.

Hollis, M. (2002) *The Philosophy of Social Science*. Cambridge: Cambridge University Press.

Holloway, S. and G. Valentine (2003) *Cyberkids: Children in the Information Age*. London: Routledge.

Home Office (2010) *CCTV and Imaging Technology*. accessed 30 March 2010.

Honneth, A. (1995) *The Fragmented World of the Social: Essays in social and political philosophy*. Albany, NY: State University of New York Press.

Honneth, A. (2007) *Disrespect: The normative foundations of critical theory*. Cambridge: Polity Press.

Hopkinson, N., R. J. M. Hague and P. M. Dickens (eds) (2005) *Rapid Manufacturing: An industrial revolution for the digital age*. Chichester: John Wiley.

Horne, A. (2002) *Seven Ages of Paris*. London: Macmillan.

Howard, E. (1960) *Garden Cities of Tomorrow*. London: Faber and Faber.

Howells, J. R. L. (2002) Tacit knowledge, innovation and economic geography. *Urban Studies*. Vol. 39, No. 5/6, pp. 871–84.

Hughes, J., P. Jenkins and R. Khalaf (2009) Dubai shockwave hits global markets. *Financial Times*. 27 November. http://www.ft.com/cms/s/0/7896cac2-db93-11de-9424-00144feabdc0.html?nclick_check=1, accessed 30 November 2009.

Hughes, M. (ed.) (2009) *Social Trends*, No. 39. Office for National Statistics. Basingstoke: Palgrave Macmillan.

Hume, D. (1998) *Selected Essays*. Oxford: Oxford University Press.

Hutchinson, D. S. (1995) Ethics, in J. Barnes (ed.) *The Cambridge Companion to Aristotle*. Cambridge: Cambridge University Press, pp. 195–232.

Inman, J. and H. Picton (2008) *Finding Official British Information: Official publishing in the digital age*. Oxford: Chandos.

IPO (2010) *Intellectual Property Office*. accessed 16 February 2010.

Ismail, A. W. and M. S. Sunar (2009) Survey on collaborative AR for multi-user in urban studies and planning. *Lecture Notes in Computer Science*. Vol. 5670 LNCS, pp. 444–55.

ITU. (2009) *Measuring the Information Society: The ICT development index*. Geneva: International Telecommunication Union.

Jacobs, J. (1961) *The Death and Life of Great American Cities*. New York: Vintage Books.

Jacobs, J. (1970) *The Economy of Cities*. London: Jonathan Cape.

Jammer, M. (1954) *Concepts of Space: The history of theories of space in physics*. Cambridge, MA: Harvard University Press.

Japan Atlas (2010) *Tsukuba Science City*. http://web-japan.org/atlas/technology/tec01.html, accessed 9 April 2010.

Japan-I (2010) *Tsukuba Science City*. http://www.japan-i.jp/explorejapan/kanto/ibaraki/tsukuba/d8jk7l000002rk35.html, accessed 9 April 2010.

Jencks, C. (1991) *The Language of Post-Modern Architecture*. London: Academy Editions.

Jenkins, S. (2008) The end of capitalism? No, just another burst bubble. *Guardian*. 15 October. http://www.guardian.co.uk/commentisfree/2008/oct/15/credit-crunch-banking, accessed 25 May 2010.

Jessop, B. (2001) Series preface, in B. Jessop (ed.) *The Parisian Regulation School*. Cheltenham: Elgar, pp. ix–xxiii.

Johansson, E. (2001) The Nobel E-Museum – A modern science education project on internet. *International Journal of Modern Physics C*. Vol. 12, No. 4, pp. 527–32.

Johnston, R., D. Gregory, G. Pratt and M. Watts (eds) (2000) *The Dictionary of Human Geography*. 4th edition. Oxford: Blackwell.

Jonscher, C. (1999) *Wiredlife: Who are we in the digital age?* London: Bantam Press.

Kahin, B. and D. Foray (2006) *Advancing Knowledge and the Knowledge Economy*. Cambridge, MA: MIT Press.

Kanniah, R. (2006) Access to knowledge in the public domain. *Consumer Policy Review*. May/June, Vol. 16, No. 3, pp. 97–100.

Kant, I. (1993) *Critique of Pure Reason*. London: JM Dent, Everyman.

Keating, D. and N. Krumholz (eds) (1999) *Rebuilding Urban Neighborhoods: Achievements, opportunities and limits*. Thousand Oaks, CA: Sage.

Keene, S. (1998) *Digital Collections: Museums and the information age*. Oxford: Butterworth-Heinemann.

Kelliher, C. and D. Anderson (2008) For better or for worse? An analysis of how flexible working practices influence employees' perceptions of job quality. *The International Journal of Human Resource Management*. Vol. 19, No. 3, pp. 419–31.

Kershaw, C., S. Nicholas and A. Walker (2008) *Crime in England and Wales 2007/08*. London: Home Office, http://www.homeoffice.gov.uk/rds/pdfs08/hosb0708.pdf, accessed 19 May 2010.

Kolarevic, B. (ed.) (2005) *Architecture in the Digital Age: Design and manufacturing*. New York: Taylor and Francis.

Kondratieff, N. D. (1935) The long waves in economic life. *The Review of Economic Statistics*. Vol. 17, No. 6, pp. 105–15.

Korotayev, A. and S. Tsirel (2010) A spectral analysis of world GDP dynamics: Kondratieff Waves, Kuznets Swings, Juglar and Kitchin Cycles in global economic development, and the 2008–2009 economic crisis. *Structure and Dynamics*. Vol. 4, No. 1, http://www.escholarship.org/uc/item/9jv108xp, accessed 1 July 2010.

Kozinets, R. (2001) Utopian enterprise: Articulating the meanings of Star Trek's culture of consumption. *Journal of Consumer Research*. Vol. 28, June, pp. 67–88.

Kuhn, T. (1970) *The Structure of Scientific Revolutions*. 2nd edition. Chicago, IL: University of Chicago Press.

Kumar, K. (2005) *From Post-Industrial to Post-Modern Society: New theories of the contemporary world*. 2nd edition. Oxford: Blackwell.

Kuznets, S. (1930) *Secular Movements in Production and Prices: Their nature and their bearing upon cyclical fluctuations*. Boston, MA: Houghton Mifflin.

Kuznetsov, E. (1992) Post-socialist transition from a Neo-Schumpeterian perspective: The case of the former Soviet Union. *Post-Communist Economies*. Vol. 4, No. 4, pp. 469–99.

Lash, S. and J. Urry (1987) *The End of Organized Capitalism*. Cambridge: Polity Press.

Latour, B. (1999) *Pandora's Hope: Essays on the reality of science studies*. Cambridge, MA: Harvard University Press.

Latour, B. (2005) *Reassembling the Social: An introduction to actor-network theory*. Oxford: Oxford University Press.

Latour, B. and S. Woolgar (1986) *Laboratory Life: The construction of scientific facts*. Princeton, NJ: Princeton University Press.

Lazzarato, M. (1996) Immaterial labour, in P. Virno and M. Hardt (eds) *Radial Thought in Italy*. Minneapolis, MN: University of Minnesota Press.

Le Corbusier (1971) *The City of Tomorrow, and Its Planning*. London: The Architectural Press.

Le Corbusier (1978) *Towards A New Architecture*. London: The Architectural Press.

Le Corbusier (1987) *The City of Tomorrow and Its Planning*. London: The Architectural Press.

Le Grice, M. (2001) *Experimental Cinema in the Digital Age*. London: British Film Institute.

Leadbeater, C. (1999) *Living on Thin Air: The new economy*. London: Viking.

Lee, J. Y., D. Seo, B. Y. Song and R. Gadh (2010) Visual and tangible interactions with physical and virtual objects using context-aware RFID. *Expert Systems with Applications*. Vol. 37, No. 5, May, pp. 3835–45.

Lees, L. and D. Ley (2008) Introduction to special issue on gentrification and public policy. *Urban Studies*. Vol. 45, No. 12, pp. 2379–84.

Lefebvre, H. (1991) *The Production of Space*. Oxford: Blackwell.

Lehrer, K. (1974) *Knowledge*. Oxford: Clarendon Press.

Leibniz, G. (1979) The relational theory of space and time, in J. J. C. Smart (ed.) *Problems of Space and Time*. New York: Macmillan, pp. 89–98.

Leicester City Council (2010) *Cultural Quarter*. http://www.leicester.gov.uk/your-council-services/ep/regeneration/regenerationnews/culturalquarter/, accessed 21 April 2010.

Ley, D. (1996) *The New Middle Class and the Remaking of the Central City*. Oxford: Oxford University Press.

Liberty (2010) *Privacy*. http://www.liberty-human-rights.org.uk/issues/3-privacy/index.shtml, accessed 30 March 2010.

Lipietz, A. (1987) *Mirages and Miracles: The crises of global Fordism*. London: Verso.

Lipietz, A. (1992) *Towards a New Economic Order: Post-Fordism, ecology and democracy*. Cambridge: Polity Press.

Lipietz, A. (2003) Rethinking social housing in the hour-glass society, in A. Madanipour, G. Cars and J. Allen (eds) *Social Exclusion in European Cities*. London: Routledge.

Locke, J. (1979) Place, extension and duration, in J. J. C. Smart (ed.) *Problems of Space and Time*. New York: Macmillan, pp. 99–103.

Logan, J. and H. Molotch (1987) *Urban Fortunes: The political economy of place*. Berkeley, CA: University of California Press.

Lösch, A. (1954) *The Economics of Location*. New Haven: Yale University Press.

Loukaitou-Sideris, A. and B. Tridib (1998) *Urban Design Downtown: Poetics and politics of form*. Berkeley, CA: University of California Press.

Lynch, K. (1979) *The Image of the City*. Cambridge, MA: MIT Press.

Lyotard, J.-F. (1984) *The Postmodern Condition: A report on knowledge*. Manchester: Manchester University Press.

Ma, L. J. C. and F. Wu (eds) (2005) *Restructuring the Chinese Cities: Changing society, economy and space*. London: Routledge.

MacIntyre, A. (1980) Epistemological crises, dramatic narrative, and the philosophy of science, in G. Gutting (ed.) *Paradigms and Revolutions: Appraisals and applications of Thomas Kuhn's philosophy of science*. Notre Dame: University of Notre Dame Press, pp. 54–74.

Madanipour, A. (1996) Urban design and dilemmas of space. *Environment and Planning D: Society and Space*. Vol. 14, pp. 331–55.

Madanipour, A. (1996) *Design of Urban Space: An inquiry into a socio-spatial process*. Chichester: John Wiley.

Madanipour, A. (1999) Why are the design and development of public spaces significant for cities? *Environment and Planning B: Planning and Design*. Vol. 26, pp. 879–91.

Madanipour, A. (2001) How relevant is 'planning by neighborhoods' today? *Town Planning Review*. Vol. 72, No. 2, pp. 171–91.

Madanipour, A. (2003) *Public and Private Spaces of the City*. London: Routledge.

Madanipour, A. (2005) Value of place, in CABE (ed.) *Physical Capital: How great places boost public value*. London: Commission for Architecture and the Built Environment, pp. 48–71.

Madanipour, A. (2007a) *Designing the City of Reason*. London: Routledge.

Madanipour, A. (2007b) Social exclusion and space, in R. LeGates and F. Stout (eds) *The City Reader*. 4th edition. London: Routledge, pp. 158–65.

Madanipour, A. (2009) City identity and management of change, in C. Vallat, F. Dufaux and S. Kehman-Frisch (eds) *Pérennitéurbaine, ou la ville par delàsesmétamorphoses*. Paris: L'Harmattan, Volume III, pp. 217–234.

Madanipour, A. (2010a) Living together or apart: Exclusion, gentrification and displacement, in T. Banerjee and A. Loukaitou-Sideris (eds) *Companion to Urban Design*. London: Routledge.

Madanipour, A. (ed.) (2010b) *Whose Public Space? International case studies in urban design and development*. London: Routledge.

Madanipour, A. (2010c) Newcastle upon Tyne: In search of a post-industrial direction, in J. Punter (ed.) *Urban Design and Urban Renaissance*. London: Routledge, pp. 132–47.

Madanipour, A. (2011) Ghetto, in Susan Smith (ed.) *International Encyclopedia of Housing and Home*. Oxford: Elsevier.

Madanipour, A., G. Cars and J. Allen (eds) (2003) *Social Exclusion in European Cities*. London: Routledge.

Maffesoli, M. (1996) *The Times of the Tribes*. London: Sage.

Magnusson, L. (1993) *Evolutionary and Neo-Schumpeterian Approaches to Economics*. Boston, MA: Kluwer.

Makagon, D. (2004) *Where the Ball Drops: Days and nights in Times Square*. Minneapolis, MI: University of Minnesota Press.

Malairajaa, C. and G. Zawdie (2008) Science parks and university – industry collaboration in Malaysia. *Technology Analysis and Strategic Management*. Vol. 20, No. 6, November, pp. 727–39.

Maloutas, T. (2004) Segregation and residential mobility: Spatially entrapped social mobility and its impact on segregation in Athens. *European Urban and Regional Studies*. Vol. 11, No. 3, pp. 195–211.

Mannheim, K. (1968) *Essays on the Sociology of Knowledge*. London: Routledge and Kegan Paul.

Manovich, L. (2001) *The Language of New Media*. Cambridge, MA: The MIT Press.

Markosian, N. (2002) Time, in E. N. Zalta (ed.) *The Stanford Encyclopaedia of Philosophy. Winter 2002 Edition*. http://plato.stanford.edu/archives/win2002/entries/time/.

Marshall, T. (ed.) (2004) *Transforming Barcelona*. London: Routledge.

Martin, R. (ed.) (1999) *Money and the Space Economy*. Chichester: Wiley.

Martin, R. and P. Sunley (1998) Slow convergence? The new endogenous growth theory and regional development. *Econ. Geogr.* Vol. 74, pp. 201–27.

Martindale, D. (1966) Prefatory remarks: The theory of the city, in M. Weber *The City*. New York: The Free Press.

Marx, K. (1967) *Capital*. Vol. 1. New York: International Publishers.

Marx, K. (2008) *The Poverty of Philosophy*. New York: Cosimo Classics.

Matlin, M. (2005) *Cognition*. 6th edition. New York: Wiley.

McCloskey, D. W. and K. Leppel (2010) The impact of age on electronic commerce participation: An exploratory model. *Journal of Electronic Commerce in Organizations*. Vol. 8, No. 1, pp. 41–60.

McCracken, G. (1986) Culture and consumption: A theoretical account of the structure and movement of the cultural meaning of consumer goods. *Journal of Consumer Research*. Vol. 13, June, pp. 71–84.

McLuhan, M. (1964) *Understanding Media: The extensions of man*. London: Routledge and Kegan Paul.

Melucci, A. (1996) *Challenging Codes: Collective action in the information age*. Cambridge: Cambridge University Press.

Mensch, G. O. (1979) *Stalemate in Technology: Innovations overcome the depression*. Cambridge, MA: Ballinger.

Michie, J. and M. Sheehan (2003) Labour market deregulation, 'flexibility' and innovation. *Cambridge Journal of Economics*. Vol. 27, pp. 123–43.

Millenson, M. (1997) *Demanding Medical Excellence: Doctors and accountability in the information age*. Chicago, IL: University of Chicago Press.

Miller, K. (2007) *Designs on the Public: The private lives of New York's public spaces*. Minneapolis, MA: University of Minnesota Press.

Millham, R. and C. Eid (2009) Digital cities: Nassau and Bologna – a study in contrasts. *2009 IEEE Latin-American Conference on Communications. LATINCOM '09*. Conference proceedings. Article number 5305144.

Minkowski, H. (1979) Space and time, in J. J. C. Smart (ed.) *Problems of Space and Time*. New York: Macmillan, pp. 297–312.

MIT (2003) Boston's 8 research universities provide 7B annual boost to the regional economy. *MIT website*, accessed 1 February 2005.

MIT (2004) *Annual Town Gown Report*. Cambridge, MA: Massachusetts Institute of Technology.

Modelski, G. (2001) What causes K-waves? *Technological Forecasting and Social Change*. Vol. 68, pp. 75–80.

Mokyr, J. (2002) *The Gifts of Athena: Historical origins of the knowledge economy*. Princeton: Princeton University Press.

Mumford, L. (1954) The neighbourhood and the neighbourhood unit. *Town Planning Review*. Vol. 24, pp. 256–70.

Mumford, L. (1961) *The City in History*. London: Secker and Warburg.

NASA (2009) *The National Aeronautics and Space Administration*. http://www.nasa.gov/ accessed 17 August 2009.

National Atlas (2009) *Population Change and Distribution: 1990 to 2000*. http:// nationalatlas. gov/articles/people/a_popchange.html, accessed 27 July 2009.

Nayar, P. (2010) *The New Media and Cybercultures Anthology*. Oxford: Blackwell.

Nelson, K. (2008) *Teaching in the Digital Age: Using the Internet to increase student engagement and understanding*. Thousand Oaks, CA: Corwin Press.

Nerlich, G. (1994) *The Shape of Space*. 2nd edition. Cambridge: Cambridge University Press.

Newman, O. (1996) *Creating Defensible Space*. Washington, DC: US Department of Housing and Urban Development, Office of Policy Development and Research.

Nicholas, D. (2000) *Assessing Information Needs: Tools, techniques and concepts for the internet age*. London: Aslib Information Management.

Nietzsche, F. (1998) *Beyond Good and Evil: Prelude to a philosophy of the future*. Oxford: Oxford University Press.

Nietzsche, F. (2007) *Ecce Homo: How to become what you are*. Oxford: Oxford University Press.

Njenga, J. K. and L. C. H. Fourie (2010) The myths about e-learning in higher education. *British Journal of Educational Technology*. Vol. 41, No. 2, pp. 199–212.

Obama, B. (2005) *Literacy and Education in a 21st-Century Economy*. 25 June. http://obamaspeeches.com/024-Literacy-and-Education-in-a-21st-Century-Economy-Obama-Speech.htm, accessed 6 July 2009.

O'Brien, T. and H. Hayden (2008) Flexible work practices and the LIS sector: balancing the needs of work and life? *Library Management*. Vol. 29, No. 3, pp. 199–228.

ODPM (Office of the Deputy Prime Minister) (2005) *Planning Policy Statement 1: Delivering sustainable development*. London: ODPM.

OECD (1996) *The Knowledge-Based Economy*. Paris: Organization for Economic Cooperation and Development.

OECD (2000) *Is There a New Economy?* Paris: Organization for Economic Cooperation and Development.

OECD (2006) *Conference on Globalization and the Knowledge Economy: Issues paper*. Conference on 'Globalisation and the knowledge economy'. 9 October. Paris: Organization for Economic Cooperation and Development, Directorate for Science, Technology and Industry (STI).

OECD (2008) *Factbook 2008*. Paris: Organization for Economic Cooperation and Development.

OECD (2008) *Growing Unequal? Income distribution and poverty in OECD countries*. Paris: Organization for Economic Cooperation and Development.

Onanuga, T. (2010) Emergency Budget: George Osborne's speech in full. *Guardian*. 22 June. http://www.guardian.co.uk/uk/2010/jun/22/emergency-budget-full-speech-text, accessed 2 August 2010.

Ong, S. K., Y. Pang and A. Y. C. Nee (2007) Augmented reality aided assembly design and planning. *CIRP Annals – Manufacturing Technology*. Vol. 56, No. 1, pp. 49–52.

O'Sullivan, A. (2003) *Urban Economics*. 5th edition. New York: McGraw-Hill Higher Education.

Owen, R. (1991) *A New View of Society and Other Writings*. London: Penguin.

Pappas, G. (2008) Internalist vs. Externalist Conceptions of Epistemic Justification, in E. N. Zalta (ed.) *The Stanford Encyclopedia of Philosophy (Fall 2008 Edition)*.

Park, R., E. Burgess and R. McKenzie (1984) *The City*. Chicago, IL: University of Chicago Press.

Parkins, H. (ed.) (1997) *Roman Urbanism: Beyond the consumer city*. London: Routledge.

Parkinson, M. (2006) *State of English Cities*. Volume 1. London: Office of the Deputy Prime Minister.

Pastuszak, Z. (2010) Use of the e-business reception model to compare the level of advanced e-business solutions reception in service and manufacturing companies. *International Journal of Management and Enterprise Development*. Vol. 8, No. 1, pp. 1–21.

Perez, C. (1983) Structural change and assimilation of new technologies in the economic and social systems. *Futures*. October, pp. 357–75.

Pessoa, A. (2009) Kuznets's hypothesis and the data constraint. *Applied Economics Letters*. Vol. 16, pp. 813–18.

Pevsner, N. (1963) *An Outline of European Architecture*. 7th edition. Harmondsworth: Penguin Books.

Piore, M. and C. Sabel (1984) *The Second Industrial Divide: Possibilities for prosperity*. New York: Basic Books.

Plato (1993) *Republic*. Oxford: Oxford University Press.

Platt, C. (1976) *The English Medieval Town*. London: Secker and Warburg.

Platt, C. (1990) *The Architecture of Medieval Britain: A social history*. New Haven, CT: Yale University Press.

Pointer, G. (2005) *The UK's major urban areas*. http://www.statistics.gov.uk/downloads/theme_compendia/fom2005/03_FOPM_UrbanAreas.pdf, accessed 27 July 2009.

Polanyi, M. (1958) *Personal Knowledge: Towards a post-critical philosophy*. Chicago, IL: University of Chicago Press.

Polanyi, M. (1983) *The Tacit Dimension*. Gloucester, MA: Peter Smith.

Portalés, C., J. L. Lerma and S. Navarro (2010) Augmented reality and photogrammetry: A synergy to visualize physical and virtual city environments. *ISPRS Journal of Photogrammetry and Remote Sensing*. No. 65, pp. 134–42.

Poster, M. (2001) *Jean Baudrillard: Selected writings*. Stanford, CA: Stanford University Press.

Potter, D. (1995) *A History of France, 1460–1560: The emergence of a nation state*. Basingstoke: Macmillan.

Powell, W. and K. Snellman (2004) The knowledge economy. *Annual Review of Sociology*. Vol. 30, pp. 199–220.

Pratt, A., R. Gill and V. Spelthann (2007) Work and the city in the e-society: A critical investigation of the sociospatially situated character of economic production in the digital content industries in the UK. *Information, Communication and Society*. Vol. 10, No. 6, December, pp. 922–42.

Pred, A. (1966) *The Spatial Dynamics of US Urban-Industrial Growth, 1800–1914*. Cambridge, MA: MIT Press.

Pritchard, D. (2006) *What Is This Thing Called Knowledge?* London: Routledge.

Punter, J. (ed.) (2010) *Urban Design and the British Urban Renaissance*. London: Routledge.

Quah, D. (2000) Internet cluster emergence. *European Economic Review*. Vol. 44, pp. 1032–44.

Quah, D. (2002) Matching demand and supply in a weightless economy: Market-driven creativity with and without IPRS. *De Economist*. Vol. 150, No. 4, pp. 381–403.

Quinn, M. (2005) *Ethics for the Information Age*. Boston: Pearson/Addison-Wesley.

QUT (2010) *Overview*. http://www.Ciprecinct.qut.edu.au/about/, accessed 21 April 2010.

Ratinho, T. and E. Henriques (2010) The role of science parks and business incubators in converging countries: Evidence from Portugal. *Technovation*. Vol. 30, No. 4, April, pp. 278–90.

Raymer, M. (2009) *The Silicon Web: Physics for the Internet age*. London: Taylor & Francis.

Reeve, C. D. C. (1992) *Practices of Reason: Aristotle's Nicomachean ethics*. Oxford: Clarendon Press.

Reilly, P. and S. Rahtz (eds) (1992) *Archaeology and the Information Age: A global perspective*. London: Routledge.

Ricoeur, P. (1995) *Oneself as Another*. Chicago, IL: Chicago University Press.

Riewoldt, O. (1997) *Intelligent Spaces: Architecture for the information age*. London: Laurence King.

Right to the City (2009) *The Right to the City*. http://www.righttothecity.org/, accessed 1 March 2009.

Romer, P. (1986) Increasing returns and long-run growth. *Journal of Political Economy*. Vol. 94, No. 5, pp. 2–37.

Rorissa, A. and D. Demissie (2010) An analysis of African e-government service websites. *Government Information Quarterly*. Vol. 27, No. 2, pp. 161–9

RSA (2009) *Russian Federal Space Agency*. http://www.roscosmos.ru/index.asp?Lang=ENG, accessed 17 August 2009.

Saalman, H. (1968) *Medieval Cities*. London: Studio Vista.

Sabel, C. and J. Zeitlin (eds) (1997) *World of Possibilities: Flexibility and mass production in Western industrialization*. Cambridge: Cambridge University Press.

Salem Partnership (2007) *The Innovation Agenda: Growing the creative economy in Massachusetts*. www.Creativeeconomy.us/documents/Final_Report_and_Action_Plan.pdf, accessed 21 April 2010.

Sareika, M. and D. Schmalstieg (2007) Urban sketcher: Mixed reality on site for urban planning and architecture. *2007 6th IEEE and ACM International Symposium on Mixed and Augmented Reality, ISMAR*. Article number 4538821.

Savage, M. (2009) Against Epochalism: An analysis of conceptions of change in British sociology. *Cultural Sociology*. Vol. 3, No. 2, pp. 217–38.

Schacht, R. (1996) Nietzsche's kind of philosophy, in B. Magnus and K. Higgins (eds) *The Cambridge Companion to Nietzsche*. Cambridge: Cambridge University Press, pp. 151–79.

Schorske, C. (1981) *Fin-de-Siècle Vienna: Politics and culture*. New York: Vintage Books.

Schumpeter, J. A. (1942) *Capitalism, Socialism and Democracy*. New York: Harper and Row.

Schumpeter, J. (2003) *Capitalism, Socialism and Democracy*. London: Taylor and Francis.

Schutz, A. (1962) *Collected Papers I: The problem of social reality*. The Hague: Martinus Nijhoff.

Schutz, A. (1970) *On Phenomenology and Social Relations, selected writings*. Chicago: The University of Chicago Press.

Schutz, A. and T. Luckmann (1974) *The Structures of the Life-World*. London: Heinemann.

Scott, A. J. (2006) Entrepreneurship, innovation and industrial development: Geography and the creative field revisited. *Small Business Economics*. Vol. 26, pp. 1–24.

Searle, J. (1995) *The Construction of Social Reality*. London: Penguin.

Searle, J. (1998) *The Mystery of Consciousness*. London: Granta.

Searle, J. (1999) *Mind, Language and Society: Philosophy in the real world*. London: Weidenfeld and Nicolson.

Sellers, J. (2002) *Governing from Below: Urban regions and the global economy*. Cambridge: Cambridge University Press.

Sendov, B. and I. Stanchev (eds) (1986) *Children in an Information Age: Tomorrow's problems today*. Oxford: Pergamon Press.

Sennett, R. (1993) *The Conscience of the Eye: The design and social life of cities*. London: Faber and Faber.

Sert, J. L. (1944) *Can Our Cities Survive? An ABC of urban problems, their analysis, their solution*. Cambridge, MA: Harvard University Press.

Shapiro, C. and H. R. Varian (1999) *Information Rules: A strategic guide to the network economy*. Boston: Harvard Business School Press.

Shibata, T. and H. Takeuchi (2006) *Japan, moving toward a more advanced knowledge economy*. Washington, DC: World Bank.

Simmel, G. (1950) *The Sociology of Georg Simmel*. New York: The Free Press.

Simmel, G. (1978) *The Philosophy of Money*. London: Routledge and Kegan Paul.

Simmie, J. (2003) Innovation and urban regions as national and international nodes for the transfer and sharing of knowledge. *Regional Studies*. Vol. 37, No. 6 and 7, pp. 607–20.

Simmie, J. and S. Strambach (2006) The contribution of KIBS to innovation in cities: An evolutionary and institutional perspective. *Journal of Knowledge Management*. Vol. 10, No. 5, pp. 26–40.

Slater, T. (2006) The eviction of critical perspectives from gentrification research. *International Journal of Urban and Regional Research*. Vol. 30, No. 4, pp. 737–57.

Smart, J. J. C. (ed.) (1979) *Problems of Space and Time*. New York: Macmillan.

Smelser, N., W. J. Wilson and F. Mitchell (eds) (2001) *America Becoming: Racial trends and their consequences*. Washington, DC: National Academy Press.

Smith, A. (1993) *An Inquiry into the Nature and Cause of the Wealth of Nations*. Edited by Kathryn Sutherland. Oxford: Oxford University Press.

Smith, A. (1997) *The Emergence of a Nation State: The commonwealth of England, 1529–1660*. London: Longman.

Smith, E. and S. Kosslyn (2007) *Cognitive Psychology: Mind and brain*. Upper Saddle River, NJ: Pearson Prentice Hall.

Smith, N. (1996) *The New Urban Frontier: Gentrification and the revanchist city*. London: Routledge.

Smith, N. (1998) Giuliani Time: The revanchist 1990s. *Social Text*. Vol. 16, No. 4. pp. 1–20.

Sörlin, S. and H. M. C. Vessuri (2007) *Knowledge Society vs. Knowledge Economy: Knowledge, power, and politics*. Basingstoke: Palgrave Macmillan.

Sosa, E. (2001) Human knowledge, animal and reflective. *Philosophical Studies*. No. 106, pp. 193–6.

Southall, A. (1998) *The City in Time and Space*. Cambridge: Cambridge University Press.

Spear, A. (1967) *Black Chicago: The making of a negro ghetto, 1890–1920*. Chicago, IL: University of Chicago Press.

Squicciarini, M. (2008) Science parks' tenants versus out-of-park firms: Who innovates more? A duration model. *Journal of Technology Transfer*. Vol. 33, No. 1, pp. 45–71.

Standing, S., C. Standing and P. E. D. Love (2010) A review of research on e-marketplaces 1997–2008. *Decision Support Systems*. Vol. 49, No. 1, pp. 41–51.

Stehr, N. (2001) *The Fragility of Modern Societies: Knowledge and risk in the information age*. London: Sage.

Steup, M. (2006) The analysis of knowledge, in E. N. Zalta (ed.) *The Stanford Encyclopedia of Philosophy (Spring 2006 Edition)*. http://plato.stanford.edu/archives/spr2006/entries/knowledge-analysis/

Steup, M. and E. Sosa (eds) (2005) *Contemporary Debates in Epistemology*. Oxford: Blackwell.

Stiglitz, J. (1999) *Public Policy for a Knowledge Economy*. Washington, DC: World Bank. http://www.worldbank.org/html/extdr/extme/jssp012799a.htm, accessed 6 July 2009.

Storper, M. (1997) *The Regional World: Territorial development in a global economy*. New York: Guilford Press.

Sturrock, J. (ed.) (1979) *Structuralism and Since*. Oxford: Oxford University Press.

Sudjic, D. (2009) *The Language of Things*. London: Penguin.

Sutton, D., S. Brind and R. McKenzie (eds) (2007) *The State of the Real: Aesthetics in the digital age*. London: I.B. Tauris.

Sylaiou, S., K. Mania, A. Karoulis and M. White (2010) Exploring the relationship between presence and enjoyment in a virtual museum. *International Journal of Human-Computer Studies*. Vol. 68, May, No. 5, pp. 243–53.

Tedjokusumo, J., S. Z. Y. Zhou and S. Winkler (2010) Immersive multiplayer games with tangible and physical interaction. *IEEE transactions on systems, man and cybernetics*.

Part A. Systems and humans. Vol. 40, No. 1, January, Article number 5306180, pp. 147–57.

Terranova, T. (2004) *Network Culture Politics for the Information Age*. London: Pluto Press.

Thomas, M. (2008) Digitality and immaterial culture: What did Viking women think? *International Journal of Digital Culture and Electronic Tourism*. Vol. 1, No. 2/3, pp. 177–91.

Thompson, J. (2005) *Books in the Digital Age: The transformation of academic and higher education publishing in Britain and the United States*. Cambridge: Polity Press.

Thompson, P. (2009) The German Left, the Berlin Wall and the Second Great Crash. *Debatte: Journal of Contemporary Central and Eastern Europe*. Vol. 17, No. 1, pp. 41–54.

Toffler, A. (1970) *Future Shock*. New York: Random House.

Toffler, A. (1981) *The Third Wave*. London: Pan Books.

Tönnies, F. (1957) *Community and Society*. New York: Harper and Row.

Torretti, R. (1984) *The Philosophy of Geometry from Reimann to Poincaré*. Dordrecht: D. Reidel Publishing.

Touraine, A. (1995) *Critique of Modernity*. Oxford: Blackwell.

Townshend, T. and A. Madanipour (2008) Public space and local diversity: The case of Northeast England. *Journal of Urban Design*. Vol. 13, No. 3, October, pp. 317–28.

Tredinnick, L. (2008) *Digital Information Culture: The individual and society in the digital age*. Oxford: Chandos.

Trout, A. (1996) *City on the Seine: Paris in the time of Richelieu and Louis XIV*. New York: St Martin's Press.

Tsai, W.-H., Y. Purbokusumo, M.-S. Julian and N. D. Tuan (2009) E-government evaluation: The case of Vietnam's provincial websites. *Electronic Government*. Vol. 6, No. 1, pp. 41–53.

UN (2009) *The Digital Divide: ICT Development Indices*. http://stdev.unctad.org/themes/ict/dd.html, accessed 17 August 2009.

UNESCO (2005) *Towards Knowledge Societies*. UNESCO World Report. Paris: United Nations Educational, Scientific and Cultural Organization (UNESCO).

UNESCO (2009) *Creative Industries*. http://portal.unesco.org/culture/en/ev.php-URL_ID=35024&URL_DO=DO_TOPIC&URL_SECTION=201.html, accessed 27 November 2009.

UNESCO (2010) *Science and Technology Park Governance*. http://www.unesco.org/science/psd/thm_innov/unispar/sc_parks/parks.shtml, accessed 8 April 2010.

Urban Task Force (1999) *Towards an Urban Renaissance*. London: E & FN Spon.

US Census Bureau (2009) *New Orleans was Nation's Fastest-Growing City in 2008*. Press Release, 1 July. http://www.Census.gov/Press-Release/www/releases/archives/population/013960.html, accessed 27 July 2009.

US Census Bureau (2010a) *Households by Type and Size: 1900 to 2002*. http://www.census.gov/statab/hist/HS-12.pdf, accessed 18 May 2010.

US Census Bureau (2010b) *Housing Units – Historical Trends for Selected Characteristics: 1940 to 2000*, accessed 18 May 2010.

US Census Bureau (2010c) *2002 Economic Census: Comparative Statistics for United States Summary Statistics by 1997 NAICS*. http://www.census.gov/econ/census02/data/comparative/USCS.htm, accessed 18 July 2010.

US Census Bureau (2010d) *Annual Value of Construction Put in Place 2002–2009*. http://www.census.gov/const/C30/total.pdf, accessed 18 July 2010.

US Department of Commerce (2008) *Press Release: Gutierrez calls for government, private sector, and academic actions on innovation measurement.* 18 January. Washington, DC: Office of the Secretary. http://www.innovationmetrics.gov/press_releases/011808PressRelease.pdf, accessed on 16 October 2009.

van den Berg, L. (2005) *European Cities in the Knowledge Economy: The cases of Amsterdam, Dortmund, Eindhoven, Helsinki, Manchester, Munich, Münster, Rotterdam, and Zaragoza.* Aldershot: Ashgate.

Van Geenhuizen, M. and D. P. Soetanto (2008) Science parks: What they are and how they need to be evaluated. *International Journal of Foresight and Innovation Policy*. Vol. 4, No. 1–2, pp. 90–111.

van Roon, G. (1981) Historians and long waves. *Futures*. October, pp. 383–8.

Van Winden, W., L. Van den Berg and P. Pol (2007) European cities in the knowledge economy: Towards a typology. *Urban Studies*. Vol. 44, No. 3, pp. 525–49.

Veblen, T. (2007) *The Theory of the Leisure Class*. Oxford: Oxford University Press.

Vergara, C. J. (1999) *The New American Ghetto*. New Brunswick, NJ: Rutgers University Press.

Vertova, G. (ed.) (2006) *The Changing Economic Geography of Globalization: Reinventing space*. London: Routledge.

Walby, S. (2007) *Gendering the Knowledge Economy: Comparative perspectives*. Basingstoke: Palgrave Macmillan.

Wall, D. (2007) *Cybercrime: The transformation of crime in the information age*. Cambridge: Polity Press.

Wallerstein, I. (1974) *The Modern World System*. New York: Academic Press.

Wallerstein, I. (1979) *The Capitalist World Economy*. Cambridge: Cambridge University Press.

Wang, X., R. Chen, Y. Gong and Y.-T. Hsieh (2007) Experimental study on augmented reality potentials in urban design. *Proceedings of the International Conference on Information Visualisation*. Article number 4272036, pp. 567–72.

Webber, M. (2003) The Post-City Age, in R. LeGates and F. Stout (eds) *The City Reader*. 3rd edition. London: Routledge, pp. 470–74.

Weber, M. (1966) *The City*. New York: The Free Press.

Weber, M. (1978) *Economy and Society: An outline of interpretive sociology*. Berkeley, CA: University of California Press.

Weber, M. (1998) *The Agrarian Sociology of Ancient Civilizations*. London: Verso.

Webster, F. (2006) *Theories of the Information Society*. 3rd edition. London: Routledge.

Whitehand, J. W. R. (1992) *The Making of the Urban Landscape*. Oxford: Blackwell.

Whitrow, G. J. (1972) *What is Time?* London: Thames and Hudson.

Willets, D. (2010) *Science, Innovation and the Economy*. London: Department for Business, Innovation and Skills. http://www.bis.gov.uk/news/speeches/david-willetts-science-innovation-and-the-economy, accessed 21 July 2010.

Williams, N. (2005) UK is limited on flexible working practices. *Personnel Today*. 7 June. http://www.personneltoday.com/articles/2005/06/07/30191/uk-is-limited-on-flexible-working-practices.html, accessed 23 May 2008.

Wirth, L. (1964) Urbanism as a way of life, in A. Reiss (ed.) *Louis Wirth on Cities and Social Life: Selected papers*. Chicago, IL: The University of Chicago Press, pp. 60–83.

Wirth, L. (1964) *On Cities and Social Life: Selected papers*. Chicago: University of Chicago Press.

Wolf, M. (2005) *Why Globalization Works*. New Haven, CT: Yale University Press.

World Bank (2007) *Knowledge Economy Index (KEI) 2007 Rankings*. KAM (Knowledge Assessment Methodology). http://www.worldbank.org/kam, accessed 28 January 2008.

World Bank (2008a) *Knowledge for Development (K4D)*. http://go.worldbank.org/94MMDLIVF0, accessed 28 January 2008.

World Bank (2008b) *The Four Pillars of the Knowledge Economy*. http://go.worldbank.org/5WOSIRFA70, accessed 28 January 2008.

World Bank (2009) *Knowledge Assessment Methodology*. Washington, DC: World Bank. http://go.worldbank.org/JGAO5XE940, accessed 19 October 2009.

World Intellectual Property Organization (2010) *Understanding Copyrights and Related Rights*. Geneva: WIPO.

World Intellectual Property Organization (2010) *What is Intellectual Property?* http://www.wipo.int/about-ip/en/, accessed 16 February 2010.

World Trade Organization (2010) *TRIPS (Trade-Related Aspects of Intellectual Property Rights)*. http://www.wto.org/english/tratop_E/trips_e/trips_e.htm, accessed 16 February 2010.

Wymbs, C. (2004) Telecommunications, an instrument of radical change for both the 20th and 21st centuries. *Technological Forecasting and Social Change*. No. 71, pp. 685–703.

Yang, C. H., K. Motohashi and J. R. Chen (2009) Are new technology-based firms located on science parks really more innovative? Evidence from Taiwan. *Research Policy*. Vol. 38, No. 1, pp. 77–85.

Index

Note: page numbers in **bold type** refer to illustrations.